On Motherhood:
Fireflies to First Dates

On Motherhood:
Fireflies to First Dates

A Collection of Planet Mom Essays

Remember that it is the harvest of tiny moments that matters most...

Melinda L. Wentzel aka Planet Mom :))

Melinda L. Wentzel, aka Planet Mom

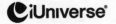

ON MOTHERHOOD: FIREFLIES TO FIRST DATES
A COLLECTION OF PLANET MOM ESSAYS

iUniverse books may be ordered through booksellers or by contacting:

iUniverse
1663 Liberty Drive
Bloomington, IN 47403
www.iuniverse.com
1-800-Authors (1-800-288-4677)

Because of the dynamic nature of the Internet, any web addresses or links contained in this book may have changed since publication and may no longer be valid. The views expressed in this work are solely those of the author and do not necessarily reflect the views of the publisher, and the publisher hereby disclaims any responsibility for them.

Any people depicted in stock imagery provided by Getty Images are models, and such images are being used for illustrative purposes only. Certain stock imagery © Getty Images.

ISBN: 978-1-5320-7162-1 (sc)
ISBN: 978-1-5320-7161-4 (e)

Library of Congress Control Number: 2019903565

Print information available on the last page.

iUniverse rev. date: 04/04/2019

All of the essays that appear in this work were originally published both in print and online in the Webb Weekly newspaper column, Notes from Planet Mom. Some pieces have been edited specifically for the publication of this book.

Select essays in this work (list to follow) were published both in print and online in the Khaleej Times Newspaper, Dubai, UAE. Some pieces have been edited for the publication of this book. "Sweet Dreams," "The Twelfth of Never," "The Grass is Always Greener Somewhere Else," "Dear Diary," "Eggs, Toast and a Side of Cynicism," "Mommie Dearest," "Dances with Carts," "Nightmare on Mom Street," "Dear Departed Summer," "Hands Upon My Heart," "Ode to Embarrassment," "The Value of Permanence," "Seven Things Parenthood Has Taught Me," "Food for Thought," "Building a Reader," "The Road Less Traveled," "Fitness for Dummies," "Worms Fail Me," "Ode to Oblivion," "A Sacrilege of Sorts," "The Beauty of Mismanagement," "Necessity is the Mother of Clean Closets and Tidy Drawers," "Fixing What Isn't Broken," "Be Careful What You Wish For," "The Color of Bizarre," "Ode to Odor," "Juneuary," "A Kinder, Gentler Sort of Summer," "Vacation Schmacation," "The Seven Habits of Highly Defective Parents" and "Training Wheels".

The essay "Romance for Dummies" was published in print and online in Mountain Home Magazine entitled as "Love Notes." It has been edited for the publication of this book.

Grateful acknowledgment is made to Brooks Permissions, Chicago IL for permission to reprint an excerpt from the poem, "The Womanhood X," from Blacks by Gwendolyn Brooks, which appears in the essay, "Exhaust the Little Moment."

"Exhaust the little moment. For soon it dies. And be it gash or gold it will not come again in this identical disguise." Reprinted By Consent of Brooks Permissions.

Caricature by Simon Ellinas.

For Mel,

My sunshine, my rock, my everything...

For Sadie, Taylor and Sara,

Forever and always, I'm so grateful to be your mom...

For *Webb Weekly*,

Thank you for having faith in me and for giving me the opportunity to author the newspaper column, *Notes from Planet Mom*...

ADDITIONAL PRAISE FOR ON MOTHERHOOD: FIREFLIES TO FIRST DATES

"Wentzel will have you nodding your head in solidarity and grinning like a fool while you read! Heartwarming and funny!" (Robin O'Bryant, NYT bestselling author of *Ketchup is a Vegetable and Other Lies Moms Tell Themselves*)

"When I'm having a challenging day at work I slip on over to Planet Mom for a break and to remember who/what is really important in my life...my family! Your site grounds me!" (Steph Kocher Skilton, New Tripoli, PA)

"(Planet Mom), I have read and enjoyed your column for years. It just really hits home for me. It's what all moms are thinking and feeling and dealing with on a daily basis. I love how straightforward and honest you are about the ups and downs and everything in between, and you make even the most boring everyday stuff hilarious! It helps us moms to know we're not the only ones!" (Sharon Steinbacher, Cogan Station, PA)

"Planet Mom is a REAL mom…the kind we all hope to be." (Ruth Fidino, Kennewick, WA)

"I can SOOOO relate to your words. I laughed out loud. Thank you for capturing the insanity we all live in…" (Brenda Holmes-Stanciu, Manitou Springs, CO)

"Parenting is an unbounded experience spanning years, a million different moments encompassing unique challenges and providing unexpected gifts. No one knows this better than Melinda Wentzel, aka Planet Mom, whose touching essays illuminate so many of these experiences." (Garrett 'Neanderdad' Rice, author of *Neanderdad*, San Mateo, CA)

"(Planet Mom), I love your easy humor. I was a huge bookworm growing up and went through a huge Erma Bombeck phase. You channel her for me." (Susan Weissman, author of *Feeding Eden*, New York, NY)

"I love Planet Mom…it's where we all live." (Lisa Novotny, Pennsylvania)

"Your words brought me back. Thanks for reconnecting me with my past." (Joanne Laverty, Glenshaw, PA)

"(Planet Mom), you rock!" (Robert Wilder, author of *Daddy Needs a Drink*, *Nickel* and *Tales From the Teachers' Lounge*, Santa Fe, NM)

"(Planet Mom), may your windows be closed and the neighbors away the next time the kids give you reason to yell." (Kelli Wheeler, author of MOMSERVATIONS ®: *The Fine Print of Parenting*, Sacramento, CA)

"(Melinda), …I discovered your writing on Planet Mom and told my husband, 'I have found a treasure chest.' Nearly every day since I have been reading, sometimes enjoying a laugh or sometimes crying. We need your column here in the *Arizona Republic*. We have not had such a heartwarming and humorous column since Erma Bombeck." (Carol Cary, Tempe, AZ)

"(Planet Mom), I love the passion with which you write…and share your personal journey." (Jodi Moore, children's author of *When a Dragon Moves In, When a Dragon Moves In Again* and *I Love My Dragon*)

CONTENTS

PREFACE

I'm not especially sure that I was meant for mothering—with all its rigors and responsibilities, and those insufferable shades of gray. Simply put, I'm just not wired for it. I much preferred being able to place chunks of my life into tidy little squares, where I could tend to them separately and manage my world at will. Becoming a mother changed all that. I learned that children don't do the tidy little square thing. In fact, they don't do the tidy little *anything*, nor are they built for confinement of any sort. I also learned that there is no logical formula in existence for raising teenagers. I only knew that I'd need to tie on my sneakers.

And as I look around at other women who were thrust into the role for one reason or another, I think, "Wow. They've really got it all together—ferrying their kids here and there without missing a beat, sprinkling their beloved charges with balanced meals and an abundance of feel-good blurbages, oozing patience and composure at every juncture in life, no matter how harried the schedule or demanding the pace." Nothing, it seems, rattles them, even when they discover one of many cruel truths of parenthood: that they don't get to choose their children's friends—a control freak's living nightmare.

They stay on top of things, too, these supermoms—like homework and school functions, birthday parties and soccer leagues—and of course, all the really important stuff like remembering ballet slippers, shin guards and library books for the right child on the right day of the week. They also recognize the importance of filling minds with wonder and lunchboxes with love. My paltry lunch pail offerings (i.e. "I love you" notes scrawled on scraps of paper and tossed in with a sandwich and crackers) are at best hastily prepared, pitifully cliché and often faded and crumpled from recycling. "Have a great day, Hon!" is pretty much all my frazzled brain is capable of churning out on the fringes of my day. The lunches themselves are dreadfully dull, too, which is perhaps a sad reminder of how horribly inadequate I sometimes feel as a mom—notes or no notes.

Indeed, motherhood is overwhelming—a seemingly insufferable, plate's-too-full collection of moments that, when taken together or viewed within the prism of the unattainable ideal, beat us into submission, the thrum of parental failure ringing in our ears. That said, there's nothing quite like comparing oneself to the façade of perfection—holding our harried selves up against those who appear to be getting it right, the moms who keep all the plates spinning as if flawless extensions of themselves.

That said, becoming a parent means accepting one's flaws. It also means a humbling loss of identity to some extent, punctuating the uncertain nature of our so-called significance in certain circles. We are simply so-and-so's mom now—maker of sandwiches, applier of sunscreen, gracious recipient of dandelions. But somehow the title feels right, as does finding a pretty vase for the dandelions.

In the pages that follow I've tried to depict my own personal journey of motherhood—a journey that I hope is as candid as it is relatable, and as heartwarming as it is edifying. Most importantly, I've shared some of what my children have taught me along the way—that extraordinary often lives deep within the ordinary, that it is the harvest of tiny moments that matters most and that the discovery of a teensy-tiny wad of paper—one that has been painstakingly folded and carefully tucked within a pocket, wedged beneath a pillow or hidden inside dresser drawer—is akin to being granted psychic powers. Everything a parent needs to know about his or her child will likely be scrawled upon said scrap of paper.

While it's true, I'm a seasoned columnist and I'd be lying if I said this wasn't immensely cathartic to write, mostly I'm just a mom, sharing her story with a community of other moms who are just trying to get through each day—moms who are wholly invested in the important business of nurturing tiny humans who will hopefully wind up being kind and compassionate individuals—moms who are grateful beyond all measure because someone on this planet calls them mom.

Planet Mom: It's where I live.

CHAPTER 1

Sweet Dreams

Sweet Dreams

Putting a child to bed at a reasonable hour has never been my forte. Okay, it's at the bottom of the list, hovering slightly above ice sculpting and changing a flat tire. Admittedly, I am pitiful when it comes to the bedtime routine thing. For me it represents yet another mommy arena in desperate need of improvement—that, and remembering to dab sunscreen on that little spot on the tops of my children's heads.

I suppose it's the chore-like feel of the whole rigmarole that gets to me. And the fact that I have to bark those tired orders each and every night like some sort of tyrant: "Brush your teeth!" "Put on your pajamas!" "Use the bathroom!" "Enough with the television already!" and "Quit fooling around in there and GO TO SLEEP!"

Quite frankly, I'm spent at that hour and I can't stand having to *work* when I'm already maxed-out on the exhaustion scale myself. But then again, mommies don't punch a time clock.

Their shifts never truly end. And downtime is nothing but a myth—unless, of course, you count the smidgen of time spent alone in the shower or those precious moments locked within the solitude of a closet, where the din cannot follow and where the world can wait until we're reunited with our marbles—yet again.

So it's nothing short of remarkable when the nightly *change* finally occurs—that indescribable transformation within me that takes place shortly after books are read, tuck ins are complete and the sandman officially arrives. Gone is the sense of urgency and frustration. Erased is the tension that once filled the air. Dulled and diluted is my shameful volatility, hissing like the air that leaves a balloon.

None of it matters now. My tiny bundles of energy and neediness are lost in the Land of Dreams. Sweet ones, I hope. No matter what the hour…no matter how sapped the day has made me…no matter how infuriated I am about the stringy clumps of whateverness forever welded to the carpet, or the pinkish yogurt drippings, still clinging like sap to the edge of the coffee table—I feel compelled to watch them as they sleep. Silent and still, at long last.

I tousle their hair, study their tender hands, now supple and yielding as they lay in mine, and soak up the trace of lavender bubble bath, lingering in those sun-streaked locks. Our breaths mingle intimately as I draw nearer to steal yet another good night kiss, awed by the peace washed over their faces and rugged little bodies. Even their pea-shaped toes are finally at rest, tucked snugly beneath their bottoms, which rise and fall with each restorative breath.

For me, each night's agenda is nearly the same: to commit to memory every minute detail—to freeze the moment in time so that I might return to it at will decades from now. The curve of their lips, their smallish frames, the warmth of their tiny fingers and the way their eyelashes lay like petals against their cheeks—these are the things I want to remember. Not how their endless chatter, unbearable bickering matches and miles of raucous galloping over hill and dale drove me berserk. And certainly not my ogreish bedtime routine. I'd like to erase that altogether—or perhaps amend it.

Watching closely, I can't help but be reminded of how they used to be; and for a wistful moment I wish they were back—needier than ever, scooching around the place, babbling on about whatever it is that babies babble on about. But I'm a realist at heart. I know there is no going back.

So as a rule I push the rewind button to review the day's events, thankful for having had those moments. I try to recall our special conversations and think of what we did together, who we saw and where we went. Of course, I dwell on the mistakes I made as a parent, and vow to be a better mommy tomorrow.

It's a promise worth keeping.

Planet Mom: It's where I live.

I've Got Those Potty-Training Blues

Exasperating. I cannot think of a single more befitting word to describe one of the most trying challenges of early parenthood, bar none. And I'm a veteran. You'd think I'd have this potty-training thing down. Nope. It's got ME down.

Lately, I've felt as though the whole ordeal has been an exercise in futility, something destined to fail from the very start. And I find little comfort in the knowledge that thousands of toddlers successfully use the bathroom each and every day. Basically, it's because my own pride and joy-bringers, otherwise known as the twin trainees, are not among this elite group—not just yet anyway.

It's certainly not for a lack of enthusiasm or know-how on their part. I've never met more eager or capable candidates— Democrat or Republican. They know WHAT to do, and perfectly well WHERE to do it. But as is often the case with campaign promises, follow-through seems to be the problem. Consistency, too.

Furthermore, it's not as though they haven't been rewarded for their achievements—limited as those instances might have been. I've encouraged. I've cheered. I've coaxed and cajoled to the nth degree. Hell, I've even resorted to bribery—and it's getting costly. We even purchased special underwear for the occasion, in hopes that favorite cartoon characters would spur them on to victory. Disappointingly, they were mild motivators at best.

What's more, I think those highly revered training pants, advertised nearly every waking moment, cost more and do less.

They're nothing more than glorified diapers. Even my toddlers know this. They're not stupid, just soggy much of the time.

It seems we've tried nearly everything, to no avail. Together we've discussed the many virtues of using the potty. "It's not as messy!" "You get to flush!" "You never have to worry about that unsightly bulge again!" Well, maybe the first two promises mean something to them—as if I were actually selling the idea. My objective is to deliver a perfectly polished sales pitch (highlighting key potty benefits) in ten seconds or less—because, of course, my audience possesses the attention span of a fruit fly. Trouble is, they're not buying. In fact, some days they don't even answer the door. Definitely two of the toughest customers I know.

We've tried reading about the topic together, too. Volumes, in fact. They know all about Prudence and her new potty (Alona Frankel), they understand and accept the idea that *Everyone Poops* (Taro Gomi) and were absolutely thrilled beyond compare to receive a book that flushes (*It's Potty Time for Girls* by Ron Berry and Chris Sharp). How ingenious. But despite it all, we've made little headway. Perhaps if Eric Carle's *Very Hungry Caterpillar* character had visited the outhouse after his colossal binging session, we'd be getting somewhere by now. It's a thought anyway.

Maybe the problem is that I expect too much. Or quite conceivably, I've been impatient with the pace of their progress, painfully slow that it's been. One thing's for certain, I'm tired of the near misses, less-than-specific aim and no-where-near-the-target doo-doo placements. No doubt, I've single-handedly kept the makers of wipes in business these past few months. Likewise, the endless treks to the bathroom to try and try again are wearing me down. By my calculations, nature calls about every eleven minutes in this household, unless fluids have been consumed—then it's a mere twenty-nine seconds.

Furthermore, the daily task of collecting soggy underwear discarded here, there and everywhere has been slightly maddening. And the living room potty-chair, (yes, LIVING ROOM potty-chair) has lost its luster—and novelty. Not to mention, it clashes horribly with our couch.

I've had it up to HERE (about a foot above my head) with the inadvertent tinklings and sprinklings—on the carpet, on the furniture and once, even on their beloved stuffed animals. Nineteen of them, in fact. I counted. "Unbelievable," was all I could manage to mutter to myself, positively too stunned to curse.

But mostly, it's the regression that gets me down. Just when the flame of hope begins to glow brightly with the promise of a new day, someone pees on it.

Figuratively speaking, of course.

Planet Mom: It's where I live.

I Flung It!

I flung it. Out the door and into the yard—for the whole blasted world to see. Yep, that's what I did. I launched it as far as any half-crazed parent who has had to deal with one too many bathroom disasters ever could fling a seven-pound rug soaked to its core. I probably set the record—for distance, for arc, for number of mid-air, end-to-end, roof-splattering rotations and quite possibly for hang time.

My husband can vouch for me. Probably neighbors too. Last night's tub-time soakfest ranks right up there with all the other ruinous pranks my infamous charges have been guilty of lately. Perhaps it wasn't as calamitous as the salt shaker incident. Nor was it as disastrous as the time we found our twin cherries buck naked and perched underneath our refrigerator water dispenser—"filling" their sandals—and the basement. But it came dangerously close. And it was certainly worthy of an exuberant rug fling.

As is always the case, I had stepped out of the room for a mere nanosecond, which was plenty of time for the duo to open the floodgates of hell. Sure, I heard plenty of splashing. Giggles and your typical garden variety of silliness, too. Even bits and pieces of their conversation filtered to my ears. It was the meat and potatoes portion of their discussion I missed, however. If only I could push the rewind button…or demand a do-over….

Now that I think of it, one of the banshees was hollering, "Mommmmmmm! She's getting me wet! She's splashing me, Mommmmm!" At the time, I thought nothing of it since I detected unmistakable glee in her tone and figured it qualified

7

as the day's forty-third episode of crying wolf. Besides, WET HAPPENS in the tub, right? Plus, the banshee thing is pretty much a given beneath THIS circus tent—especially between bath and bedtime. No red flags popped up. No little voice in my head warned me of impending doom. Even my mommy intuition failed to send a reliable signal.

It's probably faulty anyway.

Apparently, the splashee was NOT in the tub after all, but on the toilet—being repeatedly pelted (bombarded, actually) with voluminous amounts of water—HUGE CUPFULS, to be more specific. The splasher was merrily hurling round after round of punishing ammunition from her home base—the tub. Hence, the splishes, the splashes and the giggles. Good God. What a time to be oblivious.

When I finally decided to investigate, it was far, far too late. The damage had long been done. I first laid eyes on the splashee/drowned rat, who sat cowering and shivering atop the loo in a futile attempt to preserve any speck of dryness that happened to remain. The poor kid had been soaked to the bone—her matted hair lay plastered against her head and great pools of water dripped from her toes. The toilet looked as if it had survived a hurricane. I wondered how the culprit would survive *my* wrath, never mind a deluge.

"Mommy, I'm sorry I did a bad thing, but I was a fish and I had to splash and splash like this!"

I can't even begin to describe the fin-like, arm-flippy-swirly thing she demonstrated—purely for my benefit. It's amazing

I even REMEMBER what she said at all. Rage tends to cloud my memory.

It also triggers within me the urge to fling. That growing list would include completely saturated bathroom rugs or whatever items my unruly urchins happen to have destroyed. So that's precisely what I did. I yanked the seven-pound dripping mess off the floor, raced to the bottom of the stairs with it, flew past my adoring husband (who knew better than to question what I was doing), threw open our back door and...flung it.

I'll be the first to admit that it was immensely cathartic. The judges gave it a 9.7 in spite of my unorthodox approach and colorful expletives.

Planet Mom: It's where I live.

Assume Nothing When it Comes to Toy Assembly—and on Christmas Eve, Even Less

It has been said that you can tell a lot about a person simply by looking at how they handle three things in life: a rainy day, lost luggage and tangled Christmas lights. No doubt, "toy assembly" could easily be added to that list. Even more telling—toy assembly WITHOUT INSTRUCTIONS on CHRISTMAS EVE. Yep, WAY telling.

Needless to say, my husband and I learned plenty about one another last year on the night before Christmas as we struggled to remain calm despite the plight that befell us. Let's make that *volumes* we learned. Hell, it was an EDUCATIONAL FEAST.

At precisely three p.m. that day we made what could only be described as a horrifying discovery: One of the toys we had purchased—a multi-level, fifty-six-inch, 197-piece, treehouse-style doll house—had NO instructions. That's right. NONE. Zip. Zilch. Nada. We know this to be true since we nearly destroyed the box in our frantic search for said directional material, to no avail. And no matter how many times we shoved our heads inside the box, tipped it on end and meticulously examined each little packet that poured out, we were faced with the same grim reality: THERE WERE NO INSTRUCTIONS. And no amount of wishing would have made them appear, although at one point I seriously considered calling the North Pole to make a special request. I may as well have.

As one might expect, we tried contacting the store where we bought the blasted thing. No luck. It just so happened to be the last one on the shelf so we couldn't drive there to make an exchange, nor could we tear into another box to peek at the instructions. *Hey, we were desperate.* We then called the manufacturer, whose kind, caring and oh-so-compassionate answering machine wished us a politically correct "Happy Holidays!"

"Lovely—just lovely," we thought. Perhaps it's best that we didn't leave a message. It would have been ugly.

We even got online in hopes that those elusive assembly guidelines would be available for downloading. Perish the thought. Too sensible. In lieu of that, we *were* able to view photos of the wretched thing—fully assembled, I might add. All 197 pieces. Together. As one. Indivisible. Earnestly I studied that picture. Somehow it just didn't seem plausible that it had once been a jumbled mass of wooden thingies. Duct tape and/or glue *had* to have entered the picture at some point, although I was hoping they wouldn't be a part of our solution that night.

Meanwhile the clock kept ticking. We were due in church soon and after that we had tentatively planned to WRAP EVERYTHING since we live at Procrastination Central. Needless to say, using that precious time to assemble what had become a monstrosity of a toy was out of the question. It was now or never. Do or die.

So the two of us pooled our meager resources—common sense, manual dexterity, mechanical ability and patience—and met the challenge head on. After two full hours of heated debate, we emerged from the basement victorious. The monstrosity had been assembled—totally without the aid of duct tape, glue or a single marriage counselor. Unquestionably, the picture on the box had saved us. Had it not appeared there in such fine detail, I am certain that we would have been the proud owners of 197 distinct wooden thingies.

I suppose we could have presented the stupid thing unassembled, as one of those colossal gift projects. You know, "the gifts that keep on frustrating…." Granted, it might not have been completed till now, but it would have certainly lived up to its claim: PROVIDES HOURS OF ENTERTAINMENT. For sure, it would have been entertaining, but it's likely I wouldn't know as much about my spouse.

Then again, I've seen him handle tangled Christmas lights.

Planet Mom: It's where I live.

Oh, Those Pitiful Pit Stops!

There are several, all right MANY, aspects of parenting that just plain stink. Our only option: Endure the agony and pray for the ugliness to pass.

That said, much of childrearing I'd like to have skipped entirely, or at the very least, fast-forwarded through to the good parts. Currently, topping my list of not-so-favorite parental rites of passage is the fine art of instructing my preschoolers to use a public restroom. I hate it. I hate it. I hate it. I'd almost rather get on my hands and knees with a toothbrush and scrub from top to bottom the most repulsive restroom on the face of the earth than teach my kids how to use the blasted things. Undeniably, it qualifies as a dirty job and I can't stand being the somebody who has to do it. Not that my husband shirks any responsibility. He does his part by dutifully leading our little ladies to the men's room where he is often strapped with the task of explaining the purpose of a urinal. Some guys have all the luck. But it's just as difficult from where I sit. No pun intended.

First off, every public facility possesses a certain degree of grunge. I don't care if it's located in an upscale restaurant, your run-of-the-mill movie theater, a favorite campsite or in a fly-infested, weed-choked gas station where a guy named Bubba hands you a key chained to a two-by-four bearing the words, THE CAN. In my mind, they *all* register somewhere on that infamous cootie scale.

Personally, I'd rather not even think about such places, teeming with all sorts of disgusting microorganisms, littered with soggy wads of toilet tissue and paper towels and plastered with a myriad of sordid notes and numbers. As a bonus, I get to explain why such X-rated, hedonistic hieroglyphics even exist—which is tough since my charges have only recently accepted the idea that coloring on walls is NOT a good thing.

But of course, I can't help but dwell on the filth that lurks within most public restrooms—particularly knowing how Seek and Destroy (or is it Lewis and Clark) generally operate. There are toilets to touch, puddles to stomp in, faucets to fiddle with, trashcans to inspect, soaps to dribble and an entire armada of electric dryers to set off in chorus. And without question, the lure of abandoned cups, straws and gum wrappers (especially those that have been trampled upon all day) is almost too great to resist—they MUST be examined. It's no wonder I bark instructions: "Don't touch THAT!" "Don't step THERE!" "Please keep your UNDERWEAR off the FLOOR!" and my favorite, "Use more SOAP!" Porta-potties and outhouses make me bark even louder, all for naught, usually.

As if avoiding germs isn't challenging enough, I must also endure unparalleled embarrassment within such confines. The little magpies simply say and do things that are mortifying. They peek at our "neighbors" in the next stall, carry on conversations with them and have even tried to crawl under and visit once or twice. The door never stays locked (or even shut) and commentary related to bodily functions flows like a river. Of course, when anyone (even three stalls down) experiences "success," rousing cheers and applause usually follow while newcomers receive a deluge of encouragement for their efforts.

What's more, spontaneously created toilet tunes (which possess absolutely no rhyme and even less reason) fill the air, as do conversations that feature complete and utter giddiness. Heated debates take place, also—over who gets to go first, whether the clothes come off or stay on and which method of toilet paper usage is best—wadded into a giant, misshapen clump, or folded neatly into a perfect square. The jury is still out on that one.

No wonder herds of people vacate when they see us coming. Those seeking entertainment, however, pull up one of many available seats.

Planet Mom: It's where I live.

Puuuurfect Pancakes

PREPARATION TIME: Significantly longer than it takes to prepare entrée *without* a feline helper—or without assistance from children drunk with amusement over said feline and his asinine antics.

SERVES: As many poor souls who dare to partake—despite knowing all the facts.

INGREDIENTS:

> 1 cup dry pancake mix
> ¾ cup milk
> 1 T oil
> 1 egg
> Dash of saliva, eau de pussycat
> Tuft or twenty of black fur (see above)
> Trace of cat breath (don't ask)

INSTRUCTIONS: Combine dry pancake mix and milk in a bowl. Set aside on counter. Instruct children not to blow on flour-like heap or to stir clumps of milky mixture with their fingers—no matter how tempting that might be. Search high and low for oil and fresh egg, employing great care not to trip over children or ravenous cat in the process. Set egg and oil on counter and begin search for measuring spoon. Warn children (hand on hip and finger wagging is optional) not to spin or juggle egg—no matter how tempting *that* might be.

Become thoroughly engrossed in some inane activity like talking on the phone (with husband who SHOULD be home helping with dinner), checking e-mail or responding to 324th child-generated question of the day. Set table. End activities and return to pancake disaster-in-the-making. Work self into frenzy upon sighting cat on counter with head totally immersed in bowl. Throw both hands up in the air and then on top of head (hair pulling is optional) while giving children patented incredulous how-could-you-NOT-tell-me-he-was-in-the-batter?!! type of look.

Really go ballistic when eye contact is made with little black bastard, now abundantly bedecked from nose to tip of whiskers with flour/milk mixture. Begin fuming profusely from the ears when cat nonchalantly blinks and licks his lips as if to say, "It's simply marrrrrrvelous." Bolt in the direction of furry four-legged miscreant, screaming louder than when he shattered favorite butter dish and shredded children's school calendar—just because. Chase wily little demon around the house like a madwoman bent on thrashing his sorry patootie, while simultaneously launching a lengthy and colorful tirade, recounting each and every misdeed for which he was responsible and all that could have possibly been WRONG with the decision to ADOPT said cat. Kick and pummel self repeatedly for having caved to kids' begging and whining for cat, for becoming attached to his fuzzy little face in the first place and for ever thinking his ridiculous pranks were cute.

Catch breath and regain composure while dismissing feelings of utter rage and loathing toward cat. Give up on locating him for the time being. Vow to thrash him next time. Accept the fact that THERE WILL BE A NEXT TIME. Return to kitchen. Reassure ashen-faced children that you haven't killed their pretty new kitty. Instruct them not to repeat the words Mommy shouldn't have said—no matter how exciting that might be during Show and Tell.

Warm griddle or fry pan to medium-high heat or until a few drops of water sizzle upon contact—with pan *or* with furrowed brow. Remove tufts of fur from flour/milk mixture. Add remaining ingredients to bowl. Mix well. Convincingly explain that all those silly cat germs—now housed in the batter—will surely be killed once we "...put it on the stove and cook the tar out of it."

Pour batter onto heated surface (in desired shapes and sizes), ignoring children's persistent requests to "Make him one, Mommy! Make *him* one!"

SERVE & ENJOY: Resist the urge to noticeably inspect pancakes for traces of fur, etc. and deny all claims that "Mr. Binx helped us make pancakes, Mommy! I think I can smell his breath in here!"

Heaven forbid you give him that kind of satisfaction.

Planet Mom: It's where I live.

Nothing Miniature About THIS Headache

I have come to the conclusion that miniature golf just isn't my thing—at least when it comes to instructing my progenies on the finer points of proper stance, technique and etiquette. Naturally, they'd much prefer digging little holes and whacking everything in sight (read: unsuspecting patrons, each other, available flora and fauna, etc.) with those insanely impractical clubs that come up past their nipples and whose rubberized coatings do little to protect those in the line of fire—least of all, someone's teeth. They're also far more interested in messing with the funky-looking obstacles planted all over the course than in the game's so-called object. What's more, I think they get a real thrill out of asking me ridiculous questions I can't answer in public.

"Mommy, how do you know this humungous thing we have to hit it past is a boy cow and not a girl cow? It doesn't have any antlers, you know."

"That would be 'horns,' not 'antlers', and for Pete's sake can't you see its dangling…go ask your father how I know it's a boy—I mean a bull. I'm busy fishing your sister's putter out of the pond."

"Now then, let's try and gently hit the ball toward that leeetle hole waaaaaaaaaaay down there, through those teensy weensy doors on the lighthouse, over that decrepit-looking bridge and past the windmill that's spinning out of control. You can do it, Honey! I know you can!"

"But Mommy, Mommy, I *can't*! Can you help me pleeeeeeeeeeeease?" (cute head tilt, pout and irresistible puppy-dog eyes included).

This, of course, leads to what can only be described as an exercise in futility and frustration. "Okay, come stand over here…no, no on THIS side of the ball, please. What's with your feet now? Could you possibly un-cement them? Thaaaat's right, now place them shoulder-width apart. No, not *my* shoulder-width, *your* shoulder-width. Hey, don't whack that ball YET! And keep your putter down, or I'll slap you with a high sticking penalty. Switch your hands, please. No, the other way. What are they—GLUED to the silly club?! Loosen up already! It's like you've got rigor mortis or something!"

Basically what follows is that I lift and cumbersomely position each miniature duffer behind her ball—as if she were an enormous chess piece or unyielding wedge of granite—then we swing the club together with the adeptness and grace of a walrus. Correction: a one-armed walrus with a nasty slice. We then chase down the ball and repeat, until we get to within about four feet of the hole. At that point, I generally turn them loose (because I'm ready to wrap my putter around someone's neck) so that they can begin the process of wielding their clubs like hockey sticks or pool cues, depending upon the lie.

My poor husband and I are then relegated to stand by idly and watch them do whatever it takes to sink the putt, including (but not limited to) shamelessly sweeping, raking or even depositing by hand the tiny dimpled orb to which they have grown so fond. Quite frankly, I find the whole business painful to witness. And it's a fool's errand besides.

Strangely enough, it probably wouldn't be half as agonizing if we weren't golfers ourselves. Mediocre ones, mind you, but golfers just the same. Perhaps then we could gain genuine pleasure from watching our children sit in the middle of an adjacent fairway, totally oblivious to those who might like to tee off sometime this century. "Isn't that adorable, Honey; they're rolling the ball to each other." "No they're not—they're befriending those cute little ants." "Awwwww...."

Undoubtedly, we could also spare ourselves a ton of grief by dropping the idea that our lessons in etiquette actually serve some sort of purpose. Comments such as: "Stop digging trenches with that putter right now!" "Quit bouncing that ball off your sister's head!" and "Get your arm out of that paddle-wheel this instant!" would be a thing of the past. No longer would we fret over such trifles and we could simply feast on the splendor of the moment.

It's possible, I suppose. Not likely. But possible.

Then again, maybe I should just hand them hockey sticks and be done with it.

Planet Mom: It's where I live.

The Land of Kindergarten

My youngest charges start kindergarten this year—where they'll learn everything they'll probably ever need to know in this life, or so it has been stated time and again. It hardly seems possible that the time has finally arrived, given that just yesterday we were graduating from the bassinet to the crib and from primitive utterances like "Want milky!" to "I'd like a bologna and mustard sandwich with the mustard on the bologna not the bread, Mommy, 'cause it'll drip out the holes, three pickles, five black olives, some chips and an apple with no skin. Chocolate milk, too, please." My, how things have changed—only I've struggled to keep pace with those changes more than just a little.

Part of me wants them to stay right where they are—smallish and dependent, malleable and pure, curious and full of wonder, innocence and hope. No pride or prejudice to sully their paths. No real world influences to crush their spirits. Safe and sound in this tiny corner of the globe called home. Maybe that same part of me is reluctant to embrace the whole growing up thing because the world no longer feels cozy or warm, much less— familiar. Or perhaps it's because the future seems uncertain at times, for all of us—or because I can't imagine anything more vulnerable than a kindergartener.

Quite conceivably though, I cling to what is and what was because they'll be the last to leave the nest—marching forward on that infamous quest for knowledge and independence. Lunch boxes in hand. Bus numbers memorized. Sponge-like minds ready and willing to soak up all there is to know, and then some.

Ready or not, however, that big, yellow beast-of-a-thing will soon come lumbering up the hill and around the bend, its tired engine groaning all the way to our stop. It'll then whisk my beloved cherubs away to the Land of Kindergarten—the place where they've longed to be ever since they laid eyes on the cool monkey bars and the "...toilet that's just our size!" At least two somebodies I know are eager for the transition.

In all honesty—me too—at least to a degree. I admit I'll probably do something outlandish when the time finally arrives—after the tears and irrational fears subside, of course. This memorable occasion certainly deserves some sort of formal commemoration—like a toast or a few thousand cartwheels across the lawn. It's not every day that one becomes reacquainted with his or her long lost liberties, doused with more freedom and autonomy than one who has spent the better part of five years cooped up with a couple of wily imps can reasonably handle. So I suppose I should recognize and fully appreciate the moment.

It'll be grand for sure, and I'm quite certain I won't know how to act—at first anyway. But I'll get the hang of it. Really, I will. Except when I'm sick with worry—about them getting left behind on the bus, trampled by a herd of first graders or lost within an endless maze of corridors. Or worse yet, they'll get hurt on those blasted monkey bars—with no one to kiss the boo-boos. It's what moms do best. That, and worry too much.

Anxieties aside, the year ahead should be a wonderful experience for all of us, and one that I'm sure we'll treasure for a long time to come. So let the adventures begin—to the Land of Kindergarten and beyond!

Rest assured, I was a kindergartener once myself—so there's at least a glimmer of hope that I'll be able to keep pace.

Planet Mom: It's where I live.

The Saint

Our school bus driver has a secret life—according to our vastly imaginative kindergarteners anyway. Who knew?

"Where's your regular bus driver," I probed one afternoon as they clambered down those Godzilla-sized steps—the ones better suited for Gulliver than for my ungainly Lilliputians. Then again, I load them up like a couple of pack mules every morning and make them wear snappy new sneakers over which they trip roughly fourteen times an hour. It's no wonder they have trouble getting on and off that big, yellow beast-of-a-thing.

As we crossed the road and began hiking through the lawn together, I inquired again, "So where is she? Do you know what happened to her?"

"She likes to go on *dates*," Child #1 whispered with a smirk and a sidelong glance at the bus.

"Oh reeeeeeeeally," I commented, stuffing a sleeve in my mouth so as to stifle the spillage of chortles. "*Dates*, huh?"

"Yeah, Mommy," Child #2 added. "She said she had an *outbreak*."

"An *outbreak*?!" I asked completely puzzled now, but more intrigued than ever. "What sort of *outbreak* did she have?" (I was afraid even to think.)

"Well, maybe it was a *breakout*, Mommy. Yeah, it was a BREAKOUT," she explained further.

Instantly I envisioned this poor woman revisiting adolescence, giddy and pimply all rolled into one.

"A breakout you say?" I pressed further, going for that staid and genuinely concerned look I've been honing ever since they started sharing with me really important stuff—like which six-year-olds they intend to marry and how soon they plan to visit the moon. "Wow, a *breakout*, huh? Sounds serious."

"Yep, a breakout…I think…or maybe it was a *break*. Yeah, she said she needed a BREAK one time when we asked her why she wasn't our bus driver that day that Bus Driver Bob forgot to stop at our stop and all the kids screamed and screamed until he finally stopped." (A day which will live in infamy….)

"So your bus driver needed a *break*?" I offered tentatively.

"Yeah," they both chimed in. "She gets tired of just sitting and sitting. Sometimes she needs a break so she goes home and does stuff and then Bus Driver Bob brings us home."

"Well, that explains it," I agreed, happy to have been enlightened for the 467th time that day. Who wouldn't need a break from my two magpies now and then? The woman deserves a medal—or at the very least, to be sainted. In my humble opinion, she possesses more patience than six people ought to. Translation: I could never drive a school bus. Never. She tolerates all sorts of weirdness too—like my propensity to videotape and photograph nearly every Kindergarten Moment involving my children and the silly bus. Climbing on the bus. Off the bus. Walking toward the bus. Away from the bus. And most recently…SLEEPING on the bus. Couldn't resist that one. Of course, she kindly invited me aboard to preserve the moment for posterity. Or maybe she just wanted me to hurry up and haul my drooling, sweat soaked charges and their eighty-pound backpacks away. Far away.

Further, she-who-should-be-sainted also graciously accepts each and every "gift" those gregarious creatures in question bestow upon her—to include rocks, handfuls of gravel, wet leaves, twigs and to date, a plethora of drawings and indecipherable notes. Like I said, the woman's a saint. She just smiles and quietly tucks them away in a pocket or on the dashboard. Always grateful. Never rushed. Mindful at all times of their feelings. Forever interested in their beloved offerings—which is more than I can say much of the time. *There are just so many wilted dandelions and speckled leaves I can take in one lifetime.*

But not her. Nope. My guess is that she'll continue to warmly receive each and every useless bit of tripe that my charges hand her till doomsday—thereby brightening their days and making a difference in their world. A world in which many have forgotten how important it is just to be nice. How refreshing and comforting it is to know that one such individual is out there day in and day out, delivering that invaluable message to *my* beloved offerings—and, no doubt, to scores of others'.

Thanks, Helen.

Planet Mom: It's where I live.

The Learning Curve

Well, we made it through those first crucial weeks of kindergarten. Ten days. Two hours. And sixteen minutes. But who's counting? No one was abandoned on the bus, abducted by aliens, locked in a closet or swallowed by a third grader. By all accounts, the transition proceeded quite smoothly, aside from our collective exhaustion. Although it could just be that their tiny bodies are still in a state of shock and their brains haven't fully processed the information. Had the proper processing occurred, they might then realize that THEY SHOULD BE MISSING MOMMY MORE. Way more. Instead, they're off each day making friends, kibitzing in the hallways and doing all sorts of fun stuff with scissors, glue and "smelling-good markers"—three things I'd have banished from the curriculum till Jr. High if it were up to me.

In essence, *I'm* the one who has an array of adjustment issues. At times, I'm a pitiful creature who suffers needlessly and miserably with the pangs of separation—the I-miss-my-kids-even-though-they-make-me-crazy sort of malady. But I expected as much. At least in the beginning. I worry about this, that and the other stupid thing, driving myself insane in the process. My husband can readily attest: "Hey, don't pack hot dogs in their lunches! Don't you know their friends will make them laugh and they'll choke to death?!" Like I said, he can attest to the ridiculous nature of my concerns.

Maybe the term ridiculous isn't adequate. I watch the clock more than I'd care to admit, flip through the television channels pausing wistfully on their favorite programs and wonder what they're doing at noon and at one o'clock and again at two-thirty. Confession: I wonder what my little urchins are doing from the instant the bus rounds the bend and fades from view in the morning until it reappears in the afternoon with dozens of tiny faces pressed against the glass, wordlessly revealing what the day had brought to each and every rider.

Quite frankly, my curiosity gets the best of me. More than once I've fought the urge to stuff myself inside a backpack and tag along for the day. Safely tucked away, I could spy without ever being discovered—shamelessly satisfying my desire to know what really goes on in the life of a kindergartener. Oh, to eavesdrop on their conversations over the course of a day. I can't imagine anything more telling—or delicious. Of course, imagining is about all I can do at this point—because thus far they've been less than cooperative in the information-sharing arena.

Maybe it's because I'm viewed as an outsider now—a meddlesome mommy with a hidden agenda. Or maybe it's because they're veritable zombies when they first get home, stunned by the tsunami-sized day they probably had. "Mommy, you ask too many questions. I just don't want to talk right now." So we empty backpacks in the middle of the kitchen floor, together sifting through the day's artifacts—my only clues as to what went on there in the Land of Kindergarten. And from what I can gather, most of it is good—which makes me feel good.

There are half-eaten lunches and prized drawings, books and crafty things galore "...that we made all by ourselves!" and strange-looking tidbits of memorabilia stashed away for keeps—like the pebble "...I tucked inside my sock so I could add it to my collection, Mommy" and "...the penny I found on the floor today!"

But there are tears, too, in the telling of "Mommy, I missed you so I cried a little bit," and the bumps and bruises and behemoth-sized bandages with which skinned knees were patched—lovingly, I might add. "The nurse is really nice and she gave me this be-U-tiful brown bandage! I'm leaving it on for-EVER!" Three days certainly came close.

And there are warm remembrances too. "I love my bus driver... and the girl in the yellow shirt with blonde hair helped me find the nurse's office...and the tall girl with purple butterflies on her shirt hugged me so I'd stop missing you at lunchtime...and my teacher always makes me feel all better, Mommy."

Maybe this transition thing is going even better than I thought. As for me, I'm still on the learning curve wagon, trying to figure it all out and get over myself besides.

Planet Mom: It's where I live.

CHAPTER 2

Nooks and Crannies

It's the Great Pumpkin, Charlie Brown!

I've often thought that the art of raising children is a lot like carving a pumpkin. In both instances, I brought home a rotund little bundle of neediness, fumbling and stumbling over myself just to get it out of the car and safely inside. I then set it down, took a step back and stared—marveling at its inherent uniqueness and at its wealth of complexities, most of which I had yet to discover. A *"Now* what?" comment fell from my lips shortly thereafter as I contemplated my next move. Anxiously I paced the floor, studying this newish thing from every angle imaginable—careful not to overlook so much as a dimple or a distinctive feature upon its ruddy face. I then wrestled endlessly with self-doubt and indecision, fully and completely acknowledging the challenges that lay ahead.

At once, I also considered the endless potential this wonder of wonders possessed, pondering the remarkable role I would undoubtedly play in the days to come. I prayed for insight and wisdom, and for the ability to make its spirit glow and its face shine brighter than bright. I loved and nurtured it unconditionally, shaped and molded it tenderly yet purposefully, pouring forth every single ounce of knowledge, creativity and patience I could muster, in hopes that one day my little *pumpkin* would stand on my doorstep straight and tall, illuminating my world forevermore—a beacon in the night for all who would pass.

But no one ever told me there would be muck in the middle—a slippery, slimy mass of gloppage with which I have had to contend, time and again, in order to move forward. My hands don't lie. They've been mired deep within this monstrous task for an eternity. And it shows. I am worn and weary, doused with sticky remnants of the chore. There have been a multitude of tricky corners to navigate with precision and grace, and unforeseen lumps and bumps to address along this winding path of growth and development. Countless hours have been spent scooping out and whittling away that which is undesirable and stubbornly rooted—the gunk that would surely detract from inner beauty.

Desperately, I have sought the counsel of others. I've searched long and hard for guidance—for some sort of pattern to follow so that I could avoid a minefield of mistakes and make the right impression in the end. Heaven forbid I mismanage so much as a solitary stroke of my efforts.

What I find both completely frustrating and strangely wonderful about the whole process, however, is that despite the planning and the commitment and the intensity with which I have approached it all, the end result is virtually unknown until I lay down my tools, step back from my work and light the flame within. Only then will I learn how well I've done my job—when my pumpkinish creation stands before me, glowing on its own amidst a sea of ink. Mere glimpses of what will be are all I have been afforded along the way. But glimpses, nonetheless.

Happy Halloween to all those makers of little jack-o'-lanterns, whose work is truly a labor of love and whose efforts are worthy of high praise—regardless of the outcome.

Planet Mom: It's where I live.

Juggling Act

I'm not especially sure that I was meant for mothering—with all its rigors and responsibilities, and those insufferable shades of gray. Simply put, I'm just not wired for it. I much preferred being able to place chunks of my life into tidy little squares, where I could tend to them separately and manage my world at will. Becoming a mother changed all that. I learned that children don't do the tidy little square thing. In fact, they don't do the tidy little *anything*, nor are they built for confinement of any sort. I also learned that there is no logical formula in existence for raising teenagers. I only knew that I'd need to tie on my sneakers.

And as I look around at other women who were thrust into the role for one reason or another, I think, "Wow. They've really got it all together—ferrying their kids here and there without missing a beat, sprinkling their beloved charges with balanced meals and an abundance of feel-good blurbages, oozing patience and composure at every juncture in life, no matter how harried the schedule or demanding the pace." Nothing, it seems, rattles them, even when they discover one of many cruel truths of parenthood: that they don't get to choose their children's friends—a control freak's living nightmare.

They stay on top of things, too, these supermoms—like homework and school functions, birthday parties and soccer leagues—and of course, all the really important stuff like remembering ballet slippers, shin guards and library books for the right child on the right day of the week. They also recognize the importance of filling minds with wonder and lunchboxes with love. My paltry lunch pail offerings (i.e. "I love you" notes scrawled on scraps of paper and tossed in with a sandwich and crackers) are at best hastily prepared, pitifully cliché and often faded and crumpled from recycling. "Have a great day, Hon!" is pretty much all my frazzled brain is capable of churning out on the fringes of my day. The lunches themselves are dreadfully dull, too, which is perhaps a sad reminder of how horribly inadequate I sometimes feel as a mom—notes or no notes.

Occasionally I fail to summon the humor and flexibility needed to approach such an impossible task, as well as the wisdom to accept that some battles as a parent just aren't worth fighting—especially those that involve six-year-olds and mashed potatoes or teenagers and five-year plans. "Let it go," I need to remind myself again and again. Certainly, there are more important issues with which to concern myself—like the beefy toad I found on the coffee table recently, warts and all. And the mouse-tail stew that had apparently been concocted in the garage/laboratory and subsequently smuggled into the kitchen. God only knows how long it had been brewing there and what other bits of foulness had been added to the stagnant pool of repulsiveness. Color me oblivious, yet again.

Kidding aside, I'd like to know how other moms do it. How do they keep all the balls in the air? All those plates spinning—as if flawless extensions of themselves? Maybe it has something to do with my multitasking skills—or lack thereof. Simply put, I stink in that category—which contributes greatly, I think, to the whole woefully-inept-mommy thing. Over the years, I've been forced to develop just enough juggling proficiency to get by—enough to get me through a day's worth of kid-related chaos to include the morning frenzy to catch the bus and the after-school circus, when backpacks are emptied, bellies are filled and the air is inundated with multiple conversations, all of which I am expected to attend to meaningfully. The homework gig is yet another monstrous challenge for my sorry set of skills, mostly because I try to do everything SIMULTANEOUSLY. Because that's what moms do best—at least the good ones, equipped with a multitasking gene.

I'm sure much of the ugliness would go away if I were capable of turning off or at least filtering the noise in my head so that I could focus on each task individually—instead of trying to absorb and act upon everything that floats across my radar screen. I'm doing one thing perhaps—like driving the kids to ballet, but I'm thinking about the last six things I've done, critiquing myself to death in the process, while catapulting forward to the next seventeen things I will do before bed, all the while fielding inane questions like "How can people buy invisible dog fences if nobody can see them, Mom?"

It's no wonder that I sometimes wind up at the soccer field curious as to why my kids are wearing tutus and not cleats.

Planet Mom: It's where I live.

Hari-Kari is Just a Phone Call Away

I hope that by the time my youngest kids enter college, I will have had at least one phone conversation in their presence completely devoid of alleged bathroom-related calamities, deafening and mysterious crashes in the living room and assorted brawls over squirt guns, sand shovels and completely idiotic stuff like who gets the cereal bowl with the dinosaurs on it. Just one measly—yet gloriously uninterrupted—phone conversation. That's all I ask.

Sadly, I doubt that day will be arriving anytime soon. The elfin creatures in question are far too needy. I can tell because they still yank on me relentlessly and/or attach themselves to my appendages on occasion (usually a leg), forcing me to hobble around the place with a phone wedged under my chin and one or more barnacle-like children cemented just below the knee.

What's more, there are thousands upon thousands of ridiculous this-just-can't-wait-till-Mom-gets-off-the-phone types of questions that they evidently feel compelled to pose. And just when I think I've responded sufficiently to the last, "Mom, can you get chickenpox from touching chickens?" type of query, another follows closely on its heels. "What do clouds taste like, Mommy?" And another, "Why can't they just call saliva 'drool'? I know what *drool* is, Mom."

None of it, apparently, can wait until I hang up. Answers to those innumerable and impossible questions must be provided without delay. Hence, my frustration and colorful tirades. "Unless your hair is on fire or you've fallen into the toilet up to your armpits, don't BUG me when I'm on the phone!! Understood?!"

Naturally, their responses often do nothing but frustrate me more. "Mommy, how come my hair would be on fire?" Good grief.

Likewise, it seems that there is a vat of earth-shattering news that must be reported to me immediately or sooner each time I pick up the horn. For instance: Did I know that so-and-so got a wicked nosebleed in gym class today or that another so-and-so threw up in the cafeteria (and he had PIZZA, Mom!) or that yet another so-and-so lost a tooth on the bus?! And was I even aware that our birdie friend who crashed into the window moments ago made a full recovery and is no longer flopping around like a fish?! Surely, this qualifies as vital information without which I would be doomed.

Interestingly, I have been able to make fairly accurate predictions with regard to specific wants and needs that occur within my household while I'm on the phone. I can almost guarantee that within the duration of any conversation involving said device, someone's shoes will need to be tied, a request for a glass of chocolate milk will be made or an emphatically delivered statement such as, "Mommy, come quick and make the cat stop eating his vomit!" will find my ears. Joy.

I often wonder what the people on the other end must think. It can't be good. They probably peg me as one of those high-strung helicopter parents with a propensity for shrieking at the slightest hint of domestic turmoil. Or as a pushover who allows her charges to run amuck day and night and to forage for candy before dinner.

Quite frankly, I don't know how my mom ever managed. Her calls must have been rife with the same sort of maddening little interruptions for years; although she had a phone cord to deal with, too—an unruly, anaconda-like twisted piece of coated wire that not only tied her to the general vicinity of the kitchen and swept lamps and such onto the floor, but also lured curious cats and toddlers who found the whirly, twirly wonder to be fascinating. At least I can flee the mayhem and lock myself in a closet if need be. Don't laugh. I've been there on more than one occasion. Ostensibly, it is the most perfect hideout on the planet, serving as a great refuge for frazzled parents.

Oddly enough, that's what a *phone* is supposed to do.

Planet Mom: It's where I live.

Nooks and Crannies

Killing time is a completely foreign concept to my children. Completely. Foreign. It's absurd actually—to think they'd deliberately destroy or somehow devalue so much as a solitary second of that delicious commodity. Quite frankly, it's unthinkable. To them, the notion of being granted an extra nugget of time on this wonder-filled planet—whether measured in minutes, hours or days—is like stumbling upon a package that's been shoved behind a thicket of boughs under a Christmas tree, all but forgotten, waiting to be discovered, brimming with endless possibility. It's a gem through and through, and wasting its sparkle is simply not an option. Not for them, anyway. Time is far too dear.

Even the sandman encroaches upon their beloved daily allotment. "But Mommy, if I go to sleep, I'll miss something." I suppose he encroaches upon everyone's share of the pie to some degree—as does the host of responsibilities we cram into each slice, almost without thinking. Oddly enough, some of us actually *believe* that if we scrawl the details of upcoming events into a bunch of little squares and then prominently display them on our refrigerators, we can, in fact, attend said events. All of them. Even the ones that overlap, are insignificant or are logistically impossible.

Without question, harried schedules breed harried lives. No surprise there. Jammed calendars and bulging-at-the-seams planners are nothing new under the sun. People have been trying to stretch days and squeeze every last drop from the Almighty Clock for eons. It's practically a national pastime. Going here. Going there. Doing this. Doing that. All at a horrendous pace. We joke about being overburdened with obligations as a way of life, casually sharing our collective plight at dinner parties and picnics. Just for fun, we compare notes and then award prizes to those who, ostensibly, are three barbecues, two reunions and one kid-themed birthday party short of complete lunacy. When all is said and done, precious few pockets of time remain—time that isn't already spoken for.

Interestingly, it's those unclaimed gaps that my kids truly relish, the time wedged between rigidly structured events and penciled-in plans—the nooks and crannies of life. Like those priceless moments spent at the bus stop each morning, where they pass the time without so much as a hint of boredom or complaint. Sometimes we read. Sometimes we talk. Sometimes we chase snowflakes and leaves, other times—woolly caterpillars and hapless ants. Sometimes we huddle together under an umbrella, with soggy shoes and drippy noses or battle the biting winds and subzero temps of January, snuggling ever closer, our breaths mingling in the frigid air. Even still, the time is thought to be rich and delicious.

It's the same scenario in the waiting rooms of our doctor and dentist, at the supermarket checkout, in line at the bank and while gnarled in traffic. In restaurants, while fiddling with spoons and drawing silly pictures of giraffes and elephants on our napkins and placemats. Before the sun sets, the fireflies fill the night sky with yellowish flickers of light and the fireworks begin at long last. And in the theater, during that eternal block of time before the lights dim and the film finally starts, when we consume a hefty portion of our popcorn and soda—that's when we share secrets, giggle just because and make memories that last. Whiling away the hours at Grandma's viewing three weeks ago was no exception.

I have no doubt that she would have been pleased to see them whirling about the church parlor in their fluffy dresses, weaving colorful stories with their dolls, completely absorbed in the world of make-believe as they held their tiny horses and made them gallop gently across the backs of cushiony pews— just being kids. Taking advantage of yet another opportunity to seize the day—words their grandmother lived by, and died fulfilling. Words that perhaps were an inspiration to do more than just kill time—but to savor it—especially those nooks and crannies.

Planet Mom: It's where I live.

Organized Chaos

I must have rocks in my head—or something pebble-ish anyway—to think that it made perfect sense to sign up my kids for an organized sport even before they could blow their own noses. Clearly, I had been playing "the assumption game" at the time, which is precisely why I was able to entertain such a ridiculous notion in the first place.

Case in point: I *assumed* my charges were capable of grasping at its most elementary level the object of the game of basketball. I *assumed* they inherently possessed (or could readily acquire) enough drive and determination to compete with other smallish creatures who, likewise, tend to dawdle for days on end. Furthermore, I *assumed* they'd each embrace the idea of being a team player, that they could take direction at least as well as a piece of driftwood and that they could concentrate for more than seventeen seconds at a time. I also *assumed* that they could (and would) refrain from playing *London Bridges* at half-court during a game.

I couldn't have been more delusional in my thinking had I tried.

Snippets of conversation at the last game went something like this: "Yes, those are my two cherubs out there and yes, it does appear as though they are playing *London Bridges*."

"No, I didn't teach them to do that." I *wanted* to say, "No, you fool! Can't you see I'm dying of embarrassment here?! Stop telling me how giddified and cute my children are. I know they're giddified and sometimes they're cute—just not now. Their *father* is the wired one. Go ask him about *London*

Bridges, *Duck, Duck Goose* or whatever else strikes your fancy. I'll be over here hiding behind the scoreboard."

Let's face it; the whole concept of organized sports for the five-and-under set is just plain ludicrous. It's got oxymoron slathered all over it. Sure it's great for making friends and developing those much-heralded social skills. And it's particularly beneficial with regard to improving fitness levels, building upon gross motor coordination and establishing healthy lifestyle habits. But when it comes right down to it, expecting a motley crew of nose-miners to understand the overall point of a particular sport—as well as to perform as a cohesive unit for what seems like an eternity—is like asking a pile of glitter to get back in the bottle. Most of the uniformed Lilliputians in question are about as organized and disciplined as a bunch of gnats.

By and large, kids at this stage are a little more distracted than many of us are probably willing to admit—especially during that all-important game-time. They're into whirling and twirling around in circles till they collapse, racing and chasing end to end with arms outstretched and hair blowing in the breeze, building towers with water bottles on the sidelines and stopping on a whim just to hug someone or to lug them around the court "…because I'm really strong, Mom!"

Of course they gallop, too. And skip. But you knew that.

It's not because the coaches have failed them—or us. Day in and day out those heroic men and women do all that is humanly possible to bring order to the chaos that lurks deep within each and every little imp placed in their care. They quell disturbances, tie shoes, wipe noses and tears, reassure moms and dads, boost morale and harness the boundless enthusiasm and energy each child brings to the table. Anyone who volunteers for such a position deserves to be sainted forevermore. At the very least they should receive a T-shirt emblazoned with the words: I Coach Kids Who'd Rather Be Playing with Their Trucks, Therefore I Am.

All that aside, I should have known better when the sign-up sheet was thrust under my nose. I've traveled this path before. T-Ball was the culprit some thirteen years ago when I decided my kindergartner ought to be wearing a glove and wielding a big bat like everyone else. All those skinned knees and grass stains had to be good for something, right? Why else would droves of parents (obviously thrilled to the core) hang on the fences and stand in the bleachers cheering for their children?

To watch 'em pick dandelions and dig in the dirt, of course. Some things never change.

Planet Mom: It's where I live.

The Warm Fuzzies

As I write this, the promise that Christmas Day holds for my family has yet to be realized. The halls are decked and our stockings now hang—empty, yet pregnant with hope. The mistletoe waits patiently, as does the tree, aglow with the holiday spirit of all who helped trim it. The doors open wide to welcome family and friends who will soon come to call. Notes to Santa have been carefully crafted, plans for preparing his feast of sugary treats have been finalized and last minute wishes have been whispered ever-so-earnestly in his ear.

I can only imagine the warmth I'll feel come Christmas morning. Or during Holy Communion the night before, moved by the wonderment and intimacy surrounding the event. Like every other year in the time leading up to Christmas Day, I am still deeply immersed in this tide of tides, wrapped up in all that the season embodies—hope, remembrance and the spirit of unconditional giving.

As you read this, that special day has already passed. The time has since come and gone. But hopefully some semblance of the warmth lingers—like that of a sun baked stone, long after the shadows of evening have consumed it.

I think that's what matters most to me this time of year— that the warmth of the Yuletide continues beyond December and well into the new year, despite the blazing crescendo- type ending defined by our calendars and the torrent of post- holiday sales. Moreover, I want the same for my family. I want the true spirit of Christmas to endure in their hearts at least till the Canada geese return, if not longer. But that's a particularly tall order these days. Society demands that we charge swiftly forward to the next major holiday or seasonal event, paying no mind to that which has already passed. "Sift through the remnants of chintzy cologne and bedroom slippers already, and move on to heart-shaped boxes of chocolates! Valentine's Day is just around the corner!" advertisers would likely suggest.

I'd prefer to linger here awhile, however, to soak up the goodness that surrounds me and to delay the crushing finality of it all, which hits me squarely like a sack of sadness as I pack up the ornaments and good cheer—shoving them deep in the recesses of my attic, forsaking both for a time. That's what I hate most about the holiday—and about myself. The warmth, it seems, is only temporary. Maybe that's why I adopted a silly little tradition of giving each of my children fuzzy pajamas for Christmas—to remind us of the warmth of that morning, of that season, of the people in our lives.

Maybe I do it because I sometimes feel as if it's the only way I can fight the almighty clock. At least symbolically, I can wrap my beloved charges in a cottony embrace and hold on to them—today and always—or at least until they outgrow my fleecy offerings. But I can always buy more. Larger and perhaps trendier versions of the same thing. Year after year, for decades theoretically. And whether they sport reindeer, or snowflakes or elves with stupid-looking hats matters little. In my mind, a snuggly pair of PJs will forever be considered a gift worth giving and worthy of receiving, despite the chorus of gripes and grumbles my motley crew is sure to deliver.

"Mom, you gave us jammies—AGAIN!" the youngest ones will grouse. "How lame," my twenty-something will likely protest.

"Pshaw! (You ungrateful twerps) I gave you something of boundless value—something that shouts 'I love you!' from the hilltops—something that captures the true essence of the warm fuzzies! What on earth could be better?!"

Of course, this was—and continues to be—a rhetorical question.

Planet Mom: It's where I live.

The Twelfth of Never

My refrigerator is the center of my universe, the heart and soul of my very being and without question, the hub of all that defines my world. Not because of the mince pie, Jack cheese and leftover potato salad contained within. But because of the Almighty Calendar that hangs on its shiny surface—eye-level, next to the school lunch menu, surrounded by tiny scraps of paper upon which I scrawled phone numbers I need to know but will never remember. And like a lot of well-worn items in my household, it looks as though it belongs there—wedged comfortably between favorite photos, prized artwork, a colorful array of magnetic letters A to Z and those all-important memos and appointment cards without which I would most certainly shrivel up and die.

Each perfect square on that grand and glorious grid of events represents a chunk of precious time. And it must—I repeat, it MUST—have something scribbled within it. Someone's birthday. A holiday mealtime. A veterinary appointment. An eye exam. New tires for the car. A vacation destination. A reminder to return the kids' library books. Something. Anything. Except nothingness—which would imply a sort of nothingness about me, I suppose, or perhaps that downtime actually exists in my harried world. Perish the thought.

There are swimming lessons, birthday parties and play rehearsals to attend. Basketball games, haircuts and doctors' visits galore. Empty blocks simply do not reflect the reality that is mine. Besides, the voids make me feel guilty—as if I have nothing better to do than sit around and watch bits and pieces of modeling clay dry and crumble while the kids are at school. Calendars crammed to capacity with details of this or that planned affair give me a real sense of purpose, of direction, of connectedness with the outside world—linking me to all the goings-on I have chosen to include (willingly or not). And they provide a healthy dose of structure and truckloads of predictability, too—both of which are sorely lacking beneath this circus tent. In sum, calendars bring a smattering of order to my otherwise disordered world. I shudder to think where I'd be without mine—mired in some muddled state till the twelfth of Never, no doubt.

Some days the world simply spins too fast for me (as my friend, Ruth, has so often quipped). Nothing could be closer to the truth. But my oh-so-wonderful, tangible timeline-on-the-fridge helps me hold it all together, to keep everything in its proper perspective and to effectively answer questions like, "What are you doing next Tuesday the sixteenth?"

Quite frankly, I wouldn't have a clue unless and until I consulted the calendar. At least I know my limitations—one of which involves not straying too far from the Master Schedule. Another: writing small enough so that everything is neatly and completely contained within its designated block—an impossible task to say the least.

But I love calendars, despite my personal limitations in dealing with them. I especially enjoy receiving a crisp, new one for Christmas (a traditional wish list item in this household) and spending a lazy afternoon in January slathering its pristine little blocks with all sorts of important dates and times to remember. Every syllable precisely placed, of course. Even more thrilling: adorning my organizational wonder with cool reminder stickers that are sometimes included as a bonus. I'm quite certain that for a day or two following said ritual, I fool a myriad of individuals into believing that I'm impeccably organized. Even *I* believe it for a time, until that dastardly interloper with whom I reside adds *his* appointments, meetings and countless other chicken scratchings to the revered framework I so meticulously and thoughtfully crafted.

Shortly thereafter, the frenzied pace of the world returns and information starts spilling from those neat and tidy little squares into the narrow margins. Stuff gets scribbled out or transferred to other squares in haphazard fashion and big, ugly arrows are drawn across what was once an unsullied masterpiece of time management—which is a lot like life, I suppose.

It's subject to change.

Remarkably, most of us manage to muddle through the madness with a few reroutings and derailments here and there, which builds character, I'm told. Maybe that's what makes the month-by-month journey worth journeying—even if it's just to the fridge.

Planet Mom: It's where I live.

The Grass is Always Greener Somewhere Else

Practically every kid on the planet has done each of the following at some point during his or her tenure: marred something of immeasurable value with an impossible-to-remove substance, tried flushing something that's decidedly unflushable and/or threatened to run away from home for one seemingly absurd reason or another. Of course, the world is full of overachievers in this particular realm, as many will attest to having surpassed the gold standard of misguided behavior. I am no exception.

My guess is that much of what kids do stems from an unquenchable thirst for information and a great longing for independence. Further, I'd surmise that much of their internal dialogue begins with phrases like, "I wonder what would happen if..." and includes impassioned statements like, "If I were king, there'd be no more...bedtimes, baths, rules, etc. like at so-and-so's house."

Indeed, the grass is always greener somewhere else.

Back in 1970, I for one believed it to be so—just two doors down, in fact. A lovely couple, whose children were long since grown, lived there in a quaint little brick house with a sprawling back yard and the most enormous shade trees I had ever known. That's where my four-year-old brother and I found George and Bernice, in the haze of mid-summer— lolling in cavernous chairs when day was done, enjoying what breeze could be summoned as the sun inched toward the horizon, watching and waiting as the shadows lengthened and the crickets prepared for their nightly symphony.

Invariably, she'd wear a light, cottony dress with a floral pattern and generous pockets for clothespins and whatnot. He wore woolen pants, a plain, white t-shirt and work boots. Suspenders sometimes, too. Cookies were involved, as I recall, as was lemonade. There were countless treks through their garage, their magnificent garden as well as their home because, of course, it was their pride and joy and they seemed genuinely pleased to show us every inch of the place—from the cavernous ceramic sink in the kitchen to its stiflingly hot, yet obscenely tidy, attic. *God, I loved that attic and could picture myself living there comfortably—heat or no heat.*

All the while we learned where each knickknack came from, who was pictured in the portraits on the walls, the make and model of their extraordinarily well-cared-for car (an Olds, I think) and how to keep rabbits from nibbling at lettuce. But mostly, we sat under the tall trees and talked. Their aging beagle, Lady, that hobbled even more than they did, stayed close. Cool grass and good company were precious commodities. Even my brother and I knew that. Especially on the days we packed our bags and ran away from home— frustrated beyond words with our parents, fed up completely with this or that perceived injustice, eager to find something better under someone else's roof. George and Bernice's seemed just fine.

Oddly enough, they tolerated our gripes and grumbles. They listened intently as we told of the insufferable nature of living in a home where an eight-year-old might be expected to take out the trash or set the table from time to time. They nodded understanding and offered quiet solace as we voiced our rage against the powers that be. But they had to have been laughing inside—remembering a time when their own children had run away, hauling lumpy sleeping bags and peanut butter sandwiches across the neighborhood.

Looking back I now see the tours and the talks for what they truly were—cleverly implemented diversionary tactics, designed to defuse our anger and redirect our attention. They were just neighbors being neighborly. Givers of guidance. An instrument of good.

Time and again, my tag-along brother and I wised up and headed home. Darkness was encroaching, mosquitoes had begun to bite and our dear companions, fear and worry, had come calling. *Would those who had helped us pack actually search for us?* Besides, I missed my dog and it was soon time for our favorite television shows.

Indeed, it was time to admit defeat and return to the home we knew best—although it was fun to taste a bit of independence and to partake of the seemingly greener pastures just two doors down.

Planet Mom: It's where I live (bracing for the infamous I'm-gonna-run-away phase).

Trial by Fire

I should have listened to the little voice inside my head—the one that warned of impending doom as it relates directly to slumber parties and other foolishness to which parents subject themselves voluntarily. But proving yet again that my idiocy knows no bounds, I barreled ahead, boldly making plans for four giddified first graders to join Seek and Destroy in celebrating their seventh birthday. "With any luck," I thought, "I'll want them to see their eighth birthday."

Clearly, I had been stricken stupid in the process. At the very least, I had experienced a weak moment (read: I caved) as evidenced by my willingness to proclaim to my beloved charges, "Alright already. You can have a sleepover. On your birthday." And with those seemingly innocuous words, I had sealed my fate.

What a creampuff.

I then spent roughly two light years devising what I believed would be the treasure-hunt-to-end-all-treasure-hunts, complete with catchy little rhymes, a bevy of thought-provoking clues and a clever ploy for getting even the ditsiest of participants to work as a team instead of the warring factions they would likely become. Silly me. The whole thing was over in less than twelve minutes with little or no fanfare—aside from the rapture the girls exuded while tearing from one post to the next, all the while waving their arms overhead and screaming like a bunch of banshees. Blissfully, I might add. The treasure itself was apparently less than impressive, producing a collectively unenthused look of, "Eh, is that *it*?"

Next time, everyone will get a pony.

As the evening progressed I distinctly recall wanting to leave—the planet. Of course, I couldn't hide out in the attic. My husband had already claimed that coveted space. After he had sopped up dog urine (in which at least one partygoer had stepped), prepared the made-to-order mini pizzas in rapid-fire succession, popped a vat of popcorn and delivered the thirty-seventh piece of cake, he was spent. It's no wonder the notion of retreating to something closet-ish carried such appeal.

But it was the unspeakable din and the relentless flurry of activity that got my goat. Mind you, no one was hurt, no one went missing and no one bickered over so much as a kazoo. By all accounts, it appeared as though everyone had a terrific time. But I have to admit, in the throes of it all, my mind kept returning to the same theme: "Lordy, how do primary teachers stay sane day in and day out?!" If nothing else, the experience cultivated within me a new level of respect for what they do, as well as a deeper understanding of how kids (i.e. the needy little creatures I send to school each day) conduct themselves when grouped together. Good grief.

That being said, the madness abounded for what seemed an eternity—to include blowing of horns and harmonicas, banging of keyboards and tambourines, clacking of castanets and strumming of guitars. Moreover, a fair number of couches were leapt upon, a bazillion toys were strewn EVERYWHERE IMAGINABLE and a sizable chunk of time was spent terrorizing our hapless cat. Never mind the dress-up circus, which enthralled one and all and led to a fashion parade the likes of which had never before been seen.

Not surprisingly though, nothing went as planned. One child didn't like chocolate cake, another ate exactly NOTHING from the time she made landfall and still another had sneezes that could have been measured by a Richter scale. No one wanted to sit through the movie we had chosen and the vast majority of kids were spooked by the backup movie—as evidenced by the cluster of pajama-clad waifs cowering behind the couch. Thankfully, everyone agreed on another flick we had on hand. The gods were smiling, if only fleetingly.

But when it came time for the *slumber* component of the slumber party, no one was particularly interested. Except the adults. So into the wee hours of the morning we journeyed, our voices adrift over a tangle of sleeping bags, pillows and smallish bodies that refused to be still.

"Mrs. Wentzel, I can't sleep. I'm not even tired yet."

"So-and-so's sleeping bag is in my space. Can you make her move it?"

"I'm thirsty…I'm hungry…I have to pee…again…."

Eventually, the whining intensified.

"Mrs. Wentzel, I can't get to sleep with all that coughing and coughing and with Mr. Wentzel's SNORING and what's that thumping sound I hear?" Translation: One of my birthday girls barked like a dog ALL NIGHT—which would have been exceedingly difficult for *anyone* to tune out, least of all a seven-year-old jacked on a truckload of sugar.

My husband did, in fact, snore TO EXCESS while camped on the couch and the mysterious thumping sound—well, the dog apparently felt compelled to scratch himself, beating his wretched little leg on the floor to the point of distraction. Like I said, I wanted to leave. I could get more rest bedded down in the lawn.

Instead, I carried the barker to her bedroom, ordered the husband to snore elsewhere and remedied the dog's itchiness issue—at least temporarily. Sleep had finally come to one and all. A mere five hours later, however, the fun began in earnest once more. I suppose creampuffs like me deserve as much. In the truest sense, it was a trial by fire.

Planet Mom: It's where I live.

Augustember

As August wanes and September draws ever nearer, I can't help but dwell on the notion of my freedom—and how utterly delicious it will soon be. But by the same token, I am also reminded of how horribly unprepared I am for all that heading back to school entails. My charges are no more equipped for the first day of second grade than I was for the first hour of motherhood. It's shameful, really. To date, I have amassed next to nothing in the realm of kid gear and gotta-have-it-garmentage for that special square on our calendar. The square now gloriously bedecked with stickers and messages like, "The BIG Day!" and "Yea! The first day of SCHOOOOOOL!!"

If I had my druthers, another thirty-day chunk of time would be added to the year, smartly sandwiched between the eighth and ninth months. Say, "Augustember," or "Pause" (which would be more of a directive than anything). We *march* into spring; why not *pause* before forging headlong into fall? Such a godsend would give people like me time to breathe, time to warm up to the idea of letting summer go, time to rummage around for the soccer cleats that by now probably don't fit anyone anyway.

I've never been one to embrace change. More often than not (and if all is well), I like things just the way they are—the same. It's simply too much work to adapt to something slathered with newness. That being said, I abhor drastic transformations. Dead asleep to total wakefulness. The mildness of spring to the oppressiveness of summer. *At* the lake. *In* the lake. Not pregnant. Pregnant. I need generous windows of transition for such things. Time to adjust. Time to switch gears. Time to brace myself for the tsunami-sized wave of change sure to thrust me forward—ready or not.

While it's true we are on the cusp of yet another promising school year with its sharpened pencils, bright yellow buses and characteristic swirl of excitement enveloping virtually everything and everyone in its path, part of my joy is swallowed up because of what and whom I must become as a result. The bedtime enforcer. The tyrant of tuck-ins. It's a brutal role of parenthood and one that I hate with a passion.

I much prefer gathering my wily charges in from the great outdoors long after the brilliant clouds of pink, orange and crimson have faded to plum, gray and eventually an inky blue-black. There is much to relish between dusk and darkness, when the moon hangs clear and bright, begging to be plucked from the sky and the stars greet the earth one by one, gradually painting the heavens with a milky glow.

At once, the night air is filled with a symphony of crickets, peepers and barefoot children whacking at Wiffle balls, racing and chasing each other through the cool grass, already laden with dew. Shouts of "Marco...Polo! Marco...Polo!" emanate endlessly from the pool next door along with the muffled thwunks of cannonballs, instantly taking me back to my own youth—the one where Frisbees were thrown until no one could see, where nails were hammered in forts till the woods grew thick with darkness and alive with mosquitoes, where lemonade flowed freely, the pool beckoned and the rules for tag were rewritten more than once.

And all was well—much like this good night.

Fireflies are everywhere now, hugging the trees and the darkest spots in the lawn, blinking here…and a moment later, there—signaling would-be mates and captivating all who give chase with mayonnaise jars in hand. Add the crackle of a campfire, the sweet aroma of toasted marshmallows and the thrill of eavesdropping on children in the midst of any number of conversations and I'm perfectly content. It pains me to put an end to their fun. To rain on their parade. To say goodnight to the Big Dipper and to our constant companions—the lightening bugs.

Naturally, my popularity wanes. Sleep, they must.

But in the end, all is forgiven. Tomorrow is a new day. And there will be more Augusts to savor and a lifetime of moments to give pause.

Planet Mom: It's where I live.

Don't Ask, Don't Tell

My kids send me into a panic for lots of reasons these days—like when they hurl their smallish bodies into oblivion, when they careen out of control on those precarious scooters, or when they giggle uncontrollably while stuffing their mouths as full as humanly possible with marshmallows or macaroni. But mostly, I live in fear of what my progenies will say in school as a matter of course—the telling bit of detail that will raise as many flags as eyebrows in the teachers' lounge this year. More specifically, it's the completely spontaneous and utterly uncensored snippets of speech that worry me to the point of distraction—revealing the glut of dysfunction present in our home.

And now that the let's-get-to-know-our-classmates phase of school has begun in earnest, my trepidation has grown to a level roughly three times what it was just a few short weeks ago—when I stressed over what drivel Seek and Destroy might be inclined share with fellow camp-goers, instructors and swimming chums. At least in those venues, I could present my side of the story, if not defend my ineptitude as a parent.

Quite literally, I cringe when I think of the boundless opportunities for embarrassment and shame (mine, of course) that exist from the moment my charges make landfall in their classrooms till the moment they return home. During Show & Tell (if second-graders still enjoy such an activity), my gals are likely to produce a fistful of worms or the petrified wad of chewing gum that together they harvested from the bleachers at basketball camp this past summer. A treasured memento for certain, along with the photo of a dashing, twenty-something-ish coach they both vowed to marry "…when I get big, Mom."

Likewise, I want to crawl under a rock when I imagine the pall that will undoubtedly be cast over their teachers upon learning that my dear children are more than just a little familiar with stand-up comedy routines that glorify irreverence. Or that I once laundered seventy-four pairs of underpants in one day (we counted). Or that all who reside under my roof believe that ketchup is an actual food group and ice cream, the nectar of the gods—qualifying as a legitimate meal in all fifty states. Or that I've fed my brood dinner in the bathtub more than once—to compensate for my less-than-stellar (read: abysmal) performance in the getting-to-bed-on-time arena.

I shudder also to think of the shock and horror my blithesome bunch might engender in the cafeteria should they inadvertently quote the aforementioned comedians if they suddenly felt the compelling desire to entertain the troops. Worse yet, they could repeat with remarkable accuracy each and every syllable of what I shouldn't have said while shrieking at the dog who had just gnawed an entire leg off a plastic cow—and before that, a plastic dinosaur—and before that, a plastic pig.

What's more, I envision stunned silence (followed by riotous laughter) when one or both shoot a hand in the air, eagerly volunteering the word "poop" as a perfect example of a palindrome. Or the circus that would ensue upon their use of the word "pathetic" in a sentence: "My mommy thinks the president is *pathetic*." It's only a matter of time before that gem of commentary bubbles to the surface, fueling all sorts of classroom discussions—both welcome and not-so-welcome. Perhaps I should just apologize now.

There's no doubt about it; dysfunction lives here.

Planet Mom: It's where I live.

Dear Diary

Two years ago, when my youngest daughters turned seven, I gave them each a diary—a scrumptious chunk of blank space within which they would reveal their innermost hopes, fears and desires—to the world, or to no one. A place where thoughts could be poured onto paper without hesitation or shame. A 234-page sentinel-of-secrets, complete with its own tiny lock and key—a decidedly priceless feature I am told. A canvas upon which my charges could portray mommy in horrific detail.

Of course, I bought said diaries ~~because I so greatly enjoy being maligned~~ because I am perfectly incapable of resisting that which is certain to thrill my brood beyond all imagining. Translation: Anything thought to celebrate the notion of secrecy makes my kids drunk with joy. Further, I was shamed into buying them. That said, the silly things beckoned to me from the shelf where they sat, insisting that I act immediately— lest my dear progenies be robbed of happiness forever.

"Isn't it about time you encouraged a little self-expression in your children?" whispered a diary infused with a beautiful medley of blue hues (Child One's favorite). As I wended my way through the stationary aisle, fumbling with calendars and whatnot, I heard more of the same—only a bit louder this time, seemingly emanating from an adorable little log that boasted a delicious shade of bubblegum-pink (Child Two's favorite). "Have you not thought about cultivating more introspection among your impressionable charges?" it probed with an air of haughtiness.

"Have you not felt the need to nurture your kids' inner-Thoreau?!" both diaries chided in unison.

Slack mouthed and dumbfounded I just stood there, feeling horrible about having deprived my children—staring back at the bookish entities that spoke the undeniable truth.

"*Thoreau? Good grief, who's Thoreau?*" I muttered to myself.

"Put us in the cart, you simpleton," they ordered. And so I did. The medley of blue and bubblegum-pink. One for each child to voice all-that-is-deliciously-personal. One for each girl to revere more than life itself.

"This is so awesome! I get to keep secret stuff in here that no one else can see—even *you*, Mom," I've been reminded again and again.

Indeed, everyone needs some sort of venue for chronicling life's events, for reflecting upon everyday occurrences, for delving deep into the most intimate of affairs—like ensuring there's a tangible record of current love interests as well as detailed accounts of classmates' exceedingly annoying habits involving one's nose (not that I've been privy to such information). It's also a marvelous place to grouse about perceived injustices, to gather expletives by the bushel and to put into words how completely dreadful it is to be filled with angst. Even for third graders. Perhaps *especially* for third graders.

But said journal-ific wonders are also capable of capturing the essence of goodness—through sketches and prose filled with happiness, pride and gratitude for all that is right in one's world. Keepers of diaries would be wise to dog-ear such pages and refer to them often. Even third graders. Perhaps *especially* third graders.

I, too, worshiped and glorified the notion of privacy, having stuffed a diary beneath my bed as a third grader and beyond. Better still, I had a top-secret clubhouse in the basement, a multitude of forts nestled deep in the woods and a cat with whom I shared classified information on a daily basis. Strange, but true. I hid notes in hollows, carved stuff in trees and scrawled upon rocks—although I'd be hard pressed to say whose initials were paired with mine and which particular grade school tragedy was spelled out in horrific detail on page seventy-three of my dear diary.

I suppose, it's neither here nor there at this late date. The essential thing was having some sort of space within which I could voice what mattered to me at the time. As it should be.

Planet Mom: It's where I live (wondering where I hid my damn diary—even still).

Dear Santa

Dear Santa,

Please believe me, oh great giver-of-gifts, I know you love my children dearly and that you'd do almost anything to make them happy this Christmas. You're a kind and generous soul. And make no mistake about it; I've recognized (with the help of countless reminders) how hard my heathens have tried to be good, grateful and well mannered these past 357 days. But in the interest of preserving what remains of my sanity, would you please give some consideration to the following bit of information?

1. For the record, I don't need any lizards or llamas, bats or birds, real live chicks or even eggs that will hatch. Nor do I have any desire whatsoever for an ant farm and an accompanying anteater ("...in case it breaks open and ants are crawling EVERYWHERE, Mom!"). Furthermore, I have absolutely no use for a potbellied pig or a goat for that matter. Are we perfectly clear on that? NO POTBELLIED PIG. NO GOAT. Also, please ignore all future requests— maddeningly incessant as they might be—for another cat. Seriously. Perish the thought.

2. Additionally, please take note: It is totally unnecessary to spoil my charges by spending fifty-four dollars (EACH!) on flimsy pajamas that happen to match those worn by the very dolls they begged for last year. That's simply ludicrous. Get a grip, Santa. Give Mrs. Claus a new nightie or something instead.

3. Moreover, bear in mind that I have yet to summon the strength necessary to parent those who thirst for danger. More specifically, those who would willfully and gleefully ride a skateboard, a motorcycle or roller skates down an impossibly sheer slope. Blindfolded. On fire. During an earthquake. I have enough trouble tolerating the wretched scooters they so adore. Perhaps by next year I will have purged from memory my own horrific skateboarding disaster (i.e. the face plant I made one summer afternoon on a gravelly patch of pavement at an inordinately high rate of speed). But who could forget eight stitches? They were purple. And stubbly. And infinitely intriguing to all my friends who wanted to touch the freakish goatee I had seemingly sprouted from my chin. That being said, please refrain from delivering any of the aforementioned instruments of evil.

4. Also, if you must darken my door with all-that-makes-noise (I mean music), I beg of you that each sinful device (read: trumpet-kazoo-recorder-drum-keyboard-microphone-guitar-tambourine-maraca-like piece of idiocy) be suitably equipped with soundproofing, some sort of on/off switch or at the very least a volume control thingy. Thank you, in advance.

5. Also, kindly be advised that my humble abode lacks the space necessary to house a grand and glorious, five-story cat house that my kids have been whining about since the middle of summer. Honestly, it is outlandishly opulent, highly impractical and offensively massive. If you so much as *think* about bestowing such a monstrosity upon us, I will have no choice but to forego the cookies next year. You can count on broccoli instead, you silly little elfin man.

6. What's more, I would be immeasurably displeased to discover a pile of pretend dog poop in anyone's stocking. Enough said.

7. Furthermore, Santa, read my lips: NO MORE SILLY@$$ ELECTRONIC GADGETRY. I am appallingly inept when it comes to programming any and all gizmos of a technological nature. I hereby resign from said post effective today.

8. And for the love of God, NO MORE WATER BALLOONS, GLITTER OR BATHTUB TOYS. They are the bane of my existence.

9. And sweet Jesus, please, please, please don't bless us with another puppy this Christmas—at least not one that routinely gnaws on furniture, pees indiscriminately, consumes chew toys, destroys leashes (four and counting), eats holes in the carpet, nibbles on plastic Army men and Barbie doll shoes, considers deer droppings a delicacy and is entirely bent on causing bodily harm during jaunts in the great outdoors— via our garrote- like tether coupled with a frenzied demeanor and the pirouette dance I have grown to know and loathe. I simply cannot handle another floppy-eared bundle of joy. Not now. Not ever.

10. I would, however, be thrilled to receive an indestructible dog leash and maybe a ridiculously huge cardboard box. Empty, of course. The one you so graciously left for my brood three years ago was far and away the most fabulous item under the tree. It was the gift that kept on giving—till early spring, as I recall.

Sincerely,

Planet Mom

November's Sweet Indulgence

I'm not particularly fond of November—that dreary block of time wedged between the fullness of fall and the magic of winter. As calendars go, it is the dead zone for me. Except for evergreens, the landscape will soon grow barren and its naked forests and fields will be nearly devoid of life. The arrival of spring seems all but impossible in the doom and gloom of November.

Not surprisingly, as the skies gray, the chill of winter looms large and wayward leaves of oak and maple gather en masse outside my doorstep, I find myself drawn to the warmth of a good book. Simply put, if it's a solidly written work of nonfiction and a topic worthy of my time, I'm smitten from word one till the bitter end. Think: *USA Today's* columnist, Craig Wilson (*It's the Little Things*) and Betsy Lerner (*The Forest for the Trees*). A novel, however—especially one that is palpable, plausible and profoundly irresistible—is a different animal altogether, tending to woo me for a host of reasons. Think: Jennifer Weiner (*All Fall Down*) and Katherine Center (*The Bright Side of Disaster*).

Maybe I'm charmed to death by a particular narrative's cast of characters, intrigued by its wealth of unpredictability or awed by the author's sheer brilliance as it relates to the telling of tales. Perhaps the language itself sings to me or more often than not, its message hits me squarely where I live.

Or maybe, just maybe, my passion for all-things-bookish stems plainly from this: For a few delicious and utterly decadent moments, solitude is mine. The harried pace and unrelenting hustle and bustle of my child-filled world fades to black as I sink deeper and deeper into the pages of a literary gem. There, in the glorious window of stillness just before the house begins to stir, and in the quiet of night when day is done, I refuel and recondition, sipping the honeyed words of giants like Anna Quindlen, Mitch Albom and Anne Lamott. Indulgence like that is sinfully satisfying—yet in a good-for-me sort of way. After devouring as little as a passage or a page (never mind something as grand as an entire chapter) I often feel a tinge of guilt—as if I've stolen a nap or a head-clearing walk amidst the falling leaves and crisp air, thick with the scent of autumn—a walk completely devoid of meandering tricycles, tangled dog leashes and less-than-attentive-to-traffic children.

Better still, books transport me beyond the realm of bickering matches and breakfast cereal dishes. Upon my return I'm refreshed, restored and genuinely grateful for having been granted a slice of time to collect my thoughts, to reflect on someone else's or to simply dissolve into the woodwork of life. I'd like to think I emerge as a better parent, or at least as one who is less likely to go ballistic upon discovering yet another unflushed toilet or yogurt surprise.

Admittedly, I savor the chunks of time spent in lounges and waiting rooms, even those littered with chintzy toys, wailing children and a hodgepodge of germ-ridden magazines. But only if I've remembered my own scrumptious reading material— such as *Furiously Happy* (Jenny Lawson) or *Let's Explore Diabetes with Owls* (David Sedaris). Likewise, I'm happy to be huddled (half frozen) on a playground bench or stuffed behind my steering wheel at a soggy soccer field if armed with one of many delectable titles I have yet to complete (twenty-three and counting). Confession: I fantasize about being holed up in a forgotten corner of a bookstore, swallowed by a cozy chair and forced to read 200 pages of literary goodness in one sitting. Not surprisingly, I've lingered more than once in the aforementioned venues, yielding to the power of a page-turner. That being said, the notion of consuming a memoir like *Dry* (Augusten Burroughs), curled up like a cat on my couch is unthinkable. Okay, *intoxicating*.

In sum, books are my refuge from the torrents of parenthood, an intimate retreat from my inundated-with-Legos sort of existence and a source of pure salvation not unlike becoming one with my music, bathing in the sweet silence of prayer and journeying to the far shores of slumber—where the din cannot follow, the day's tensions are erased and the unruly beasts within are stilled...during my less-than-favorite month of November, or anytime.

Planet Mom: It's where I live (where both books and Halloween candy beckon).

CHAPTER 3

It's the Little Things That Make Life Sweeter

Eggs, Toast and a Side of Cynicism

For whatever reason, the gods of morning madness have been smiling upon me these past few weeks. And like any good cynic, I keep waiting for the bottom to fall out. With every ounce of my being, I fully expect my petulant children to return, brimming with an abundance of snarky commentary regarding breakfast cereal choices (or the lack thereof), eager to display the alarm clock-inspired rage to which I've grown so accustomed and to bring to the fore their lovely penchant for bickering with one another at dark-thirty. Joy. Likewise, I presume the frenzied packing-of-lunches-and-backpacks thing coupled with shrieks involving the very real possibility of missing the bus will resume shortly as well.

If nothing else, it would feel familiar. Quite frankly, I am suspect of the degree of calm that has befallen my home of late. Mornings are no longer intolerably hectic, which I find fairly disturbing since it's all I've known since the days of kindergarten. There are no shouting matches to speak of, no monumental crises related to bedhead or perceived fashion offenses and, incredibly, no one has become enraged over wrinkles in socks or the gunkiness of toothpaste for days on end. *Gasp!*

It's all so alarmingly alien—this death of disorder and dissent. So naturally, I greet it with cool skepticism, assuming that a conspirator has somehow snatched my ill-tempered brood and left me with a delightful pair of third graders who get up on time, dress for school without complaint and exhibit an obscene amount of good cheer all morning long. Imposters, I am sure, are among us.

Or perhaps my fortuitous situation has arisen as a direct result of the plan my husband so shrewdly devised and skillfully implemented. Translation: The man is a genius. That said, he pulled our charges aside one day and explained how our ~~shameless bribe~~ new morning routine would work. The seed was planted thusly.

"If you get up and get dressed as soon as your alarm goes off," he purred, "and haul your sorry selves to the kitchen by six thirty, I'll make you WHATEVER HOT BREAKFAST YOUR LITTLE HEARTS DESIRE. And," he sweetened the pot, "I'll even let you crack eggs and stir stuff." To date, the immaculately prepared entrées have included pancakes (with faces!), French toast and waffles (to die for!), eggs (infinitely varied!), bacon (impossibly crisp!) and a vat of drool-worthy, bathed-in-olive-oil fried potatoes I felt compelled to appraise. Again. And again.

In sum, he made a *deal* with the unwitting pair. A wickedly clever, painfully simple, non-negotiable agreement—one that is likely responsible for the glowing success we've experienced thus far on our journey to the Land of Hassle-free School Mornings. Note to self: Cold cereal nourishes the body, but hotcakes (and other breakfasty-type foods with irresistible aromas) inspire action of the bounding-out-of-bed variety.

But perhaps the motivation runs deeper than that. Part of me suspects that under the surface lies a host of benefits aside from the obvious. Like the delicious sliver of time during which we snuggle together before anyone heads to the kitchen. All four of us, looking as much like sardines as anything, burrow beneath a sea of blankets in our big, oak bed—the place where toes are warmed and whispers are shared in the waning moments of still and darkness.

"Here I am, your little alarm clock," they each announce as they crawl in with us, a different stuffed animal tucked under their arms each morning. To my utter amazement, both kids have already dressed, fulfilling their end of the bargain. I shake my head in disbelief.

The plan is working.

A few minutes later, they clamber downstairs to the kitchen and confirm with the cook their menu choices for the day. Chairs are then shoved against counters, eggs are cracked and batter is stirred—fulfilling the other end of the bargain.

As the sun crests over the hillside and begins pouring into the house, a steaming, hot breakfast is served—as promised. Syrup and cinnamon, juice and jam look on as chatter fills the room. There is talk of disjointed dreams, of library books and of plans for playing with a favorite friend at the bus stop. Everything that follows is sunny side up.

Once again, I shake my head in disbelief. The plan is *still* working—despite my side of cynicism.

Planet Mom: It's where I live (wondering when the novelty will wear off and hoping like crazy that's *never*).

Mommie Dearest

Always and forever, I am blown away by the seemingly trivial things my kids remember about their lives. The stuff that apparently pools and coagulates in the corners of their minds, having made some sort of lasting impression upon them— good or bad.

"Like the time I ran down our front hill, tripped over the curb and got pebbles stuck in my hand. Remember, Mom?!" (*Read: the time I wanted to hurl because of the sickening thud your body made when it hit the pavement, never mind the torrent of queasiness that washed over me when I realized there were ROCKS embedded in your hand!*)

"And how about the time Dad tried to drown me in the shower?" (i.e. a date which will live in infamy during which he slathered said child's filthy face with soap, mistakenly assuming she'd have ENOUGH SENSE to rinse it off, as opposed to inhaling voluminous quantities of water).

What's more, I am completely fogged by the way my charges recite verbatim the vat of horribleness I've delivered on more than one occasion (most of which has involved orange juice spillages and missed school buses). More specifically, the shameful string of words that pour from my stupid mouth despite KNOWING how infinitely wrong and hurtful they are (i.e. the parenting tirades from hell during which the wheels fly off and *Mommie Dearest* rears her ugly head).

Likewise, I'm baffled by the intimacy my brood shares with their beloved rocks—oh my hell, *the rocks!* The ones that adorn their dressers and windowsills. The ones that spill from my

SUV's nooks and crannies. The ones now housed in my garage *forever and ever, amen*. The ones for which a special affinity has grown to a frightening degree. That said, my heathens know from whence each stone came and, perhaps, more disturbingly, *why* each particular nugget of earthy wonderfulness was harvested and hauled home in the first place, "...because my friend gave it to me and said I should keep it *forever*," "...because it spoke to me, Mom," "Each rock is a memory, you know. Why do you want to take away our memories, Mom?"

As if that wasn't enough to ensure that I will, in fact, die a slow, horrible guilt-induced death, I recently learned of another cardinal sin for which I will pay dearly.

Child: "I ate a napkin once."

Me: "You ate a *what*?! A NAPKIN?!"

Child: "Yep. A napkin. I sort of nibbled and nibbled it till it was gone." (Touches fingertips to lips, pretending to gently gnaw imaginary napkin so that I might better understand).

Me: "YOU ATE AN ENTIRE NAPKIN?! When, where and why on earth would you do such a crazy thing?! People don't eat *napkins*!" (Hands on hips, appalled by the notion).

Child: "Well *I* did. Back in kindergarten. At snack time. Besides, my friend ate a tag right off her shirt once because it was bothering her. I saw her do it. People DO eat paper-ish stuff sometimes, Mom. It's no big deal."

Me: DEAD SILENCE coupled with a look that suggested I had gone off the deep end.

Child: Continues watching cartoons, entirely engrossed in said idiocy, unaffected by my horrified expression.

Me: "But WHY?! What possessed you to *do* such a thing?!" (Thinking, of course, this HAD to have been the result of some kind of twisted dare that five-year-olds routinely engage in).

Child: "I was hungry," she said plainly.

Me: "You were *hungry*?!" (Clutches heart, gasps).

Child: "Yep. You didn't pack enough for my snack and I was still hungry, so I ate my napkin," she stated simply, as if telling me I had forgotten to fill her squirt gun, so she commissioned some other schmuck to do it.

At this, of course, I cringed—deeply ashamed of the atrocity I had unknowingly committed, wanting ever so desperately to crawl beneath a rock and die...a slow, horrible guilt-induced sort of death. One entirely befitting of Mommie Dearest.

Planet Mom: It's where I live (with an abundance of tasty napkins and an unbearable burden of guilt).

A Stitch in Time

My mother-in-law once gave me a sewing kit as a gift—one whose contents she gathered herself and chose with great care. It was the size of a shoebox and was stuffed to the very brim with everything one might imagine using for the repair of clothing and whatnot. It was bulging actually, as if it might suddenly burst at the seams, spilling forth spools of colored thread and a hodgepodge of patches.

Looking back, I couldn't help but dwell on how strange the whole thing was, given that I can't sew to save myself. Maybe she was sending me a message. *I didn't measure up. Everyone OUGHT to know how to sew.* Maybe she felt it would inspire me to delve deep into the wonderful world of thimbles and pincushions. *With an arsenal of mending wares at my side, how could I POSSIBLY go wrong?* Maybe she was just being nice and wanted her son and his family to have a wardrobe with something other than gaping holes about the knees and buttons that dangle perilously. *Besides, who would see to it to fix things when she was gone?*

Nevertheless, I resented said gift. Of course, I should have reminded myself that the woman was raised during an era in which dresses and slacks were made right at home with tissue paper patterns scattered about and the endless hum of sewing machines filling the air. Back then, people thought nothing of darning socks, of crafting their own curtains and costumes, of hemming and re-hemming pants, of resurrecting garb that might otherwise be forsaken. Indeed, it was a thoughtful—if not entirely practical—gesture to provide me with the means to remedy whatever garment-related woe might befall us.

But the whole idea of having something thrust upon me—something I have loathed since the dawn of eighth grade Home Economics—completely rankled me to the core. But I am not one to speak up in such matters. That said, I stewed in silence, dutifully fetching the sewing box whenever she visited so that she might mend what my brood had gathered since her last visit. Grandma's To-Do Pile it was soon dubbed. The place where our favorite duds (read: hideously dilapidated things we should've been ashamed to wear) were resuscitated. The place where stuffed animals came to receive lifesaving (and sometimes, largely experimental) treatments—namely stitches to repair the gaping wounds through which stuffing and pellets poured. Needless to say, our dining room table served as more of a triage center than anything, with the most critically injured patients near the top of the mountainous heap that awaited Grandma and her renowned healing powers.

Amazingly enough (and as promised) she always delivered—no matter how tedious the task or how difficult the patient. There were monkeys in dire need of lips that would stay put, lizards whose tails had been all but detached, frogs with flesh wounds, snakes without tongues (forked or otherwise) and, of course, lions and tigers and bears (oh my!) with an array of serious injuries, all of which required a surgical solution. And Grandma had just the thing. What's more, she gave play-by-play as she prepped and patched each creature, providing all interested parties and next-of-kin with gory details of the procedures performed as well as updates on vital signs and overall prognoses. Her bedside manner was stupendous to boot.

Grandma has been gone now for more than two years, leaving a void so great no one could have imagined the collective toll it would take. For a time (and against all logic and understanding), we continued to pile the clothing and wounded animals on the dining room table—a sad reminder of what was lost. Perhaps we did it out of sheer habit. Perhaps we thought it would inspire action. Perhaps it allowed us to hold on to the idea that the great and powerful repairer-of-fabric-y-things would return again, as promised.

Planet Mom: It's where I live (still mourning our loss).

Dances with Carts

Shopping carts are the bane of my existence. It seems I have an uncanny knack for choosing ones that are both germ-ridden and hideously deficient in some unforeseen manner (i.e. equipped with a smarmy handle or a pathetic set of wheels that lurch and rattle—seemingly driven to move me in any direction but straight).

For whatever reason, I initially dismiss the many and varied imperfections, foolishly thinking that they won't be terribly bothersome in the end. Moreover, the truly vexing nature of most of the rogues I choose doesn't become readily apparent until I've already journeyed halfway through the produce aisle, mindlessly fingering the fruit and considering whether we need more carrots or romaine. By then I'm committed to the match made in hell, at least until I manage to shove the aforementioned misfit-of-a-cart through the checkout line or muscle it to my car where I can finally ditch it for a better life.

To add insult to injury, I often have to endure such hardships with my brood in tow—the heathens who strive to make each and every shopping excursion more memorable. And they do—whining incessantly about this or that item (the one that the mean and horrible tyrant won't let them have), wrestling over the matter of who gets to man the cart first, showering me with pleas for sugary cereals and those gooey snack-a-ma-call-its that ought to be removed from the planet altogether.

Apparently it is not enough to be blessed with a wayward cart.

And once I make that regrettable and irrevocable decision to allow one of my miscreants to navigate the treacherous trail ahead, my fate is sealed. Someone's ankles will indeed pay the price. Likely, mine. Despite the innumerable lectures I've delivered, the live demonstrations I've provided and the vat of instructional guidance I've offered on the subject, my two charges, though well intended, are physically incapable of maneuvering from Point A to Point B without smashing into someone or something. Granted, the gunked-up wheels do little to further their cause.

Not surprisingly, at some point during each supermarket tour of duty my patience wanes with the pushing-of-the-cart ludicrousness, climaxing shamefully somewhere between the toothpaste aisle and frozen foods. As I return to the helm, attempting to pilot that which refuses to be piloted, I am met with yet another challenge: that of effectively communicating the notion of walking single file. My futile commands typically go something like this: "Okay, someone is coming toward us now. Let's walk single file."

"Hellooooooo… the aisle isn't WIDE enough for the three of us AND another cart to pass. Is any of that registering with you two?!"

Of course, neither child of mine responds, so engrossed are they with hanging on the sides of my cart and eyeing the shelves for more of that which is forbidden. I must then stop the cart and clumsily move them—as if they were a couple of small boulders, smiling apologetically to the patron now upon us. Aisle after aisle, I repeat this cart dance—this utter lunacy—both stunned and amazed that creatures capable of telling me anything and everything I might want to know about a Euoplocephalus dinosaur cannot grasp the concept of getting somewhere single file.

And let us not forget the times in the past when one or both daughters insisted upon RIDING INSIDE the cart. Naturally, there were people who found this slightly disturbing—especially when they detected a hint of movement somewhere beneath the rubble.

"Do you know there are *children* inside your cart?" they asked, alarmed by the possibility that I could have, in fact, been so clueless as to not notice a couple of stowaways.

"Yes. They're with me, otherwise known as *Dances with Carts*."

Planet Mom: It's where I live (forever dodging those ankle-biting menaces in the grocery store).

Nightmare on Mom Street

Sunday afternoons are my respite in this harried place—the sanity cocktail from which I draw sweet sustenance. That said, I lounge around doing as little as humanly possible, embracing my inner sloth. Old movies and blanket forts rule the day. That is not to say I haven't been inspired enough to haul my vacuum from the bowels of its dusky lair or to plant my sorry self in the laundry room despite my aversion to the insufferable place. Even on a Sunday. But for the most part, ambition is nowhere to be found during that glorious wedge of downtime—sandwiched between the madness that was and the madness sure to come. Last Sunday, however, was different. Havoc rained down on my world, obliterating my precious corner of calm.

Oddly enough, what led to the aforementioned began weeks ago while traipsing through a store, my cart piled high with schlock I didn't need. At every turn, it seemed, I stumbled into even MORE SCHLOCK and felt compelled to ogle it, to finger its veneer of worthiness and to toy with the notion of adding it to my ever-growing mound of that-which-I-would-one-day-regret-purchasing. And on the days during which I allow the guilt of motherhood to consume me, the mound is markedly higher. Needless to say, it was one of those days.

Indeed, the voices that drive much of my irrational behavior were especially persuasive that day, whispering words of admonishment in my ear and regaling in my grand ineptitude as a parent: "You're a HORRIBLE MOTHER. You don't SPEND ENOUGH TIME with your children. You MUST ACQUIRE this ten-dollar nugget of wonderfulness which promises to erase weeks of botched parenting." All the while I considered said nugget of wonderfulness (i.e. a two-pound chocolate cookie Halloween house kit, complete with forty-seven bats, dozens of little green candies I would later damn to hell, enough gumdrops to coat eleventy-seven teeth and an expander, a defective ghost—or rather, *segments* of insanely sweet candy suggestive of something that was once intact and specter-like—and a cauldron full of powdery mixes that were sure to deliver hours of goo-inspired, edible fun and to yield the most perfect hues of orange and purple icing on the planet).

In the end, I was shamed into buying the box of foolishness. Because that's what moms do. Just like all the other project-y stuff I haul home out of sheer guilt; never mind the techno-gadgetry thought to engender this or that brand of awe in my children. It's all about the *Is-it-as-remarkable-as-a-pony* factor and *Will-it-expunge-from-the-record-my-screw-ups-to-date?*

So I shoved the stupid thing in our pantry (good intentions and all) and forgot about it till the Halloween craze struck with a vengeance. And since the celebrated costume drama in this household was officially over, a sinful quantity of sugary treats had been stockpiled already and virtually every corner of our home had been festooned with all-that-is-Halloweenish, there was but one thing left to do—build the stupid house. So that's what we did—the three of us, while Dad cheered from the sidelines.

Several hours, two meltdowns (both mine) and a hellacious mess later, we had our two-pound Halloween house. Of course, the orange and purple mixes wound up adorning practically everything, those reprehensible little candies rolled near and far, fistfuls of trimmings were consumed with wild abandon and the icing was less than compliant as I shoveled gobs of it into pastry bags and squeezed the reluctant mass onto the house as instructed. Translation: The gloppage in question delighted in its droopiness, defiantly sliding down walls and slanted rooftops, leaving hideous-looking blobs everywhere. Even the spider webs I made sagged to the point of looking not-so-spider-webby. But because the gods of kitchen fiascos were smiling upon me, my brood rejoiced, "The droopiness makes it even SPOOKIER, Mom! You're so AWESOME!"

Well, it certainly wasn't as grand as a pony might have been; but the awe factor of this nightmarish project was evident to at least two somebodies on the planet. And perhaps that's all that matters in the end.

Planet Mom: It's where I live (admiring our droopified Halloween house).

Ode to Thanksgiving

With Thanksgiving Day mere hours away, I cannot help but dwell upon all the wonderful things for which I am grateful. It feels good, actually, to pause this fourth Thursday in November to acknowledge all the goodness in my life that I often take for granted—both tangible and not-so-tangible. With each passing year, and as the holiday looms large, I find myself slipping into the Pilgrim mode, giving thanks at the drop of a wide brimmed, buckle-bearing hat. Never mind such an accoutrement fell out of fashion nearly three hundred years ago.

That said, I am especially thankful for on the fly four-wheel drive, heated leather seats and hot cocoa in the dead of winter and for swimming pools, shade trees and succulent watermelon come July. I'm also exceedingly grateful for the ubiquitous nature of hand sanitizers that can be splashed on, sprayed on or pumped to excess into the hands of fools like me who feel the compelling desire to eradicate germs night and day. Likewise, I appreciate the monstrosity-of-a-trash-can we now own—the one that accommodates the voluminous amount of refuse my family routinely generates.

I also give thanks daily for our dog—who hasn't destroyed a leash or consumed a chew toy in months, for cats who remind me that napping ought to be a necessary and shameless activity and for the disturbingly hypnotic quality of cartoons, which have entranced my unruly brood more than once, enabling me to sound almost coherent on the telephone. Further, I am eternally grateful for unlimited texting plans and for grade-schoolers who have yet to demand cell phones.

Moreover, I am equally indebted to the makers of microwavable mac-and-cheese, for perfectly portioned kids' yogurt and for no-leak lunch boxes that promise to contain horrendous explosions involving said yogurt.

Snow delays are nice, too.

Furthermore, I have a loving family who accepts my foibles, many and varied as they are. I have friends who understand that I live in an inundated-with-sand-shovels sort of reality, which precludes me from dropping everything to go golfing and whatnot (i.e. the kids' sports schedules must first be coordinated, followed by a desperate search for a sitter and my putter). My infinitely gracious cronies also tolerate what can only be described as less-than-stimulating conversations—ones that invariably revolve around the antics of Yin and Yang, hilarious and engaging as they might be to me.

We have very kind and accepting neighbors who haven't banished us—even *after* they discovered that our cars don't always fit in the garage. Nor do they think twice about the minefield of toys and flip-flops we inadvertently leave in the yard overnight. For these things, I am highly appreciative.

What's more, I am married to an incredible man who endures my debilitating issue with time management, accepts my ineptitude with respect to cooking and cleaning and refrains from nagging me about my deplorable lack of follow-through on yard sale projects and my less-than-consistent sex drive. He also insists that I squeeze some "me time" into my schedule each day and never, ever questions my credit card balances—especially when they include foot massages and dues to the gym I have yet to visit.

Moreover, I am thankful for a twenty-something-ish daughter who, at times, forgets to make me insane with worry, reminds me of what life was like when she was eleven (read: heavenly) and understands that I cannot prepare a five-course meal for her boyfriend when he visits. And for that, I am vastly appreciative.

Furthermore, I am indescribably grateful that my youngest children refrain from inspecting dog dung under their magnifying glasses (tempting though that might be), they have yet to light anything of value on fire and they stopped bringing colonies of caterpillars into the house months ago. For these things, even a Pilgrim would rejoice.

Be sure to remember and acknowledge the special people and things that make you thankful, pilgrim—on Thanksgiving Day and always.

Planet Mom: It's where I live (thanking my lucky stars).

It's the Little Things That Make Life Sweeter

Valentine's Day is fast approaching and I can't help but be reminded of how sweet life truly is on February fourteenth as well as every other day on the calendar—with or without the chocolate-covered delectables, mawkish cards and heart shaped whateverness. Case in point, when I was home with newborn twins my husband used to pack little bags of food for me each day before he left for work, filling them with freshly peeled carrots, bunches of grapes or a handful of pretzels or cashews. Most days, there was half a turkey-on-rye waiting for me, too, abundantly dressed with lettuce, tomato and provolone. Its mate could likely be found on the same refrigerator shelf, neatly sliced and ready for instant retrieval.

However, it wasn't a job for the thin-skinned. There were high standards to be met. My slightly specific and less-than-succinct criteria: Each conveniently bagged delight had to be flavorful (yet devoid of gassiness), it couldn't be the least bit drippy or crumbly or, Heaven forbid, unwieldy. Most importantly, I had to be able to consume it using just one hand—often on the fly or holed up in a chair for God-knows-how-long nursing a grexy baby. Or two.

Needless to say, great care and consideration went into preparing such sustenance for me and I was eternally grateful—both for the man's diligence and for his abiding tolerance of my changeable mood. After all, it was the finger food that served as my salvation during that interminable stage of parenthood (i.e. the maddening era when I would have given almost anything for a hot shower or a real sit-down meal with something as fancy as a fork or idle conversation).

But the bundles of nourishment he so thoughtfully provided, though short on style, surely delivered what I needed most: the feeling of being cared for and remembered each day. It was a little thing that made my life that much sweeter.

I'd daresay the majority of what enriches my world could be categorized by most as something seemingly insignificant or ordinary at best—something perhaps unremarkable to the masses, but dear to me. Like the little notes and drawings my kids stuff inside my pockets and tape to my computer, knowing that later I'll stumble upon them and smile. Or that my oldest—beyond all logic and understanding—still confides in me and seeks my counsel. Or at the close of an especially trying day in the trenches of Parentville, when I feel like the most horrible mother on earth because I dumped someone's special potion down the drain or because I forgot to tell the yard crew not to haul away "...our eagle's nest, Mom!" or because I screamed at them over nothing or because I failed to listen yet again—I get this amazing and completely undeserved gift in the form of a breathy secret whispered in my ear at bedtime, "Mommy, I wouldn't trade you for anything. Not even for a worm."

Stuff like that makes me melt. And I'm that much surer it's the little things in life that matter most. Like the twitter of songbirds after a long, hard winter. A handwritten letter amidst a sea of emails. A yellow moon on the rise. The brackish breeze, the cries of seagulls and the soothing sound of the ocean after driving forever to get there. The way my kids' eyelashes curl and the thicket of sun-bleached hairs on the napes of their necks.

The way my grandmother traced my ears to coax me to sleep. My grandfather's firm belief that I was big enough to help him feed the cows, steer the tractor and hay the fields. Clunking around a farm in real barn boots. The warm muzzle of a horse. The company of a cat. The affection of a dog. The lullaby of crickets. The tang of autumn. The whisper of pines. The crisp scent of a novel, yet to be consumed. A distant train whistle. Fresh newsprint. Thistledown. Snowflakes. The smell of rain. Holding hands.

I often stumble upon small wonders, too, in unlikely places— like the special stones on someone's dresser, harvested from Grandma's house "…to help me remember her, Mom." And crumbs in someone's pocket—the remains of a bit of bread "…I saved for Taylor from my lunch today at school. It got all crumbly when we shared it, Mom." And heartfelt notes of apology—painstakingly folded and carefully wedged between the pages of a favorite book. "Sorry Sadie. I really love you a lot. You're the best sister ever!"

Of course, there was the strange but wonderful vine, curiously twisted into the shape of a heart, one of my dandies found while foraging in the garage last week. "Here, Mom; it's for you." But it couldn't hold a candle to the cookie she shared with my husband and me recently—the one she cleverly gnawed upon until it, too, resembled a heart.

Indeed, it's the little things that make life sweeter on Valentine's Day and every day.

Planet Mom: It's where I live (and continue to devour again and again *It's the Little Things*, by Craig Wilson, *USA Today* columnist and friend).

The Birds and the Bees—and Kangaroos, Too

Never once did I imagine calling upon my vastly deficient knowledge of marsupials to aid in providing my youngest charges with a rudimentary understanding of human sexuality. Nope. I banked on hitting the high points of the famed birds-and-bees lecture while drawing upon what little I know of how cats and dogs come into this world. Not kangaroos. Further, I had hoped for more time to mull over the intricacies of the issue and to ready myself for such an important conversation.

It's a bit fuzzy, of course, but I can picture the mother-daughter "dream chat" in my mind's eye. It would take place on a warm summer's afternoon. On a grassy knoll. DECADES FROM NOW. Each of us would be swathed in something white and billowy and richly infused with cotton. We'd find a breezy shade tree to sit under, sip lemonade from tall glasses sweating with condensation and calmly discuss the notion of how babies are made. Each of my dear children would then promise never to have sex until the age of thirty—and only *after* consulting the volumes of relationship-related advice I would have dispensed by then (read: the vat of directives only an overprotective fusspot-of-a-mother could issue).

But it was not to be. My moppets wanted information and they wanted it NOW.

Fortunately the gods were smiling upon me that day. Smirking, actually. That said, my ill-prepared discourse on the subject was at least satisfactory—having sufficiently addressed the fringes of reproductive particulars, quelling my brood's interminable curiosity for a time.

"Tell me again, Mom. Why do you have to have surgery in the place where you carried us?"

"Well, I have a...a...a...sort of problem inside and the doctor needs to fix it," I answered while patting my midsection gently, knowing full well this response would merely serve to open the floodgates of interrogation hell for my little quizmasters.

"What kind of problem?" they both pressed.

"Well...it's a mommy problem," I offered tentatively—as opposed to a *daddy* problem that we, as parents, tried and failed miserably to explain some time ago. As I recall, one of my charges wondered if a vasectomy involved removal of all or part of Daddy's brain. Naturally, I resisted the urge to field that particular question, allowing my husband to fish for an answer that would satisfy the masses—and perhaps keep me from choking on my fist.

"Oh. Daddies don't get this problem?" they quizzed.

"Nope. Just mommies. They are the only ones who have that special place in their bellies where babies grow. Sort of like a kangaroo's pouch."

"But you're not a *kangaroo*, Mom! And you don't even have a *pouch*!"

"Yes, I do." I defended. "Well, sort of. It's an inside-pouch. The one where you both grew and grew like tiny seeds. It's a pouch that you can't see—exactly. And that's where the problem is. In my pouch. Yes, that's it! I have a *pouch* problem!" I happily confessed, hoping against hope that their relentless grilling would soon fizzle out. "*End of discussion!*" I wanted to shout. "*Go torment the cat!*" I was tempted to suggest. But lo and behold (and before the famed "How do babies get in there anyway, Mom?" rolled off their tongues) they swallowed it. My analogy, crazy as it sounded, had worked. The questions stopped directly and they appeared to be genuinely content with what I had offered in explanation. Strange, but true.

So after my far-from-textbook discourse on the birds and the bees (and kangaroos, too), I was free to return to what I had been doing—brooding and stressing over the soon-to-be-scheduled procedure that would in effect end my childbearing years. And despite knowing it wouldn't be life threatening or even life altering for that matter, somewhere deep inside I felt it *would* be a life-changing event. It smacked of finality—of another chapter in my life coming to a close—of coming to terms with an inevitable truth: One day soon my womb would no longer serve as the soil in which a seed could be sown, a haven for a child that might-have-been.

That said, there is a certain sadness and unwelcome quality tied to that realization and, a sense of abruptness as well. Somewhere at the core of my being a voice shouted in protest, "But I'm not finished yet! I'm not done nurturing! Part of me still longs for a baby at my breast and the chance to nuzzle a newborn once more! *My* newborn!" Rest assured it's not as if I've seriously entertained the idea of having more children at this late date. I suppose it's the *possibility* of doing so with which I have become enamored, as foolhardy and completely unrealistic as that might be. Being with child—having a hand in the wonder of creating life—has changed me forever, just as the *pouch problem* remedy will likely do.

Indeed, as it should be.

Planet Mom: It's where I live (recovering nicely, thank you).

96

Sometimes the Sidelines are Best

Two years ago my kids swam like stones. Stones both dense and unwieldy in nature. Stones destined for the bottoms of lakes and ponds and pools. And yet, there was an uncanny barnacle-ness about them as well (i.e. they desperately clung to whatever floatation device or seemingly tallish torso that happened to be handy—namely my husband's or mine). Said buoyancy-challenged individuals were largely comfortable in swimming pools, so long as we stayed in the shallow end and refrained from making any sort of unreasonable requests—like suggesting they loosen their death grips around our necks. Heaven forbid I tuck my hand beneath their bellies and let them kick and flop around in the water like everyone else on the planet.

That said, I'm not entirely sure that my kids even *wanted* to learn how to swim. Life was perfectly perfect coiled inextricably around someone's head, neck and shoulders, their smallish bodies submerged just enough to enjoy a taste of refreshing coolness, while a goodly portion remained above the water's surface, safe and sound from the abyss below.

For a time (read: an obscenely large chunk of our children's lives), we allowed such an idiotic practice to continue, doing our level best to enable them and to accept the Island of Dependency we had inadvertently become. Of course, we fully expected a miracle to befall us. A miracle that would effectively save us from ourselves. Out of the blue, our charges would suddenly abandon their fears and start swimming like fish or, more correctly, like porpoises, plunging headlong into the murky depths in search of silvery prizes and whatever else they felt inclined to fetch from the deck of the *Titanic*. Through osmosis, our aquatic wonders would absorb every speck of knowledge and skill I had acquired as a lifeguard, and then some. They'd even be strangely adept at twirling whistles around their fingers and hauling greased watermelons across vast stretches of open water—talents that smack of impressiveness but have yet to be deemed useful.

But it was not to be. Eventually my husband and I faced the cold, hard truth. Hopes and dreams didn't make good swimmers. Lessons did. Lessons involving a lot of hard work, a boatload of skilled instructors from whom praise flowed endlessly and a vat of courage—mostly of the parental variety. That said, it takes superhuman strength and nerves of steel to idly sit back and watch one's beloved progeny flap and flounder as he or she goes about the important business of learning how to swim. It's true: Kids panic. Kids swallow a disturbing amount of water. Kids stare at you from the deep end with horrified expressions of "How COULD you?!" and "Are you *really* my mother?!"

Not surprisingly, parents twist and turn uncomfortably in their seats, wearing nervous smiles and attempting to chat casually. Yet deep inside, awash with guilt and filled with doubt, they harbor pure and unadulterated torment. Or maybe that was just me, squirming in my lawn chair in a futile attempt to silence the voices in my head that relentlessly screamed, "Your child is DROWNING for Crissakes! And all you can do is swat flies and admire your tanned toes?! What kind of parent are you anyway?!" More than anything I felt helpless—completely beside myself with the idea of being on the sidelines.

And yet, that was where I needed to be—the place where I was, in fact, most effective. I needed to have faith in the process, faith in the instructors and faith in my children's ability to succeed—in spite of the dearth of achievement I had witnessed thus far. And succeed they did. They've ditched the semblance of stones and barnacles for good and have since transformed into more guppy-like creatures, completely thrilled with their newfound ability to swim, "...even in the *deep end*, Mom!"

Aside from seeing actual results in the pool, I know this much is true because we've progressed from comments like, "I hope you know this is PURE TORTURE, Mom!" to "Can't you just LEAVE ME HERE so I could SWIM ALL DAY, EVERYDAY?!"

Yep. Sometimes the sidelines are best.

Planet Mom: It's where I live (on the sidelines).

Summer's Educational Feast

A plethora of reputable entities, educational and otherwise, have spent a good chunk of time and money prattling on about the serious nature of academic regression and whatnot, convincing great masses of parents that "the summer slide" does, in fact, exist and should be feared above all else. All seriousness aside, I'm here to proclaim otherwise. There was no *slide* that I could discern during the glorious months of June, July and August. Moreover, I'd daresay the summer epitomized an educational feast for my brood, as a host of new and exciting information was thrust upon us virtually every minute of every day.

Indeed, we were enlightened thusly:

Matter can, in fact, be destroyed (or at least it can come frighteningly close to doing so) when lawn mower blades make impact with errantly placed Wiffle balls and badminton rackets. Physicists should take note of such remarkable findings.

Considering the coefficient of friction and the gravitational pull of the Earth, flip-flops are not ideally suited for tree climbing. Likewise, and in the true spirit of experimentation, cell phones can neither swim, nor float.

With respect to Venn diagrams, not all *amusement park employees* are *amused* to be there day in and day out, collecting tickets, helping kids climb onto rides and advising patrons to keep their "...hands and feet inside at all times!" In fact, most of the joy-bringers we encountered this summer fell squarely into the category of cantankerous—only to be eclipsed by the group of dolts who were disturbingly stoic. Of course, I felt the urge to slap them senseless for failing to at least ACT THE PART of being cheery and pleasant "for the good of the children." But that would have been redundant.

Concerning the topic of animal behavior, I discovered that cats, dogs and even guinea pigs *can* be taught to type on a computer. Needless to say, I was duly impressed having witnessed said groundbreaking research conducted in the field.

As far as mathematical correlations go, I learned that the later kids stay up at a sleepover party, the earlier they will rise— demanding pancakes and bacon. What's more, the average third grader will catapult out of bed ten times faster for an unplanned and unmercifully early visit from a friend who wants to ride bikes than for the regularly scheduled arrival of a school bus.

Regarding the subject of psychology, I was reminded that children can and will defy all logic and understanding. Case in point: when they emphatically reveal that the best part of a fun-filled day at an amusement park (read: a marathon-inspired excursion involving an obscene number of rides and French fries) was purchasing a three-dollar inflatable elephant named Bob. Similarly, the most memorable thing from attending a week's worth of basketball camp might just have been "…drinking a whole can of soda so I could burp really LOUD, Mom!"

Furthermore, while field-testing a variety of hypotheses recently, I learned that it is possible to become more sodden while riding the Merry Mixer during a torrential downpour than it is to opt for a water ride on a dry day. Additionally, I found that it takes roughly three days for sandals to dry out after said rain. None of this, mind you, is especially troubling to the husband or to the children who insist that we "…just go on more rides!"

Some related summertime observations I made: When playing miniature golf, the probability of visiting an emergency room (and/or the dentist's office) increases exponentially as the number of eight-year-old participants increases. Further, it's ALWAYS a good idea to ensure that moon roofs and windows are closed overnight. Rain happens. It's also prudent to periodically check on youngsters who might do the unthinkable (i.e. blow up ants with a magnifying glass "… because they sizzle in the sun, Mom, and then they POP!" and/ or hoist the dog into the top bunk "…so he can SEE stuff up there.") Stupidity happens. Moreover, it's wise to inspect the hot tub for curiously abandoned thongs upon returning from vacation. Audaciousness happens.

Some interesting facts I gathered these past few months: Kids are more likely to retain information related to properly pitching a tent than in memorizing the sight words from kindergarten. Kids could watch a continuous loop of cartoons for an eternity—never once pausing to engage in meaningful conversation with a parent. Kids can get by with one bath a week if they frequent a chlorinated swimming pool. Kids positively DON'T CARE how fricking cold the water from the hose is. Kids will eat marshmallows till they EXPLODE. Kids will kiss worms, frogs and lick the dog—just because.

Planet Mom: It's where I live (summing up the summer).

Great Expectations

In the dark of predawn I lay in bed, tucked snugly beneath my downy comforter, sleet pinging against the windowpanes in soft yet fitful waves. Against all odds associated with parenthood, no one under the age of eight burst into the room to announce that the sky was falling. Translation: My husband and I had had the presence of mind to skip setting the kids' alarm clocks the night before, in anticipation of inclement weather almost certain to arrive by daybreak. So for a time, all was silent in this good house—except for the ticking of clocks and the tiny taps at the window.

As the not-so-surprising news of yet another school cancellation reached my ears in the wee hours that day, I was filled impossibly with hope. Hope that I would enjoy a morning devoid of the madness I had known all too well since September. Hope for a day abundant with hot cocoa, kindness and good cheer. Hope that I might finally summon the strength and ambition to take down the blasted Christmas tree. The one that has been standing very nearly straight in my living room for the past sixty-three days, mocking me on Inauguration Day as I addressed my cache of shamefully belated holiday cards.

The tree *had* to come down. It *would* come down. It was January 28th for Pete's sake. Besides, I was tired of its condescending glare, as if it were looking down its boughs at me, judging my every deficiency. Shaming my inadequate core.

Moreover, with my army of helpers that would likely be at my disposal ALL DAY (since no one wanted to frolic in the freezing rain), I banked on being able to pack up and stow away every jingle bell, snowman, Santa likeness and string of garland-y foolishness in the entire house. To reclaim my space. At least until Easter.

Needless to say, lots of people here agreed that it was high time. "Mom, you know we're going to get arrested, don't you?"

"Arrested? For *what*?!"

"Because January's almost over and we don't even have our Christmas tree down yet! We'll *all* be thrown in jail!"

"Whaaaaat?! Who's going to throw us in jail?"

"The Holiday Police."

"The Holiday *Who*?!"

"The Holiday Police. They arrest people who don't do stuff right—like taking Christmas trees down BEFORE Groundhog Day. Helloooooooooooo."

She had a point.

All I had to do was glance at the calendar and then at the muddled mess surrounding me. Remnants of the holiday season were everywhere. The Christmas lights were completely shrouded with ice and fused impossibly to the trees and shrubs outside. The stockings were still hung—and shockingly, still laden with beloved items that had been tragically forgotten since Santa's celebrated arrival. Gifts of every size, shape and hideous stage of disarray lay like carnage throughout the house and under the aforementioned evergreen, gloriously bedecked with enough ornament-age for a forest. Legions upon legions of festive-looking dishes, alarmingly bare except for the smarmy trail of cashews and the red and green fleckage of holiday candies, still rested upon my tabletops, whispering without end, "Pleeeease cleeeean meeeee." Santa's cookie plate begged to be returned to the cupboard, the crèche longed to be back in the attic and quite frankly, the mistletoe was tired of hanging around.

What's more, I noted that the kids had been swiping stuff from the tree for weeks—like the reindeer, now chummy with their toy horses and sharing a corral, and the snowmen, warmly adopted by a family of teddy bears. I even discovered a few sparkly ornaments dangling precariously from the rooftops of dollhouses. Icicles maybe?

That said, it was way past time to begin the arduous process of un-decorating. Clearly, the snow day that had been bestowed upon us was a window of opportunity and perhaps the spark that would ignite my drive and determination to succeed in spite of myself. At least that was the plan.

But it was not to be. My great expectations for the day were shot by ten a.m. and my hopes for a tidier living room were all but dashed. For all intents and purposes, the thorny pine had become rooted there, a glaring reminder of my ineptitude as a putter-away-of-holiday-hoo-ha. Instead, we frittered away the time, putting six puzzles together, littering the house with Barbie dolls and dresses, devouring books, stuffing ourselves with chocolate-chip pancakes and lounging in our pajamas till it was almost evening—at which time I sent my brood outdoors to play in the snow that had FINALLY begun to fall in big, feathery flakes. A consolation prize for my efforts.

Then again, maybe my reward was the delicious chunk of time I spent fishing for puzzle pieces with my kids, eavesdropping on their conversations with their dolls, listening to the ice hit the windows—safe and sound in this good house.

Planet Mom: It's where I live (and where the Holiday Police are destined to arrive).

CHAPTER 4

Seven Things Parenthood Has Taught Me

Dear Departed Summer

I am a poster child for parenting ineptitude. And at no time does it become more painfully apparent than during the first few weeks of school—when I look back over the vast expanse of the summer and realize that I've mismanaged a good deal of it. In spite of having the best of intentions in mid-June—with a host of events cleverly sandwiched between swim lessons, haircuts and camps galore—by the tail end of July I found myself desperately trying to cram every ounce of family fun and spontaneity into what was left of summer. The fun I promised we'd have before sliding headlong into September.

Inexcusably, it is the epitome of who I am and what I do when it comes down to the wire—when a finite number of squares remain on the calendar during which anything and everything deemed truly memorable and drool-worthy to a nine-year-old can, ostensibly, be orchestrated. In a perfect world, that is. So like a madwoman I schedule sleepovers and movie nights, plan picnics and pencil in parades, visit ball parks and theme parks and, of course, stumble over myself to accept gracious invitations to friends' homes and pools and lakeside cottages oozing with wonderfulness.

Conversely, I've tolerated a tent in my back yard for twenty-three days running—one that promises to leave a hideous, yellow square where a lovely patch of green grass used to grow. A smallish tent in which I spent an interminable night embracing all that roughing it entails, from mosquito bites and cramped quarters to a lumpy earthen mattress and a less-than-endearing quality of dankness I feared would cling to me forevermore.

Eau de Musty Tent, methinks.

I suppose, however, that it was better than a) dealing with the monstrosity-of-a-teepee that monopolized my lawn last summer b) disappointing my progenies who insisted that I camp out with them and c) the insufferable conditions that my husband (aka: Father of the Year) endured while attempting to sleep on an impossibly narrow and horribly unyielding lounge chair parked squarely in front of the zippered door. As luck would have it, he was uniquely situated and perfectly qualified to shepherd those who felt compelled to visit the loo in the dead of night. Good thing. My only lament: failing to photograph him in all his glory—mouth agape, flashlight in hand, his body entombed within a sleeping bag, his head, poking out the top, completely enshrouded within a camouflage mask I had never before seen, arms entirely enveloped by a giant mesh sack he apparently dragged from the bowels of the garage in a moment of great inspiration (aka: makeshift mosquito netting).

That said, I think it's safe to say that as parents we at least showed up for our kids this summer. Some of the time anyway. We took them places and did things together. We tolerated their abiding love of toads, their penchant for building forts, their overwhelming desire to climb to the tops of trees and their inexplicable fascination with road kill. Furthermore, we tried not to trouble our silly heads over the health and well-being of our lawn as well as the health and well-being of those who spent much of August snowboarding down our grassy front terrace. Nor did we dwell on the wanton fearlessness with which they careened hither and yon on their scooters. Barefooted, no less. So we can feel slightly good, I guess—having directly or indirectly contributed to the wellspring of memories gathered over the fleeting, albeit delicious, chunk of summer.

Looking back I now see why it was likely a success—not because of the fancy-schmanciness of this or that celebrated event, but because the extraordinary lives deep within the ordinary. It's not the double play in the bottom of the ninth they'll remember, it's the delicious medley of peanuts and popcorn wafting through the air, the distinctive shade of blue on the tongues of all who drank icy-cold, blue raspberry drinks on that sweltering summer night and the tinny clang that echoed throughout the stadium as cheering fans beat upon the aluminum bleachers like drums. Similarly, it's not the glorified picnic with throngs of people, platters of deviled eggs and eleventeen varieties of potato salad that necessarily makes a lasting impression. It's the novelty, and perhaps spontaneity, of having cucumber sandwiches and slices of watermelon on a wobbly card table in the midst of summer fun. "Thanks, Mom, now we don't have to stop playing!"

Moreover, I'd daresay that fiery sunsets and Big Dipper sightings are more mesmerizing than a summertime box office smash. That a symphony of crickets, the pungent aroma of the earth and the endless chatter of children most memorably fill a tent. That a hammock is very nearly medicinal, as is the buttery succulence of sweet corn, the shade of an oak tree and the canopy of fog at sunrise as it hangs in the valley—silent and still.

Dear Departed Summer, it's likely I'll miss your fireflies most—and the barefoot children who give chase, drinking in the moment, alive with pleasure, racing across your cool, slick grasses without end.

Planet Mom: It's where I live (lamenting the finite quality of summer and desperately searching for the rewind button).

Hands Upon My Heart

When I was nine or ten, I remember well my enthrallment with my mother's hands. They were delicate and slender, sweetly scented and rose petal-soft—so completely unlike my own nicked and scraped, callused and chafed boy-like hands that were better suited for wielding a hammer and throwing a fastball than anything else. Mine were distinctively earthy, too, largely because remnants of dirt and grass simply refused to be removed. Or at least that was the sentiment I held for much of the summer. It was a byproduct of being a kid, I suppose, literally immersed in a world of sod and soil from sunup to sundown. Never mind my fondness of forests and rocky places, which typified a deep and abiding bond with nature—one that I'm not quite sure my mother ever completely understood.

At any rate, my hands told of who I was at the time—a tomboy given to tree climbing, stealing second base and collecting large and unwieldy rocks. Everyone's hands, I'd daresay, depict them to a certain degree, having a story to tell and a role to play at every time and every place on the continuum of life. Traces of our journey remain there in the folds of our skin—from the flat of our palms and knobs of our knuckles to the very tips of our fingers. As it should be, I suppose.

For better or for worse, our hands are the tools with which we shape the world and to some extent they define us—as sons and daughters, providers and professionals, laborers and learners, movers and shakers. That said, I'm intrigued by people's hands and the volumes they speak—whether they're mottled with the tapestry of age, vibrant and fleshy or childlike and impossibly

111

tender. Moreover, I find that which they whisper difficult to ignore.

Likewise, I'm fascinated by the notion that ordinary hands routinely perform extraordinary deeds day in and day out, ostensibly touching all that truly matters to me. Like the hands that steer the school bus each morning, the hands that maintain law and order throughout the land, the hands at the helm in the event of fire or anything else that smacks of unspeakable horribleness, the hands that deftly guide my children through the landscape of academia, the hands that bolster them on the soccer field, balance beam, court and poolside, the hands that bless them at the communion rail each week and the hands that brought immeasurable care and comfort to our family pet in his final hours. Strange as it sounds, I think it's important to stop and think about such things. Things that I might otherwise overlook when the harried pace of the world threatens to consume me.

If nothing else, giving pause makes me mindful of the good that has come to pass and grateful to the countless individuals who continue to make a difference simply by putting their hands to good use. For whatever reason, this serves to ground me and helps me put into perspective how vastly interdependent and connected we are as a whole. Indeed, we all have a hand (as well as a stake) in what will be.

Equally important, is the notion of remembering what was. More specifically, the uniqueness of those I've loved and lost. A favorite phrase. A special look. The warmth of a smile or the joy of their laughter. Further, there's nothing quite as memorable as the hands of those I've lost—like my grandfather's. His were more like mitts, actually—large and leathery, weathered and warm. Working hands with an ever-present hint of grease beneath his hardened nails, and the distinctive scent of hay and horses that clung to him long after he left the barn. And although decades have passed, I can still see him pulling on his boots, shuffling a deck of cards and scooping tobacco from his pouch—his thick fingers diligently working a stringy wad into the bowl of his pipe, followed shortly thereafter by a series of gritty strikes of the lighter and wafts of sweet smoke mingling reluctantly with those from the kitchen.

Of course, my grandmothers' hands were equally memorable. One had short, stubby fingers and a penchant for biting her nails to the nub. Always, it seemed, she was hanging wash out on the line, scrubbing dishes or stirring a pot brimming with macaroni—my favorite form of sustenance on the planet. By contrast, my other grandmother suffered the ravages of rheumatoid arthritis as evidenced by her hands. To this day I can picture a set of finely manicured nails at the tips of her smallish fingers—fingers that were gnarled and bent unmercifully, although they never seemed to be hampered when it came to knitting a wardrobe for my beloved dolls.

Not surprisingly, I can still summon an image of my brother's hands, too. Almost instantly. They were handsome, lean and mannish-looking—yet something suggestive of the little boy he had once been lingered there. Needless to say, I am grateful for such delicious memories—the ones indelibly etched upon my heart.

Planet Mom: It's where I live (remembering well the hands that have touched my life).

Ode to Embarrassment

It has been said that success as a parent isn't fully realized unless and until you've become an embarrassment to your children. Apparently, my husband and I have been making remarkable progress toward that end—inadvertent though our efforts might have been. We sing in the car. We make snapdragons talk. We hurl wadded socks at one another. We scream at the TV during tennis matches. And we impersonate comedians far too often. All of which, evidently, our brood finds fairly disturbing—especially when friends come to call.

I saw flashes of it a few years ago, when our youngest kids entered the second grade. It was subtle at first—the rumblings of their discontent barely audible amidst the tumult of motherhood. At the time, their muted protests against the many and varied ways we caused them unspeakable embarrassment seemed trivial and unfounded. So I dismissed them, perhaps wrongly. Over time, however, their grumblings have become progressively louder and more insistent, swiftly sliding into the realm of that-which-is-difficult-to-ignore.

"Mom, stop sticking NOTES inside my lunch box. People will SEE them, you know. We talked about this last year, didn't we? Oh, and don't pack any more open-faced, peanut butter and chocolate chip sandwiches. So-and-so gets grossed out whenever I take a bite and then THE WHOLE TABLE looks at my stupid sandwich. It's entirely horrible."

That said, I'm starting to empathize with the smallish beings in question—who, for whatever reason of late, have adopted the survivalist mentality of Greg Heffley, the middle-schooler of *Diary of a Wimpy Kid* fame. Translation: DON'T raise your hand. DON'T use the bathroom. DON'T call attention to yourself in any way, shape or form. And most importantly, DON'T let your mother become the primary source of your embarrassment. Needless to say, there are clearly defined parameters within which I must operate so that I might be viewed as something other than the bane of someone's existence.

Evidently, the rules apply at the bus stop, too, where veritable throngs of kids might actually witness the unthinkable: handholding, goodbye kisses, a neatly folded tissue being stuffed inside someone's pocket, a bandage being hurriedly applied (with or without a dab of ointment), a threadbare monkey and/or a certain stuffed armadillo being relinquished—lest they become inadvertent stowaways for the duration of the school day.

Apparently, I'm not allowed to wave anymore either—although I've recently appealed that decision and my suggestion of "waving with a little less enthusiasm" is somewhat promising. For that, I suppose I should be thankful, and perhaps more understanding.

After all, I remember being completely mortified as a teenager when my dad would—almost inconceivably—traipse around in his underwear while my date and I sat on the couch in stunned silence. Shortly thereafter, he'd emerge from the kitchen with leftovers in hand and a big grin upon his face. Of course, he'd then amble, unabashed, down the hallway from whence he came while I very seriously considered the merits of dissolving into nothingness. It's entirely likely I make my daughters feel much the same way, although I have yet to traipse anywhere in my underwear.

I have, however, been known to read books aloud at the aforementioned bus stop, the practice of which has been met with a fair degree of resistance even though it's an ideal time and place to do so. Okay, it's been met with unequivocal refusals to listen and ardent demands that I cease and desist. "Mom, we're not babies anymore. Everyone on the bus will make fun of us if they see that book in your hand because they'll KNOW you've been reading it to us. It's *embarrassing*, you know."

Woe is me.

It's not just any old book either. Otherwise I wouldn't be so miserable. The book in question happens to be *The BFG*, a drool-worthy classic by Roald Dahl—a gift from a perfectly wonderful third grade teacher who knew I'd find it practically irresistible as a read aloud. Only it won't be happening at *our* bus stop—the place where sulkiness periodically rears its ugly head. Nope. Perish the thought.

But lo and behold, I recently learned that another perfectly wonderful individual at that very same school will soon be reading aloud that very same book to my kids in the library—a place where reading of practically every sort is celebrated. As it should be. With any luck, my charges will forget themselves and drink in every delicious syllable.

Planet Mom: It's where I live (embarrassing my children on a regular basis and getting ready to celebrate the American Library Association's annual Banned Books Week by, you guessed it, reading a banned book).

Bad Mood Munchers

Forever, it seems, my children have brought me newly created pieces of art to ogle—eager for both praise and encouragement for their Picasso-esque efforts. I'd like to hope that I've always been mindful of their feelings as they bestow upon me their most prized offerings on the planet. It could be a self-portrait destined for the refrigerator, a dachshund or a duck, lovingly wrought from a dollop of clay, or an impressive rendering of a dinosaur, hewn from a large and unwieldy sheet of poster board.

Likewise, I've been called upon to admire masterpieces that are nothing short of remarkable—like the tiny box turtle one of my progenies recently fashioned from an empty candy box, the medieval-inspired 3-D tower (with a working drawbridge!) she made from a mere sheet of paper and a bit of tape and string, or the songbird she ingeniously crafted from an acorn and a couple of feathers harvested from the back yard, "…because I wanted a pet bird, Mom, to live in the birdcage Grandma gave us."

Indeed, these are delicate matters and it is imperative that I handle the psyches of my fledgling artists with the utmost of care and sensitivity. Heaven forbid I fail to ooh and aah appropriately—providing that much-anticipated glowing review of a certain someone's work, or that I make the colossal error of misidentifying a beloved nugget of whateverness, placed in my hands for immediate appraisal. "It's a…malamute with three heads, right?"

Sometimes it's best to simply shut up and wait for my brood to inadvertently *tell me* what this or that mystery item is, so that screw-ups are minimal. Thankfully, the bulk of what comes home from school (i.e. that which hails from their amazing art teacher) is readily identifiable. Good thing.

Thus far in their academic journey my youngest charges have proffered the most endearing set of polar bears imaginable, some chunky caterpillars that I adore completely, a Canada goose whose precious neck has since been repaired, a robin redbreast that surely summoned the spring, a handsome set of Italian frescos that rendered me utterly speechless and a handful of gloriously ornate vessels for storing jewelry and whatnot—etched abundantly with love.

All I ever managed to churn out as a grade-schooler was a bunch of stupid ashtrays, which, by today's standards, would be deemed slightly appalling. Oh, and a handful of dreadfully unimaginative pot-like thingies and a deranged-looking papier-mâché rabbit for which I am hard pressed—even now—to suggest a legitimate purpose. Further, there was an embarrassment of highly unremarkable, kiln-fired blobs of clay I remember hauling home to join my shrine to bad art. At least my kids' creations possess irrefutable aesthetic value if not a preponderance of practicality. Plus, I know what the stuff is—with the exception of the *Bad Mood Munchers*.

That said, I reached into their backpacks not long ago expecting to discover yet another pair of entities to marvel instantaneously. Instead I found two fist-sized, lumps of hardened clay—ones that were warped and mangled beyond all recognition and slathered profusely with vibrant blotches of color—absolutely reveling in the quality of nebulousness. But as I examined each mass a bit more closely, I began to discern a face of sorts—a distorted rage-filled visage with deep-set eyes that seemed to pierce my very soul, a fearsome set of eyebrows that I couldn't help but trace with my finger and a maw that would forever remain agape, likely for the purpose of swallowing small children whole. In a word, it was hideous and begged the question, "What on earth IS it?"

"It's *Angry Man*, Mom. My Bad Mood Muncher. Isn't he AWESOME?! And look, I made him a castle to live in!" Child One crowed with delight.

As I stood in stunned silence, her cohort informed me that her infinitely weird-ish clay creation had been dubbed Steve, which stumped me perhaps more than anything.

"*Steve*?! Who names a monstrosity like THAT 'Steve' for crying out loud?! What's it for, anyway?" I felt driven to ask.

"It's for when I get angry, Mom. I'm supposed to find some paper and write down what I'm mad about then twist the paper and try to tear it in half, which uses up A LOT of energy and helps get my anger out. If I'm *still* angry after I try (and fail) to tear the twisted paper, I have to open it up and calmly shred it into little pieces. Then I put the pieces in his castle thingy and he EATS them. Then my bad mood is GONE! Isn't that entirely coooool?!"

Well after being enlightened on the subject, I had to admit the idea of defusing anger was slightly brilliant. And as art projects go, it was probably wicked fun besides. That said, *I* now want a Bad Mood Muncher to call my very own—one that promises to devour all that I find completely irksome on this planet.

Indeed, I'm quite sure I could feed the beast with the best of them.

Planet Mom: It's where I live (fishing bits of paper from Angry Man's mouth—some of which was twisted unmercifully, meticulously piecing the scraps together and, stupidly, reading the wrath-filled messages contained therein).

The Value of Permanence

Lots of things in this world are disturbing to me. Greed. Poverty. Heinous crime. The demise of the planet. The pervasive nature of mediocrity. Mismatched socks. Oddly enough, I include technology on that list, too—or more correctly, the alarming pace at which technological devices are mass produced, marketed to the public and propelled into the great abyss of planned obsolescence. It's as if we're cultivating a generation of people who care less about the enduring nature of things and more about the latest nugget of innovation that promises to improve society in some novel way. That said, I fear my kids will grow to devalue the permanence of things— despite the fact that on this particular day the notion seems wholly inconceivable.

That said, the hoarding tendencies of my youngest children are beyond all comprehension—as is their love of sameness. Ostensibly, their mission in life is to avoid change at all costs and to amass virtually every molecule of that which is deemed worthy of collecting—heaping it upon dressers, shoving it beneath beds and stowing it into forgotten corners of our pitifully disordered garage. Of course, they've come by this trait honestly. My husband could instantaneously produce any of the following: a receipt for a television we no longer own, a tool I have never once seen in my life, an impressive array of his artwork from the fifth grade, a prized stash of his baby teeth.

I wish I were joking.

At any rate, the hoarding gene seems inextricably present within my brood. But oddly enough, it gives me comfort because it implies there is hope that my daughters will feel compelled to hold on to the remnants of life that matter—the tangible stuff that will trigger memories long after I'm gone, serving to moor them to their childhood.

Like any good cynic, I'm skeptical that an electronic record could preserve the past on par with that which I can hold in my hands. Further, bits and bytes seem inordinately elusive to me. Ethereal almost. Not to mention, data stored in this fashion is far from safe in my charge, having managed to delete countless items to my utter dismay. My husband, too, has mourned the loss of infinitely dear morsels of remembrances, having inadvertently erased a snippet of speech from his cell phone some time ago—one that was placed there by a certain six-year-old who breathlessly told of some robins who had apparently "...lost their way, Daddy!" Her voice, filled impossibly with the exuberance of youth on that memorable January day, cannot be replicated.

Indeed, lapses in judgment happen. Computers crash. Files become corrupt or irretrievable. That which is irreplaceable can be woefully distorted or lost entirely. What's more, the digital wonders of the twenty-first century, although impressive, somehow lack palpability in my mind—especially as keepsakes go. Pictures and even video clips of my family at the shore simply cannot compare with the sack full of shells we gathered together and hauled back to Pennsylvania because someone insisted that we "...take the beach home, Mom. It'll help us remember." Even still, the briny scent of the sea hits me squarely when I open the bag to finger our bounty once more and to poke at the grains of sand that have settled to the bottom. In an instant I am back at the shore, feeling the warmth beneath my feet and hearing the gulls shriek over the waves that pound without end.

Likewise, an email doesn't possess near the charm that a handwritten letter does—especially if doodles have been scrawled in the margins or a violet has been carefully tucked within the folds of the paper. Nor can a digital photograph compete with the inherent concreteness of a grainy, black and white 35mm print. Moreover, a text message is not remotely related to a lunchbox note, or one that awaits beneath a pillow at day's end.

Color me old-fashioned, resistant-to-change—a dinosaur even. That aside, I feel connected to what's real and right for me.

Planet Mom: It's where I live (tethered forever to that which is tangible).

Romance for Dummies

My husband is a hopeless romantic. Albeit an accidental one. Of course, he's always done the stuff that hopeless romantics do. He sends me roses—just because. He writes me poetry and remembers our anniversary each November. He surprises me on my birthday, without fail and bestows upon me sinful quantities of chocolate on Valentine's Day—knowing full well that I'd do almost anything for a slab of dark chocolate almond bark. And though I love him dearly for doing so, those are not the things I find especially romantic—never mind what the world at large may opine.

No doubt, he'd be stunned by this news, and perhaps disappointed to think he'd been missing the mark all these years. But he hasn't been missing the mark. He's simply oblivious as to why I find him wholly irresistible. Indeed, he's clueless when it comes to recognizing what he does so completely right. Hence, the *accidental* component of the hopeless romantic equation.

That said, he unwittingly seizes the ordinary moments of life and somehow makes them special, which, to me, is deemed slightly wonderful and oh-so-romantic. More specifically, he leaves endearing, little notes everywhere with nary a holiday in sight. I stumble upon them throughout my day—under my pillow, in the kitchen, thoughtfully affixed to my computer screen, where I cannot help but notice—and smile. "I LOVE YOU—ALWAYS," it will read, or "I'M PROUD OF YOU." Then again, some of his messages are entirely pragmatic: "I FED THE DOG ALREADY. DON'T FEED HIM AGAIN," or mildly sarcastic: "REMEMBER TO PUT THE

FISH IN THE FRIDGE OR WE'LL ALL DIE OF FOOD POISONING."

Either way, I'm instantly charmed.

Likewise, my Romeo is liable to warm my heart by bringing me a beef and cheddar panini from town—an exceedingly delicious mid-day indulgence inspired entirely by that-which-moves-good-deed-doers-to-action. What's more, the man has texted me while perched atop the lawn mower—proclaiming his abiding love for me under the blazing sun. Or maybe it was to remind me to pick up an errant flip-flop in the lawn. I can't remember now, but I'd like to hope it was the former.

While I was pregnant he satisfied all sorts of culinary cravings, too, whipping up a shameful quantity of raspberry milkshakes and fetching dried apricots in the dead of night. He also tied my shoes, as the swell of my freakishly large belly thwarted my every effort to reach my knees, let alone my feet.

Further, the man has no qualms whatsoever in dealing with our brood when they are beyond the point of persnickety at mealtime, obscenely tired and cranky at the close of a trying day, impossibly giddified over this or that perfectly inane thing or even while hurling profusely into a big bucket—all of which I find inordinately romantic. Strange, but true. Plus, he fixes stuff that's broken. He ferries children hither and yon. He masterminds our every holiday feast. He cooks and shops and bears in mind what he'll need for meals—which isn't normal, I'm told. Not for a man. Nor is suggesting that on some lazy afternoon we should watch *Doctor Zhivago*—an epic love story in the truest sense. "What's so weird about wanting to watch a movie together?" he'll ask, puzzled by my stunned silence.

Oblivion abounds, my dear Romeo.

Lately, said oblivion has risen to a new level, giving me reason to shake my head in disbelief. Just before Valentine's Day, following an appreciable snowfall, he got up at dark-thirty to take the dog out, which necessitated shoveling a path in the back yard so that our vertically challenged pooch might not disappear altogether in a snowdrift. "How thoughtful," I mused. Some time later, I went to the window to admire what he had done. Lo and behold, he had carved a most enormous heart there in the sparkling snow—roughly twenty feet across with an arrow piercing its center. "Whoa," was all I could mouth, astounded by this wonderful thing he had surely done to woo me once more—as if Aphrodite herself had guided the shovel there in the grayness of dawn.

Naturally, I showered him with gratitude, wrapping my arms around him and pulling him closer to the window so we could gaze at this thing of beauty together, hand in hand. "How sweet and kind and UTTERLY ROMANTIC of you!" I gushed.

"Romantic?" he repeated, fumbling over the word and glancing in the direction of the window.

"Yes! ROMANTIC!" I affirmed, sure that he was merely playing dumb. "How on earth did you *do* such an amazing thing?!"

"*What* amazing thing? I shoveled a path in the snow. For the dog."

"No, no, no. That's not a *path*. That's a HEART! A GINORMOUS HEART NESTLED BETWEEN THE PINES JUST FOR ME—FOR VALENTINE'S DAY! That was so completely ROMANTIC of you!"

Stupidly, he looked out the window and back at me with an expression that clearly conveyed *the wheel is spinning, but the hamster is dead*. It was the point at which he could have *and should have* rescued himself. A simple nod of agreement and a half-hearted smile would have sufficed. But no. Not for my oblivion-minded Romeo. My (accidental) hopeless romantic.

Planet Mom: It's where I live (with my dear, sweet Romeo).

Seven Things Parenthood Has Taught Me

I've been a parent for some 8,734 days. A stunningly imperfect parent, I hasten to add. During that period of time I learned more about sleep deprivation, sibling rivalry and teen angst than I previously considered humanly possible. However, the past decade has proven to be particularly edifying. Indeed, Frick and Frack (my ten-year-old twin daughters) have provided me with a veritable feast of enlightenment. So, in the spirit of welcoming my next decade as a parent (and the vat of enlightenment sure to come), I thought it might be fitting to recap what the last ten years have taught me—at least from the perspective of a stunningly imperfect parent.

1. Beauty is likely in the kitchen. Translation: Most of the masterpieces I've collected thus far in my parenting journey are proudly displayed upon my refrigerator, where I suspect they will remain for a very long time to come. That is not to say the face of the fridge is the only canvas upon which said prized artwork hangs in all its faded glory. My home is quite literally inundated with the fledgling, Picasso-esque efforts of my brood, serving as a constant reminder of their boundless generosity and artsy flair. As it should be, I suppose.

2. The word "sleepover" is a misnomer. No one actually *sleeps* at a sleepover—including the pitiable adults charged with the impossible duty of entertaining the gaggle of impressionable youths in attendance. Furthermore, the later slumber partygoers *appear* to crash, the earlier they will rise, demanding bacon and eggs. Moreover, it is inevitable that someone's personal

effects (i.e. an unclaimed pair of underpants, a lone sweat sock, an irreplaceable stuffed animal) will be tragically lost—only to surface months later in the oddest of places.

3. When taken out of context, that-which-parents-say-and-do is often appalling. Case in point: "Stop licking the dog." "If you're going to ride your scooter in the house, wear a damn helmet." "Fight nice." In a similar vein, I've fed my charges dinner and/or dessert in a bathtub more times than I'd care to admit, I've used a shameful quantity of saliva to clean smudges off faces, I've suggested a broad range of inappropriate responses to being bullied and I consider the unabashed bribe to be one of my most effective parenting tools.

4. On average, we parents spend an ungodly amount of time reading aloud books that we find unbearably tedious. We say unforgivably vile things about the so-called "new math" and, as a matter of course, we become unhinged by science projects and whatnot—especially those that require mad dashes to the craft store at all hours of the day and night in search of more paint, more modeling clay and perhaps a small team of marriage counselors.

5. Forget wedding day jitters, the parent/teacher conference is among the most stressful experiences in life—not to be confused with the anxiety-infused telephone call from the school nurse and that interminable lapse of time wedged between not knowing what's wrong with one's child and finding out.

6. A captive audience is the very best sort of audience. That said, some of the most enlightening conversations between parent and child occur when the likelihood

of escape is at a minimum (i.e. at the dinner table, in a church pew, en route to the umpteenth sporting event/practice session/music lesson, within the confines of the ever-popular ER). Similarly, the discovery of a teensy-tiny wad of paper—one that has been painstakingly folded and carefully tucked within a pocket, wedged beneath a pillow or hidden inside dresser drawer—is akin to being granted psychic powers. Everything a parent needs to know about his or her child will likely be scrawled upon said scrap of paper.

7. Unanswerable questions never die—they simply migrate to more fertile regions of our homes where they mutate into hideous manifestations of their original forms, leaving us wringing our hands and damning our inadequate selves.

Planet Mom: It's where I live (getting schooled as we speak).

The Graduates

As a parent, I love this particular wedge of time—the infinitely delicious weeks of May during which I savor the end of the school year because I've finally gotten the hang of the wretched routine and have come to grips with the academic expectations—even those involving the dreaded partial-products algorithm that made me feel woefully inadequate. For me (this year especially), it's been a perfectly scrumptious segment of the calendar, nestled comfortably between the Land of Third Grade, during which fond memories have been gathered like seashells since the early part of September, and the celebrated Death of Structure (i.e. the warmth and wonderfulness that is summer). We're on the cusp of something grand and glorious after all, and in the name of preparing for the season of suntans and sweet corn, things have loosened up considerably—or maybe it's just me.

Come Memorial Day, I feel like less of a tyrant and more like someone who takes the inordinately-asinine-compulsion-to-stress-over-homework mantra and sets it on a shelf for a time, allowing her brood to linger outside long after the sun has set and the crickets have begun their nightly serenade. Bedtimes have been stretched to a shameful degree for weeks on end and an embarrassment of toasted marshmallows have already been consumed while crouched on the deck around a crackling fire. The only thing missing is the intermittent flashes of fireflies along the thickets and darkish places in the lawn.

Indeed, June is calling—and the long-awaited season of graduation is nigh. Time for looking forward to what the next chapter might bring. Time to reflect upon the wealth of knowledge and skill acquired while leading up to said monumental event. Time to swell with pride over the many and varied accomplishments that have been realized throughout the journey to fruition.

By the same token, *our* resident "graduates" have embraced the very same notion, boldly stepping into the realm of that which is decidedly new and different—although it has nothing whatsoever to do with progressing to the fourth grade. Oddly enough, it involves bathing—or, more correctly, showering. Because that's what they do now. They shower, "...like big kids, Mom," having renounced completely the less-than-appealing, wholly contemptible idea of washing up in anything suggestive of a tub. "Baths are for babies, Mom. Don't you know *anything*?!"

Ironically, their collective sentiment has failed to fill me with a sense of gratification, joy or the heady rush of deliverance I fully expected. I thought I'd be beside myself with glee, having no more deluges with which to deal (read: a profusion of ungainly elbows paired with WAY too many water-filled cups and saucers and bottle-like vessels poised to fall upon ill fated floors—despite the delivery of impassioned lectures on such topics). I assumed I'd be thrilled, having been relieved of the loathsome duty of fishing the remnants of broken balloons and gobs of hair from the drain. What's more, I was fairly certain there would no longer be a need to curb tub-related hostilities among the aforementioned warring factions—which would have made me slightly euphoric on any other day.

Although on this day I find myself lamenting the change. Wishing things were as they used to be. Mourning the passage of time and the birth of independence as it relates to that inexorable desire to be grown. Stupidly, I miss the rubber duckies. And the obscene quantities of suds. And the mermaids with their lithesome tails. And the gnarly dinosaurs, frozen hideously in mid-pose, their mouths agape, now languishing next to a half-empty bottle of lavender-scented whateverness. I long for a chance to eavesdrop as they sail ships hither and yon and sip tea with lizards and lions, completely engrossed in another world. Part of me regrets that I ever grew tired of washing their tangled manes and scrubbing their soiled bodies. That said, I wish I could lather their bushy heads once more—shaping and molding foamy peaks and Washingtonian-inspired dos. "Soon, they'll *want* to return to the bath," I reasoned. "The boats and bubbles and fish that squirt will call to them unremittingly."

But that day never came. Smitten are they with the almighty shower—the shower that from the very start promised to be a dreadful mistake.

I worried first about the water—as any good fusspot would. Were my children capable of remembering (and applying) the 643 crucial bits of information I had given them about the big, scary on/off knob, adjusting the temperature and shutting the damn door so as not to flood the place? Had they fully comprehended the horribleness of getting water up one's nose or soap in one's eyes? WOULD THEY EVEN KNOW HOW TO BREATHE BENEATH SAID TORRENTS?! And what of the hazards of slipping and choking on water droplets and being swallowed up by the soul-sucking monstrosity-of-a-drain?! Had any of my sage advice (and crazed thoughts) resonated?!

In hindsight, there were *other* things with which I should have concerned myself. Namely: Showers that would never end, showers that involved sinful quantities of soap (upon floors and walls and every inch of the fools in question), showers during which people would forget to wash, showers that included doodles and notes and high-fives upon glass doors, showers that became tandem in the name of saving the planet, showers that incorporated spirited games of soap hockey (don't ask), showers that featured tiny wads of toilet tissue that became fused to the ceiling forevermore.

Indeed, they've graduated. Ugh.

Planet Mom: It's where I live (lamenting the passage of time).

Still is the Night

Shortly after the big, yellow school bus groaned to a halt and deposited Planet Mom's brood at the curb, the skies grew angry and the winds began to whip, swirling all manner of leaves and debris about the place. The heavens rumbled in the distance and massive clouds moved swiftly as she and her children hurried up the grassy knoll to the safety and comfort of their home. Together they sat, perched at the northernmost bank of windows, and watched with amazement as a monstrous wall of gray swallowed the September sun as if it were a mere lemon drop. A raging storm was indeed very nearly upon them.

A sudden shroud of darkness then descended upon the land whilst towering pines swayed in the yard and lawn chairs skittered like spiders across the wooden deck, tumbling into the bushes and startling the children and their curly-haired dog. Shortly thereafter, lightning lit the skies and thunder shook the house unmercifully, causing the dog to cower in a corner—its springy, white tail hidden between its legs. Lights flickered ON and OFF and ON again while rain began to pelt the roof in fitful waves, thwarting all efforts to keep the smallish creatures in question focused on their homework. It was a school night after all.

"Are the lights going to GO OFF and STAY OFF, Mom?" one of the pair asked, a hint of apprehension in her voice. "What'll we do then?"

Their mother, not being particularly gifted in the realm of meteorological topics, shrugged her shoulders and tried desperately to think of something that might divert her daughters' attention away from the impending doom that seemed all but certain to strike.

"Get back to your schoolwork," she instructed, all the while pretending to ignore the deafening cracks of thunder and the sirens that wailed in the distance. "It's just a thunderstorm."

"But how will we *see* to do our homework if the lights STAY OFF?" the wisp of a child probed further.

"Yeah," her infinitely inquisitive counterpart added. "And how will we watch TV tonight?"

"I'll think of *something*," the mother asserted and then silently lamented the notion of being without television (*and* the computer *and* the microwave *and* so on) for what would surely seem an eternity.

Lo and behold, at some point during the ferocity of the storm, the power did, in fact, fail and legions of flashlights (many without functional batteries) were summoned from beneath beds and forgotten drawers. Cleverly, the woman lit scented candles; however it was soon determined that her progenies had mysteriously developed an incapacitating aversion to being near an open flame—despite having enjoyed countless marshmallow toasting events during the summer involving (gasp!) campfires and whatnot. "My homework will catch on fire, Mom!" So out the candles went directly, along with any bit of cinnamon-y goodness that might have emanated from said waxen devices.

Dozens of minutes elapsed and darkness fell. Soon the woman's mate returned from work and joined the anxious bunch, eager to instill calm and assurance where fear had begun to creep. Savory snacks and a multitude of shadow puppets were instantly produced to the delight of many. Needless to say, the man's offspring were mightily impressed with his skills and mesmerized by the uncommon and authentic nature of the railroad lanterns he managed to unearth from their pitifully disordered garage. His wife was equally impressed with the aforementioned feats and in return promised never to divulge the number of times he flicked light switches like a fool— because she, too, stupidly flicked switches.

Eventually, the punishing storm passed and the winds subsided, although the power outage continued. Nevertheless, an abundance of laughs were shared as were stories of parental hardship involving crippling snowstorms and great floods during which both heat and electricity were lost for days on end. "Wow! That must have been *horrible*, Dad!" (Translation: "How did you survive without cartoons, Dad?!") More importantly, the family reconnected in a way that they hadn't in a very long time. Everyone took turns recounting the day's ordinary and not-so-ordinary events. The dog's ears were gently stroked and beloved books were read within the soft glow of the lanterns as the children nestled upon their mother's lap.

At the close of each chapter, just before she began reading the next, she paused ever so slightly—and that was the moment during which a strange and wonderful thing befell them. All was perfectly still—aside from the crickets outside calling to would-be mates, the dozing dog and the breathy whispers of children completely engrossed in the deliciousness of literature. As it should be. No ever-present drone of the air conditioner could be heard. No television blared in the background. Not even the familiar hum of the refrigerator or a solitary screen saver could be detected. The sacred wedge of silence was magical, entrancing and wholly alien to those huddled upon the floor and sofa.

Just then the power returned—an abrupt and unwelcome guest. The household whirred and lurched back to life, removing all but the vestiges of ambiance and intimacy. The children blinked as if snapping out of a trance. Their squinty-eyed mother closed the book and used it to shield herself from the brightness, now everywhere. Her mate sat up suddenly, forcing himself to process the transformation. The dog awoke with a start. Shortly thereafter, everyone went their separate ways—back to the tired and the familiar. The spell had been broken, irreparably so. Or had it?

"We should do this again, Mom! We should have a fake power outage *every* week!" the children insisted at breakfast the next morning.

And so it was. Fake Power Outage Night was thereby established as a new family tradition and it was duly noted that batteries should be abundantly stockpiled.

Planet Mom: It's where I live (paying tribute to the ever-masterful Garrett Rice, aka *Neanderdad*, and his patented writing style).

CHAPTER 5

M is for Motherhood

From There to Here

Just a moment ago, my children were kindergarteners—spindly creatures with wee arms, knobby knees and tinny voices. I remember well our maiden voyage to the school's open house one afternoon late in August—to the shores of Mrs. Morehart's classroom, a warm and welcoming place at the end of the hall where my husband and I, like everyone else, crammed our oversized frames into impossibly small chairs eager to consume all that a parent of a kindergartener could possibly need to know about the year ahead. There was talk of cubbies and snow boots, art smocks and mittens. Bus schedules. Lunch lines. Recess and snacks.

Together, with our knees awkwardly pressed to our chests and our irrational fears lurking just beneath the surface, we learned about the magical nature of story time, the Puppet Lady who would come to call, the wealth of educational experiences our children were slated to have and, of course, the vastly important assurance of bathroom proximity. *God knows how dearly we valued that.* In any event, our concerns were adequately addressed as a collective sigh of relief wafted over the cozy grove of Lilliputian-inspired tables that filled the room and the brightly colored whateverness with which said room was adorned.

Indeed, Mrs. Morehart was a woman with whom we became enamored almost instantly. Her classroom promised to be a venue where impressionable minds would be nourished, creativity and curiosity would be duly celebrated and respect for others, as well as oneself, would be cultivated above all else. What's more, surnames and bus numbers would be indelibly imprinted upon the forehead of each and every five-year-old and the aforementioned godsend-of-an-educator would refrain from passing judgment on those who were wholly incapable of enforcing bedtimes as well as those who might be inclined to serve dinner in the bathtub on a school night (to, of course, remedy the not-getting-the-kids-to-bed-at-a-reasonable-hour problem).

In truth, no one's forehead was defiled in the plan to distinguish students or to ensure that the right child got on the right bus at dismissal. In any event, the curators of our precious cargo did, indeed, coordinate the logistics of transportation (and practically every other aspect of child management) seamlessly and with great aplomb. That said, the Land of Kindergarten was a place we parents could feel genuinely good about leaving our charges.

Never mind the wave of apprehension that literally consumed me the following week, when that big, yellow beast-of-a-school-bus groaned to a halt in my street and a certain couple of somebodies were expected to board and then traverse the uncertain path that would come to define their lives as kindergarteners—*without me*. Needless to say, a great deal of time has passed since then—despite the fact that it feels like mere seconds ago that I sat in one of those tiny plastic chairs, a red one I think, fretting over the exceedingly remote possibility that my children would be trampled by a herd of backpack-toting third graders or, tragically, mauled by a rogue pencil sharpener.

My charges are worldly fifth graders now—not-so-spindly creatures who positively thrive on the thrum of activity present in their school day. No longer are they overwhelmed by long lines in the cafeteria, the deafening roar of eco-friendly electric hand dryers in the restrooms or an oncoming herd of third graders for that matter. They know practically every nook and cranny of their beloved school—where favorite library books can be found, which teachers have a debilitating affinity for chocolate chip cookies and, not surprisingly, how to efficiently navigate to the nurse's office from virtually anywhere in the building. What's more, they've learned how to deal with unwieldy band instruments, lost book fair money and, occasionally, a terrible, horrible, no good, very bad day.

In that respect—yet ever so reluctantly—I acknowledge the vast chasm that exists between then and now, there and here, even though it has felt so completely fleeting.

Planet Mom: It's where I live.

Food for Thought

I'm pretty sure June Cleaver's head would explode if she knew of my pitiful and often failed attempts to gather my brood at the dinner table for a real sit-down meal—*Leave it to Beaver* style. In a word, I am woefully inept when it comes to planning, preparing and placing said meal upon the table in a timely and aesthetically pleasing manner. So much so that my kids have apparently forgotten what it's like to dine as a family within the confines of this particular circus-inspired, scheduled-to-the-max sort of establishment. Never mind that we did so for much of the summer, sweet corn having been shamelessly utilized as bait. But I digress.

"You want us to sit *here*? Together? And talk about our day?" my incredulous kids ask, clearly taken aback by the prospect of stopping whatever it is they're doing to plunk themselves at the kitchen table for twenty to thirty minutes of food and not-so-idle conversation. Of course, my gentle demands are often met with a healthy dose of eye rolling coupled with I-can't-possibly-set-the-table-if-I'm-tying-my-soccer-cleats-AND-doing-my-homework brand of snarky commentary. Par for the course in the trenches of Parentville.

Needless to say, the Gods of After School Madness rarely smile upon me and may, in fact, revel in my ineptitude, mocking my efforts to deal with the deluge of mini-crises that routinely befall our happy home at that critical juncture—that impossibly brief and patently crazed window of time wedged between the instant my charges make landfall and the race to the 437th extracurricular event of the week. As a less-than-composed parent, and seemingly without fail, *this* is the time when the wheels fly off and the bottom falls out.

That said, the phone typically rings just as the pots on the stove begin to boil over and shortly before godknowswho knocks at the door, sending the dog into an apoplectic barking seizure. Moments later, my dear progenies demand that I flit from the stove to hover nearby while they wrestle, by turns, with the concept of divisibility and the large and unwieldy vocabulary words that may or may not appear in a book I, stupidly, suggested. Granted, the experience itself is decidedly intolerable. Furthermore, it's rumored that I may know next to nothing about math and even less about adverbs. However, the ceaseless petitions for my help continue—in the midst of meal preparation, listening to a certain French horn and clarinet, answering the door and phone, conducting backpack search and rescue missions (for decomposing food) with disturbing regularity, frantically gathering whatever paraphernalia will be needed for this or that nightly venture and dealing with the occasional cat vomit surprise and/or dog-poo-on-the-bed bit of hideousness. For the record, I'm not particularly interested in learning *how* the latter occurred.

At any rate, when and if I finally succeed in shepherding one and all to the celebrated table to feast on what (hopefully) will qualify as a palatable meal, I immediately remember *why* I went to such lengths at all. Firstly, there's compelling data that links sit-down meals with a child's success, especially with respect to at-risk behaviors—so saith a team of researchers at Columbia University and Dan Harris of ABC News. Secondly, Anderson Cooper of CNN desperately wants "…to bring back the family dinner, one meal at a time" through his Sunday Supper Club and I, most assuredly, don't want to disappoint him. Thirdly, and perhaps most notably, the discussion that takes place over peas and potatoes (or whatever I managed not to burn beyond recognition) is invaluable. That alone is worth the price of admission.

Often there is talk of "bad actors" on the bus and goose poop on the soccer field, who vomited profusely in the cafeteria and which dweeb dared to drink the "mystery brew" that a host of classmates lovingly prepared. Not to be outdone, my husband brings his own brand of bizarreness to the conversation, opening a tiny window into his day as well. As it should be, I suppose.

Planet Mom: It's where I live (occasionally at the dinner table with my inimitable cast and crew).

Have You Hugged a Book Today?

We have a library in our house, which sounds slightly more impressive than it actually is. The area in question is far from a sprawling expanse littered with overstuffed chairs and an abundance of narrative gems. More correctly, our so-called library occupies a modest corner of our home—a place where a blue-checkered playpen once stood seemingly forever. Nevertheless, it is a space devoted to all-things-bookish. A small yet infinitely important enclave that exists for the sole purpose of fueling my children's passion for reading.

Almost a decade has passed since we began gathering a hodgepodge of titles and piling them into some semblance of order there upon the floor of our living room. Tallest to smallest. Favorites within easy reach. A perfect mélange of new and not-so-new tales—thanks to having traversed this parenting path once before.

Naturally, said books would spill out into the room after a certain couple of somebodies (read: Toddler One and Toddler Two) raided the cache, leaving a trail of literary goodness in their collective wake. Never mind that only yesterday pillows and great herds of stuffed animals were dragged there and commissioned for the purpose of building reading nests and whatnot. Only recently have we been able to place the prized entities elsewhere (i.e. upon the honey-colored bookshelf that now inhabits the aforementioned corner—the one that boasts a cavernous window through which the morning sun pours almost without fail).

It is perhaps a bit more special given that the shelf itself was one that my husband had designed and built back in 1969. It was the high school shop project that seemed destined never to be finished. Lo and behold, the four-tiered wonder *was* completed and for some forty years it lived in his childhood home. That's where I first ogled its glossy, maple finish—along with a handful of teakwood carvings that sat upon its top shelf. A one-humped camel and an Asian elephant with a missing tusk. Keepsakes that hailed from afar. Treasures with which my children were enamored each and every time we visited Grandma.

I guess I never really thought about the notion of my mother-in-law not being there to witness their growing curiosity. Nor did I entertain the possibility of adopting her wooden bookshelf when she died—complete with the coveted carvings. Of course, they still sit atop the shelf, nodding approval with each book selection my charges make. Grandma would be pleased, I'm sure.

Likewise, I think she'd be pleased to learn of the strides her granddaughters have made since kindergarten, and how their love of books has flourished during that same wedge of time. No longer do they reach for bedtime favorites like *Goodnight Moon*, the brilliantly penned *Where the Wild Things Are*, the infinitely tender *Guess How Much I Love You* and the exceedingly palpable *Wilfred Gordon McDonald Partridge*. Even Dr. Seuss has fallen out of favor with my brood.

Indeed, the pure and simple joy of picture books has been replaced by the all-consuming nature of chapter books— ones that invite my progenies to dwell for a time, deliciously entangled within the words on a given page. Needless to say, their tastes have grown more sophisticated, as has their command of vocabulary. That said, Child One is completely smitten with mysteries, all-things-*Harry-Potter* and that which is disturbingly terrifying while Child Two is fond of cookbooks and craft books, although she went through an interminable phase during which she would read nothing unless its plot somehow involved a godforsaken dog, a horse blessed with the ability to speak or a wretched hamster. Of course, they both feast voraciously upon the celebrated *Diary of a Wimpy Kid* series and practically anything ever written by Roald Dahl, Barbara Park or Kate DiCamillo.

All things considered, I deem my children's journey as emerging readers to have been nothing short of remarkable, and I can't help but feel indebted to those who've helped cultivate their enduring love of books—during this National Reading Month of March, and always.

Planet Mom: It's where I live (with an abundance of books worthy of hugging…and barely able to breathe ever since a request was made for Hemingway's *The Old Man and the Sea*).

Building a Reader

There are letters, phonetic elements and, of course, words to which a vast array of meaning has been assigned over the course of history. Building blocks we parents turn to as we go about the important business of raising a reader. We tap our well of instructional instincts, consider our own path to literacy and look to the experts who willingly share all that we'll ever need to know about teaching a child to read. Furthermore, we immerse our charges in literature, expose them to robust vocabulary, swear by the tried-and-true merits of repetition and, of course, read to them from the moment they become implanted within the uterine wall. Intuitively, we assume these ingredients help form a solid foundation upon which layers of understanding will take root and a lifelong love of reading will flourish. Theoretically, this is all well and good.

Enter: the unpredictable and highly diverse nature of children.

That said, for the better part of my oldest daughter's childhood, she had what can only be described as a visceral hatred of books. In sum, she gave new meaning to the term "reluctant reader." From the early days of Dr. Seuss through her interminable high school career/slightly disturbing Sylvia Plath phase, literature—even *good* literature, it seemed—was the bane of her existence.

Naturally, I was completely convinced that whatever I had or hadn't done as a parent somehow led to this sorry state of affairs. Pages, upon which writers had built a rich tapestry of words, did little to woo her within. I had failed at one of the most important assignments of motherhood—to nurture a love of books. I suppose her abhorrence could have stemmed from something far more simplistic—perhaps she found books to be pitifully uninspiring…or had yet to discover an author that spoke to her…or maybe she considered reading itself to be a horrendously taxing affair (with all that page turning and whatnot). And no matter how I tried (to reward her efforts, to involve her in summer literacy camp, to make the words on a given page come to life by reading aloud till I felt compelled to light myself on fire), it was all for naught—until she went away to college, that is. It was there that her passion for books finally blossomed. Better late than never.

In a similar vein, my youngest child was and continues to be a challenge in the truest sense of the word. For the longest time, she refused to tackle anything unless its plot involved a horse that could talk, a dog overcome by some ridiculous misfortune or a hackneyed mystery soused with exceedingly dull dialogue. And I don't know why, exactly, that sort of thing bothered me—except that I was largely responsible for reading the cussed things aloud after dinner, that is until my head lolled around as if it were tethered not to a neck, but to a spindly rubber hose. Needless to say, I remained dead asleep until my brood poked my eyelids with indiscriminate fingers, demanding to know what the stupid horse or godforsaken dog or pint-sized super sleuth had said. Thankfully, the aforementioned reader-of-that-which-is-dreadfully-banal has progressed to more thought provoking content in the titles she chooses nowadays.

In stark contrast, my middle child has a deep and abiding love of books that I did almost nothing to cultivate. In a word, she disappears into the page and is swallowed whole by the story unfolding before her. Always has. At times, I lament the fact that her sisters didn't come to reading in the same manner and with the same ferocity. Ultimately, though, I suppose what matters is that each of my children has a special relationship with books—a relationship that is as unique and individual as they are, one that will serve them well as they wend their way forward, a bond, I hope, that will enrich their lives and forever challenge their thinking. In the end, maybe that's all we can effectively do, in addition to our level best as curators of impressionable minds.

Planet Mom: It's where I live.

Write from the Heart

There is a special space in my children's baby books devoted entirely to the development and delivery of a priceless collection of words. A place where parents are encouraged to share how having a baby—*this* baby, in particular—rocked their proverbial world. A sizeable square into which moms and dads pour a bit of themselves—giving thanks, chronicling ordinary and not-so-ordinary events, articulating hopes and dreams for the future and communicating, above all else, the infinite wonder said child has brought to this place simply by being born. With any luck, most will get a glimpse of it before they become parents themselves.

And it makes perfect sense—this opportunity for crafting a message of boundless love and gratitude—to be presented when parents are fairly awestruck by all that relates to their bundles of neediness. More specifically, *before* our infants morph into toddlers and tweens, and the urge to snap photographs every hour of every day dwindles to a fleeting desire to fetch the camera when something truly extraordinary happens. Guilty as charged. We all do it, though—we attend less and fall behind more with the passage of time and with each new addition to the family. Not because we become less enamored with our children and feel that documenting every nugget of minutia in their lives is no longer necessary. It's just that we get caught up in the frenetic, nearly suffocating pace of life.

Well, at least I do. And I feel slightly horrible about my failure to record, digitally or otherwise, a goodly portion of my children's lives. Like the first time my middle child dared to fling her smallish body off a diving board and paddle to safety without a smidgeon of assistance from anyone or anything. Nor did I capture the priceless look on her face shortly thereafter, as she stood on the deck wrapped from head to toe in a beach towel, cheering on the others in her swim class. What's more, I neglected to take a snapshot of my youngest while she was missing both of her front teeth. Of course, I took dozens of pictures to preserve that memorable wedge of time for her twin sister, several of which are prominently displayed on the fridge. Let us just say that I've been reminded of said faux pas more than once. I suppose it's a moot point now, however. The endearing little gaps along her pinkish gums have long since been filled. Indeed, there's no going back.

Likewise, I failed to listen to the little voice inside my head that insisted I help my oldest move into her college dormitory. "Meet the roommates," it cooed. "Take a pile of pictures and throw them together in a collage for her birthday," it smartly suggested. Instead, like a fool, I honored my co-ed's wishes for independence, allowing her to bridge the gap from home to campus life entirely on her own. In retrospect, the lugging of boxes teeming with all-that-is-vital-to-college-freshmen was a little thing that would have perhaps meant a lot to her—no matter how desperately she wanted to feel grown. No doubt, a do-over in this instance is a virtual impossibility and no one is more keenly aware of that than I. Shame on me.

As delusional as it sounds to suggest that my brood may feel slighted or even devalued as a result of the aforementioned transgressions (never mind those I failed to mention), I still lament owning them. But at least I have their baby books—and the personalized notes I scrawled therein. Better still, I have tomorrow—to make a pledge to say what I need to say to the children who matter most to me.

Planet Mom: It's where I live (writing from the heart).

The Road Less Traveled

I remember it as if I were standing before it this very moment—the dirt road behind my childhood home that snaked through the mossy woods, carving a narrow, road-not-taken-inspired path along the base of a deep ravine, sheltered from the sun and from civilization it seemed. The place where a large and delicious chunk of my youth was spent surrounded by the pungent aroma of pine mixed with the earthy scent of decaying leaves and the ever-present drone of the creek that flowed nearby.

It was my *Secret Garden*. My sanctuary of sycamores, silver and red maples. My quiet corner of the world where I could commune with nature and collect my thoughts—one blissfully restorative trek at a time. Of course, I whiled away the hours there, exploring every inch of the road's gritty surface, the rock-strewn banks of the creek and the heavily wooded hillside that was enshrouded with a verdant canopy of foliage in the thick of summer and dappled with patches of sunlight when the wispy green of spring first emerged. Season after season, I was drawn there, swallowed whole by its quiet grandeur, inextricably immersed in the sweet salvation of solitude and unstructured play. Alone but never quite lonely. The *Last Child in the Woods*, perhaps.

Eventually, though, my brother tagged along, curious to discover what was so special about this half-mile stretch of road and haven of towering trees that lapped at its fringes. He, too, became enthralled with all that it had to offer—untold numbers of fossils to inspect and collect, intriguing salamanders and caterpillars at every turn, ideally secluded

153

spots for building clubhouses and spying on the occasional passerby, and perhaps most notably, an unforgiving and impossibly narrow footpath perched high atop a ridge where the region's entirety could be viewed with ease. Naturally, there was an abundance of tree hollows, too, perfectly suited for stowing the trappings of childhood (i.e. spare jackknives, cap guns and spears we had fashioned from fallen branches).

On the cusp of spring, when the sun had finally begun to thaw the road and its deep, frozen furrows of mud, we'd barrel down the gully—half running, half sliding through the slushy snow that stubbornly clung to the ground and to the craggy tree trunks—eager to return to our long and winding road of dirt and stone. The summers we spent there—foraging through the woods, hiding out in our ramshackle forts and letting our dog run free—were ravenously consumed, chapters of our lives that I won't soon forget. Never mind that my brother is no longer here to share such memories.

But if I could somehow turn back the time almost six years— the ones that have felt like six minutes—I'd remind him of a day in late autumn, when he couldn't have been more than nine. It was an afternoon much like those we've experienced of late—a sun-drenched, breezy, balmy Indian summer gift— only the leaves back then had long since burst with color, painting the blue skies with fiery shades of orange and red. Not surprisingly, we were on the dirt road together. Back and forth we raced and chased along our favorite stretch, the tall trees roaring and swaying in the wind, tousling our hair and casting great swirls of leaves into the air for what seemed an eternity. Leaves we desperately tried to catch before they hit the ground. Because, of course, that was the whole point.

Of all the memories I've harvested involving my brother and our beloved dirt road, it is among my most cherished.

So as I witness my own children this autumn, completely engrossed in the rapture of chasing, leaping and wildly grabbing fistfuls of sky in an attempt to cleanly snatch the leaves before they fall to the street, drunk with joy and seizing the moment, instantly I return to the place I loved as a child and to the delicious day I spent with my brother.

Planet Mom: It's where I live (remembering well the road less traveled, and recognizing that it has made all the difference).

In Praise of Turkey and Tradition

We make pot pie at our house each Thanksgiving—a savory Pennsylvania Dutch meal that features the most perfect blend of onions, potatoes, thick squares of doughy goodness and meaty strands of chicken. Only we use turkey on this festive occasion. Six-and-a-half pounds of succulent dark meat to be exact, bathing in a vat of broth that most would find fairly intoxicating. It's tradition. Or more correctly, a slight variation on tradition that serves to remind our family of the delectable dish my mother-in-law made not so long ago.

That said, in the four years since Grandma Ella's been gone, I've tried at least three times to marry the flavors of the aforementioned dish as well as she did. And although I doubt I've managed to achieve that level of culinary success, I'm guessing I've come close—which is saying a lot given my proclivity for food related disasters, making me heady with the notion that my skills are no longer thought to be among the most deplorable on record.

Tomorrow will be yet another attempt at pot pie mastery, and, of course, an opportunity for all of us to close our eyes, to breathe in the deliciousness that will hang heavy in the air and in doing so, to revisit a time when Grandma stood at the stove peering into a steamy pot, summoning her special brand of kitchen wizardry. I'll wear her rumpled apron for good measure—a speckled and storied bit of fabric flecked with tiny green leaves, now wan and threadbare from decades of use. I'll wear it because I cannot imagine surviving the ordeal without splattering inordinate quantities of the soupy potage upon myself, but also because it's tradition—or at least that is what it has become over time. Heaven forbid I disturb the delicate balance of good luck and a great recipe by offending the gods of tradition and/or flawless feasts.

With any further good fortune, I'll be able to lure my charges away from the colorful swell of parades on television, from their beloved books in the den and from the pervasive yet somehow endearing skies of gray and barren woodlands long enough to enlist their help in the kitchen. Never mind that Child One completely abhors turkey. Or that Child Two will feign interest unless and until I permit her to stand atop a chair to drop wedges of dough into a boiling sea of broth. Grandma would've let her do such a thing, mindful to teach her the importance of placing each wedge, carefully and singularly, atop a bubble as it surfaces within an impossibly brief window of time. Just as she taught me—just as I hope and envision all three of my children will one day teach *their* children. Handing it down from one generation to the next.

Again, with the tangible and treasured notion of tradition—on this Thanksgiving Day and, perhaps more importantly, on perfectly ordinary days—the ones I routinely fill to capacity with obligations of one kind or another, dismissing all too often the mundane slivers of time with my family as opportunities to connect and share that which I value. Of course, I kick myself for doing so, recognizing that it is the harvest of tiny moments that matters most. Like the delicious time I spent with my grandparents, especially my grandfather in his workshop—a place that reeked gloriously of motor oil and sawdust—a place where I became inextricably consumed time and again with saws and sandpaper, two-by-fours and tape measures. A handful of seemingly insignificant pages of childhood that somehow clung to the corners of my mind, filling me with the warmth that comes from having lived them.

I'd like to think that simple traditions (like making pot pie) are like that, too.

Planet Mom: It's where I live (in praise of turkey...and tradition).

Jingle All the Way

It's possible that I might be slightly smitten with jingle bells—more specifically, with the completely delicious and decidedly hypnotic sound they emit. A feast for the ears. A balm for the soul. A window into the past for people like me, who've harvested decades-old memories that involve horses, snow-covered cornfields and wintry afternoons spent on my grandfather's farm. As a result, I am fairly incapable of resisting the allure of a store bin filled to capacity with sleigh bells. That said, I cannot walk by without reaching in to sample each and every melodic wonder. To pluck great hordes from the array, one after another, appraising each with regard to its heft, luster and, of course, the inherent splendor of its sound. Call it a weakness if you will. Perhaps even a debilitating fixation. I have no shame.

Needless to say, there is a profusion of jingle bells in this household—both brass and silver, embossed and etched—many of which adorn our tree, several that rest near our beloved crèche, all of which are patently adored. Additionally, at least two clusters of bells, ones that are tenuously affixed to braided strands of crimson and gold, dangle freely from doorknobs so that our comings and goings, as well as those of friends and family who visit, are joyfully announced. What's more, there are bell necklaces and bell bracelets, bells on stockings and bells on sleighs. Even a pair of plump snowmen COMPOSED ENTIRELY OF BELLS are poised to welcome Christmas Day—as are the hand-painted variety that a favorite student teacher recently bestowed upon my brood.

As one might expect, I spend an inordinate amount of time each December perfectly enthralled by the chorus of ringing the aforementioned bells are capable of producing (i.e. I move from room to room, gently waggling each bell in succession, holding it to my ear so that I might savor the sound as it lingers). Some offer a mere tinkling and the suggestion of an echo, as if a tiny man were inside striking the walls with a hammer, while others resonate seemingly forever a sound so rich and so pure it can almost be tangibly held in one's hands.

The latter is my favorite and the special sort that we resurrected from my mother-in-law's estate several years ago, along with a host of ceramic centerpieces she crafted herself and a handful of wooden blocks that spell out MERRY CHRISTMAS when properly arranged. Not surprisingly, I'm drawn to the sleigh bell—a silver-plated, baseball-sized genuine collectible manufactured more than thirty years ago. Naturally, it makes a distinctive sound. And whenever I want to revisit a time when my husband's mother was here (which is often, since there are so many conversations I wish we could have), I pick up the bell—which, I suppose, is not unlike the days I find myself wandering around in search of the baby slippers my children wore so many years ago. The ones with tiny jingle bells housed inside their wooly dog exteriors, triggering fond remembrances of a pair of pajama-clad, bedtime-story-toting toddlers at will. In an instant, I can see them shuffling about, their rounded bellies protruding ever so slightly, their smallish hands clutching a toy of some sort.

Come January, as I take down the tree and unceremoniously stow away the remnants of Christmas cheer, I simply cannot bring myself to box up the bells, banishing them to the attic for an entire year. Not yet anyway. I'm not ready to say goodbye.

Long after the Moravian star is removed from its lofty perch, the garland is gathered and legions of ornaments are shrouded in newsprint for safekeeping, the sleigh bells remain. Perhaps in defiance of society's urgings that the Yuletide is over. Perhaps in spite of my longing to restore order to my hopelessly disordered world. Perhaps because of the warmth they engender, during this holiest of seasons and always.

Planet Mom: It's where I live (anxiously awaiting the sound of sleigh bells).

Countdown to Christmas

It was painful to stand there and simply watch. To idly witness, that is, a little boy, no more than three, seized by a desperate longing to ride on the horse-drawn wagon that had circled the park more times than we could readily count in the hour or so that we waited. Again and again the team of Belgians passed us in the frigid night, pausing ever so briefly along its winding path to load and unload hoards of people who had come to this festive event—to soak in some Christmas cheer, to perhaps get a glimpse of Santa in his red, velvety suit and to feast their eyes upon the spectacle of lights that blanketed the grounds, casting a warm glow upon the darkness.

The boy's frustration was palpable as he wailed in vain to his mother and to the starry sky above, arching his back and clenching his tiny fists in indignation—hot, angry tears streaming down his baby face. Inconsolable, as it were. Aside from diverting his attention from this sorrowful reality (i.e. that he was NOT sitting in the aforementioned wagon, lulled by the gentle rhythm of the horses' gait and the muted sound of their hooves as they hit the pavement), there wasn't much anyone could do to comfort him.

So many times I've watched my own children suffer through the misery of waiting for that which promises to remedy all ills, to satisfy all desires and to deliver instantaneous joy. The interminable wait for amusement park rides. The intolerable chasm between ordering a kids' meal and wrapping one's pudgy fingers around the French fries contained within said meal. The insufferable gulf that exists between falling hard on the gritty sidewalk and being swooped up into a parent's arms, where soothing assurances await.

And though they've grown immeasurably since that time, my children loathe the process of waiting even still—especially during this celebrated month of December, on the veritable cusp of Christmas. Over the years it has become tradition, shortly after Thanksgiving and perhaps before any other bit of holiday décor emerges from the depths of the attic, to haul out the handcrafted, Santa-inspired DAYS TILL CHRISTMAS thingy—the one that is cleverly outfitted with removable wooden blocks upon which numbers have been handily painted. We do this, of course, because we cannot find our Advent calendar—the endearing square of felt-like fabric filled to capacity with a crop of tiny pockets and tethered to a small, cottony fir tree intended to mark the days until the 25th. Needless to say, I had a deep and abiding love for that calendar, but sadly it disappeared—along with my girlish figure, every intact set of tumblers I once owned and the stain-free carpeting I once enjoyed.

At any rate, my charges are patently delirious over all that the Yuletide embodies, so thickly immersed are they in the important business of crafting gifts for friends and family and taking part in a good number of caroling excursions through school and church. They've also spent an inordinate amount of time composing wish lists that appear to change with the wind, instilling me with a fair amount of panic as we inch ever nearer to Christmas Day. Indeed, the ratcheting effect of the official countdown has begun in earnest. "ELEVEN DAYS TILL CHRISTMAS!" the wooden blocks seem to shout— reminding me of both the joy this season brings and of my glaring ineptitude as it relates to the enormity of the task ahead.

Cleansing breaths and great volumes of prayer are in order at such times, which, with any luck, will serve to ground me and to give me pause—especially during this grand and glorious season of hopeful expectation.

Planet Mom: It's where I live.

Fitness for Dummies

It has been said that dogs are the best brand of exercise equipment on the market. Given my penchant for failure as it relates to fitness, I guess I'm glad I own a dog. However, this leads me to question the wisdom behind a lot of my past purchases. Lately I've been wrestling with the notion of parting with my beloved treadmill—the one that has lived in my home for an eternity. And before that, in a shoebox-of-an-apartment I shared with my brother. And before that, in a house I shared with my first husband. Needless to say, the treadmill in question was far more impressive than the aforementioned apartment could've ever hoped to be. It also outlasted the abovementioned marriage and, in fact, wooed me enough to demand that it become part of my divorce settlement—so great was its ability to convince me that I couldn't possibly function without it.

More often than not, said nugget of wonderfulness was situated near a window. A practical move based upon my perfectly undocumented belief that a view of the great outdoors would somehow inspire me to exercise with more fervor and regularity. Never mind that I can't readily recall when I last used it. Or that my brood masterfully adorned it with a makeshift tightrope, time and again—designating it as a staging area for death defying trapeze acts with their dolls, as well as for storing an embarrassment of toys. Maybe that's why I find it so completely endearing even now. It holds a wealth of memories—albeit ones that remind me of my inundated-with-kids'-stuff way of life. Or maybe it's because I became enamored with the idea that the embodiment of fitness, both attainable and discreet, could be neatly tucked into a corner of my home—affording me at least some semblance of control over my vastly disordered environment and scheduled-to-the-hilt sort of existence.

Proving that I had learned next to nothing about myself as it related to ambition (or the lack thereof), years later I whined for yet another piece of fitness equipment—a recumbent bicycle. My current husband, dutiful and sweet that he is, ordered me one. A fancy-schmancy, mondo-programmable, ergonomically designed, totally unaffordable slice of heaven. A bike that promised I would look like a Greek goddess in six minutes or less—all in the comfort and convenience of my home. Or maybe it was *six weeks* of grueling workouts I'd have to endure in order to achieve such a feat. I can't be sure.

Shortly before it arrived, however, I remember relishing the thought that it would soon be MINE—to pore over and ogle to the point of delirium, to pedal and program with unbridled enthusiasm, to become hopelessly fixated with its profusion of bells and whistles which, of course, included an adjustable fan, a nifty little pair of transport wheels and comfort-fit handlebars. What's more, there was a reading rack gizmo and an ideally positioned nook for stowing one's remote control and/or wine goblet—so thoughtful and intuitive were the makers of my latest and greatest obsession.

As one might expect, we plunked said glorious piece of machinery near a window and angled it to face the television—lest I become bored while peering at the tired lawn and less-than-inspiring shrubbery outside. Sadly, tedium rained down like a scourge and the bike has since joined the ranks of every other hunk of fitness-related hype with which I allowed myself to become shamelessly infatuated (i.e. the legions of dumbbells now gathering dust beneath my couch, the gym membership I failed to use—EVER, the perfectly coiled yoga mats currently housed in a closet, unceremoniously sandwiched between someone's snow boots and a forgotten bowling ball, the aerobics DVDs).

Despite all logic and understanding, however, part of me holds out hope that one day I'll redeem myself by becoming consumed with the notion that the abovementioned items can, indeed, be resurrected. Even by someone who fails spectacularly to will herself to do much of anything—aside from walk the cussed dog.

Planet Mom: It's where I live (probably walking the dog).

April Awakening

I've always loved the springtime—especially the warm embrace of April. Of all the seasons, I'm inclined to say that it is my favorite—partly because baseball is back and the school year is drawing its last breath, but mostly because it is an era awash with newness. Almost indescribably so. Wisps of green now dot the underbrush, as if God had been handed a paintbrush and was then asked to create something slightly magnificent. Likewise, daffodils and forsythia, bathed in brilliant yellows, have been summoned from the places where shades of gray have lived for far too long. Lilac and cherry blossoms, too, are poised to burst with a profusion of muted hues and the sweet scents of spring. Armies of tulips will soon follow, standing straight and tall in the midday sun. Never mind the rain that must fall.

Indeed, the creatures of this season move me, too. The melodies of more songbirds than I can readily name fill the air along with the serenade of crickets—legions of them, welcoming each night as the woods grow thick with darkness and alive with a symphony of sound. Before long, the yellow-green flashes of fireflies will entrance my children, prompting them to give chase, mayonnaise jars in hand—but not yet. This is springtime and the earth feels soft and yielding beneath my feet, rekindling memories of running barefoot as a child, the cool blades of grass and spongy patches of moss mingling intimately with my toes. The same toes, mind you, that have begged to be reacquainted with the deliciousness of leather sandals since mid-February. The calendar assures me that the time is nigh and that the months ahead are certain to bring both warmth and goodness to the land. Springtime, it seems, is pregnant with possibility, which is yet another reason I love it so.

Or maybe it's because all three of my children were born in the thick of April. Aries babies. Tiny souls destined for equal shares of independence and optimism, despite the vast array of frailties that came with being frighteningly preterm. As one might expect, I worried about umbilical cords, fontanels and cries I had yet to decipher. I think it was there in the hospital, amidst the haze of becoming a mother again and again, where I first recognized how unspeakably euphoric this season of new beginnings made me feel. How I could look outside my window at the verdant landscape below, all the splendor of spring unfolding before me, and then marvel, in the very same breath, at the bundles of neediness I had helped create—the ones with fuzzy, sweet-smelling heads and impossibly tiny toes, the babes I would soon rock in the creaky chair that had been my great grandmother's.

Somehow, seeing the buds and the birds and the medley of green filled me with a tangible sense of hope and enthusiasm for whatever the future might bring. The sleepless nights and debilitating bouts of self-doubt I would surely encounter seemed almost manageable in the context of Mother Nature's grand awakening. Deep within, I believed that no matter how ineptly I nursed the smallish beings in question or how spectacularly wrong I swaddled said infants, all would be well. My parenting days, though stunningly imperfect, would fill my cup, bind me inextricably to my brood and leave me wondering how I could ever function without them. The spring had arrived after all, and the canvas of my world had been painted with broad strokes of vibrant color and punctuated with untold joy.

Of course, it could be the birthdays we celebrate at this time of year that make the season so special. There are four if you count my husband's—all within a span of three weeks—and

I can't help but indelibly etch in my mind all the cakes and candles, all the meals at fancy restaurants with friends and family and the countless parties with giddified bunches of little girls crowding around to see what bit of wonderfulness so-and-so happened to have unwrapped. And let us not forget the slumber parties. Lord knows I won't.

Then again, it might simply be Easter, the mother of grand awakenings, that makes this time so very dear. Egg hunts and wicker baskets. Frilly dresses and shiny shoes. Palm fronds and penitence. Spiritually stirring events that cause me to ponder the true meaning of awakening, rendering me awestruck far beyond the month of April.

Planet Mom: It's where I live (savoring every drop of spring).

Worms Fail Me

There is a routine by which my children leave the house each school day. It is a fairly logical succession of events that usually culminates with a mad dash to the bus stop, backpacks and jackets flapping as they run, their unruly manes trailing behind them. Of all the memories of motherhood I am sure to harvest, the one that features their early morning race across the lawn, a blur of gangly legs and unbridled enthusiasm, will be a favorite. It is likely, too, that I will remember the many times they paused in the street, still blackened and slick from the unending rains of spring, to rescue untold numbers of earthworms from what would appear to be certain death (i.e. either from being drowned right there on the pavement or crushed by the bus that would soon round the bend).

Quickly, yet gingerly, they scoop them up and place them where it is safe, pleased to have made a difference in a small yet meaningful way. And as I witness this determined albeit futile effort to "...rescue them all, Mom," morning after morning I am moved, inspired almost, to join in their worthy deeds. Of course, it would be cruel to utter the obvious truth: "You can't *possibly* save them all." So instead I bite my tongue and agree that worms, too, have a purpose. "They aerate and enrich the soil, Mom." Again I am reminded of the exuberance of youth and of the remarkable capacity children have for storing data sure to wow me. A decade from now, if either of them announces a plan to become somehow involved in a lifelong pursuit to save beached whales, I will not be surprised. Nor will I be disappointed.

At any rate, it goes without saying that worms lack the ability to communicate their needs and desires—no matter how compelling or dire they might be. Granted, they couldn't deliver *any* sort of message that anyone could ever hope to interpret. Crazy as it sounds, there are times that I can relate to such hapless creatures—especially as I struggle to connect with my brood via meaningful discourse. Indeed, sometimes words fail me—when weighty subjects arise, when unanswerable questions surface, when reflective listening falls flat, when my children's growing allegiance to privacy begins to rear its ugly head. But since June is Effective Communications Month, I am determined to improve the way in which we connect over the stuff that matters—as well as the stuff that doesn't particularly.

For starters (and as completely simplistic as it sounds), I've made a solemn pledge to find time on a daily basis to engage each of my daughters in conversation—to stop whatever it is I happen to be doing and tune in to their respective worlds. To find out who has a crush on whom, which item on the lunch menu is to die for these days and just how many collectible rocks it truly takes to be complete. (The jury is still out on that one). For my oldest, my curiosities would be more akin to: Which DC restaurant is her new fave, what, exactly, does one do with a graphic design degree anyway and when (oh when) will the boyfriend be getting a haircut? And although I make light of it here, I understand how important it is to have these conversations with my children. Somehow over the last decade or so I've allowed life's harried pace to take precedence over bonding in this manner—even over the seemingly insignificant happenings of life. That is precisely what I wish to change.

So aside from vowing to carve out more one-on-one time with my co-ed daughter (who is *still* away at college), I plan to call more and text more. *Thank God for unlimited texting plans.* Strangely enough, I suspect I'll even utilize our live video messaging system on a more regular basis—a concept I never once imagined myself embracing.

As for my two youngest charges, I've taken a big step forward on the path to opening the lines of communication by purchasing each of them *Just Between Us: A No-Stress, No-Rules Journal for Girls and Their Mothers* by Meredith and Sofie Jacobs (Chronicle Books). So in addition to the aforementioned one-on-one time, we now have this wonderfully interactive, perfectly confidential, writing prompt-infused means of communicating with one another—a tool that encourages us to "talk" about everything from boys and bands to wishes and worries, all within the confines of a tangible journal that we conveniently pass back and forth. Of course, it doesn't replace or devalue our customary method of conversing, but instead offers another, perhaps deeper, layer of connecting—which is a good thing.

Planet Mom: It's where I live (where worms, I mean words sometimes fail me).

The Swan Song of School

I have a love-hate relationship with the end of my children's school year (i.e. that inimitable wedge of time that is at once delicious and detestable—conveniently sandwiched between the intensity of academics and the celebrated death of structure). To most, it would seem like a fairly simple dichotomy: Either one richly embraces said collection of days during the frenzied months of April, May and a goodly portion of June or, conversely, harbors maniacal thoughts of lighting that portion of the calendar on fire. But for me, it has always been a more complex matter as I am torn between the two extremes.

Indeed, part of me completely loathes the end-of-school-year insanity—especially the frenetic pace at which we parents must perform. We dutifully ferry our charges hither and yon without complaint, cram our schedules with more events than is humanly possible to attend and go above and beyond to ensure that the infinitely numbered details of our children's lives are perfectly coordinated and expertly managed, that is until we are lulled into the lair of summer, when and where we can finally breathe. Then again, let us not forget the onslaught of camp registration deadlines that loom large, making us slightly unnerved over the uncertain nature of our so-called master plan for the coming months.

By the same token, another part of me is entirely enraptured by this particular chapter of parenthood. That said, there is a certain zeal with which my progenies now arise to greet the day on school mornings. And the greatly anticipated demise of the Homework Era alone is enough to make all concerned parties slightly euphoric. What's more, the obscene magnitude of activities slated to take place in the closing months—to include field trips and outdoor events, career days and concerts, award ceremonies and parties galore—somehow fill me with glee. Never mind the delirium-infused state my brood enjoys as a result, making it difficult for anyone and everyone in this household to get a good night's sleep prior to that which is deemed A BIG DAY. Lord knows we've experienced many such days (and sleepless nights) since the advent of spring and its characteristic ratcheting of school-sponsored events.

But the Land of Fourth Grade has been a decidedly good place, and I sometimes lament the fact that my charges will progress to the shores of fifth grade next fall, ostensibly to bigger and better things. Besides, I've grown accustomed to the routine within which my family has functioned since the early days of September. More specifically, everyone beneath this roof knows his or her role and what is expected as it relates to the business of school and learning in general. Next year, I fear, will be different and disturbingly unfamiliar, with a learning curve we have yet to even imagine.

Needless to say, there is great comfort in sameness—a predictable rhythm by which our days have been governed so very well for so very long. Part of me hates to see that disappear. Stranger still, I suspect that the laze and haze of summer will somehow deaden my children's collective passion for learning, erasing much of the progress we've made thus far and undermining the efforts of all who've had a hand in cultivating a love of books, an appreciation of music and art as well as a solid sense of self.

And yet, the summer holds a wealth of promise—as it always does. And it will have its own rhythm and perhaps a different brand of enlightenment wrapped with the merest suggestion of routine—one with rounded edges and soft spots to land come July and August. But for now, my thoughts rest on the few days that remain on the school calendar—a swan song of sorts.

Planet Mom: It's where I live (both loving and hating the end of school).

Ten Ways to Say "Thank You, Dad"

Fathers come in all shapes and sizes, temperaments and talents. On the whole, I'd daresay they are a thankless lot—often underappreciated, largely misunderstood—an entire populace of men rarely acknowledged for the many and varied ways in which they contribute as parents. Mothers, deservedly or not, garner the lion's share of recognition when it comes to the important business of raising a family. But Father's Day, with its prominently marketed golf wares, grilling must-haves and sea of manly fragrances, forces us to shift our collective sentiment and pay homage to dear, old Dad.

And as I wander the aisles in search of the perfect greeting card for my father—one that I believe captures the essence of our relationship, keys on our shared allegiance to witticism and adequately gives thanks for the sacrifices he's made and the wisdom he's imparted, I find myself settling for that which falls disappointingly short. Somehow the writers have missed the mark, along with all the other clever wordsmiths who've failed to deliver the sort of message my father needs to receive—the one that perhaps *all* fathers need to receive. So thank you, Dad, for so many things…

…for encouraging me to forge my own path instead of assuming that the paths of others would necessarily be right for me…for letting me climb to the tops of trees and to skateboard with wild abandon…for ferrying me to the ER when necessary.

…for teaching me how to throw a fastball, wield a mean golf club and sink a jump shot on command…for being my biggest advocate (even still) and for believing in me even before I believed in myself.

...for being oh-so-generous with your time...for listening intently to my wishes and worries...for considering me a worthy companion as we jogged over the back roads of town, watched doubleheaders into the wee hours and sat in scratchy lawn chairs together, completely mesmerized by the thunderstorms that rolled across the skies in the midst of July's unbearable heat, summer after endless summer.

...for letting me date boys with mustaches and muscle cars... for traipsing around the kitchen in your underwear late at night, when said boys needed reminding that it was time to go home (an infinitely mortifying experience then, but absolutely hilarious now)...for walking me down the aisle—twice—and never once saying I told you so.

...for introducing me to the concept of balancing a checkbook, as well as finding balance in my life...for teaching me to accept failure when it comes to call and to learn from my missteps... to appreciate having grandparents, a roof overhead and acres of woods all around.

...for tolerating my teenage years, for trusting me with your beloved cars even though the voices inside your head must have screamed and for resisting the overwhelming desire to share with my High School Yearbook Committee that hideous photo of me with the mumps. For that alone, I love you dearly.

...for navigating so many road trips—to distant airports, to a good number of college campuses I considered calling home, to my very first job interview in the city. Never mind that we got horribly lost in the process, but getting a glimpse of the White House at rush hour surely was grand.

...for inspiring me to be a responsible individual, to work hard and to strive to do good in this world...for illustrating the power of forgiveness, the refuge of one's church and the necessary nature of grieving our losses...for reminding me that things usually work out in the end—even when they look entirely hopeless at the start.

...for underscoring the importance of finding time for one's children, time for one's marriage and time for oneself...for helping me recognize the inherent value of ice cream sundaes, the versatility of duct tape and the irreplaceable nature of a good friend.

...for loving your grandchildren with as much ferocity as you loved me, for implanting within me the seeds of faith and for showing me the beauty of marrying one's best friend.

Planet Mom: It's where I live (giving thanks for my dad).

Ode to Oblivion

I envy my dog at times. I suppose it's because he seems perpetually happy—aside from the instances during which his neurotic little soul is seized by that which triggers a barking frenzy (i.e. when he encounters joggers with or without headbands, school buses and garbage trucks, people who ostensibly smell funny and practically every sound of undetermined origin). For the most part, however, his days are filled with the quiet contentment of gnawing on plastic dinosaurs, hauling underwear and sweat socks into the kitchen with glee and, of course, whizzing indiscriminately. In a word, he doesn't worry his fuzzy little head over much of anything— even as newscasters here and abroad deliver disturbing bulletins day in and day out as a matter of course.

Indeed, my dear dog is blissfully unaware of all the horrible things that have happened across the globe (or that may occur) on any given day. That said, he is largely unaffected by reports of natural disasters, financial ruin, personal tragedies, terrorism, heinous crimes, political upheaval and societal unrest. Never mind the special brand of *awful* that occasionally befalls our happy home. Simply put, his pea brain is incapable of processing such information; therefore he lacks the ability to catastrophize events like I do. And by *catastrophize* I mean to paint every picture with the worst-case scenario brush and to become deeply consumed with worry and dread over that which will probably never happen anyway.

Granted there are plenty of things in my life that represent legitimate causes for concern—my parents' health, my daughter having recently totaled her car and the uncertain nature of my roof and refrigerator, circa the Paleozoic Era. Need I even mention my dog's crippling affinity for hamsters coupled with an eagerness to sample the wee furry beasts—or my husband's beloved cell phone, which has been MIA for forty-two days running? Not that anyone's been counting. Alright we've been counting. And pacing. And wringing our hands in exasperation.

However the vast majority of stressing I do is patently absurd. I worry about becoming discombobulated in public, about our pet frogs reproducing to an unprecedented and unmanageable degree, about the prospect of our obscenely overloaded garage harboring some sort of immune-resistant virus involving fetid soccer cleats, about the frightening odds of our children marrying Republicans. I also trouble myself with the notion that my husband will one day wise up and leave me, opting for the greener pastures of normalcy. What's more, I fret about the contents of my kids' backpacks and whether or not they remembered to pack library books and snacks. I obsess over the color of their socks, the integrity of their bike helmets and the current state of their toenails. Coughs bother me, too. As do unexplained rashes and nosebleeds.

Admittedly, I am a fusspot-of-a-mother and I spend way too much time in a not-so-quiet state of panic over decidedly remote possibilities—like pandemics spread by way of earwax, apocalyptic wars over the fate of the new and purportedly improved social media craze and world domination by creatures (think: giant spiders) whose hideousness has yet to be fully imagined. For the record, I was all but convinced that a bus-sized chunk of space debris that was destined to fall from the sky recently would land squarely on our home. Indeed, I have issues.

Clearly I would do well to refrain from inviting fear and worry into my world. To stop thinking about all the thinking I do. To spend a moment inside my dog's carefree little mind, basking in the glory of oblivion. But perhaps what I need more than anything, as my friend Sally suggested, are stabilizers—the sort that steady ships in rough seas, providing a goodly measure of stability and assurance for all concerned. Yep. Stabilizers—for every neurotic corner of my life.

Then again, the Land of Oblivion has a certain appeal, too.

Planet Mom: It's where I live (envying my dog).

The Pretenders

It's mid-July and already there is talk of the horrors of middle school. Mind you, neither of my ten-year-old progenies will enter the sixth grade this coming fall, however the inescapable seeds of dread have apparently been sown. Chief among their concerns (aside from being stuffed inside a locker and/or trampled by a herd of eighth graders) is the notion that one's imagination tragically dies upon leaving elementary school—a date which, incidentally, will occur exactly 325 days from now. Not that anyone's counting, although I'd be lying if I denied my woeful lament regarding the finite quality of childhood. Indeed, it saddens me greatly to think of the fleeting years during which we embrace the fanciful worlds that children create. Worlds into which I am occasionally welcomed and sometimes thrust—even still. (i.e. "Hello, I'm Mrs. Snobs from London, aka Her Haughtiness, and I'll be needing your lipstick and high heels straightaway. Is that alright, Mum?")

That said, the Land of Make Believe is a very real place where kids spend a delicious portion of their lives, both emotionally invested and purposefully engaged in the important business of play. And no matter how many times I see it—a child wholly immersed within the depths of his or her imagination—I am awestruck by its palpable nature and the pure catharsis it engenders. Translation: For whatever reason, it seems that children *need* to pretend much like they need to breathe. At least mine do. I've watched it a thousand times; the here and now melts away, time is suspended indefinitely and the gateway to another dimension yawns invitingly.

That's how it happens here anyway. Legions of Barbie dolls beckon, some of which wear sequined gowns or soft, cottony dresses— ones that have been cleverly fashioned with tissues and obscene quantities of tape. Still others gallivant about the place wearing nothing at all, completely unabashed by their nakedness and entirely unaffected by their tenuously attached heads. Never mind the dolls with mismatched earrings and severed limbs. Ironically, what seems problematic to me is of little consequence to those thoroughly engrossed within an ever-emerging narrative—one that typically involves hordes of plastic people with perfect teeth and painted-on smiles.

Likewise, throngs of endearing little dogs, miniature ponies and other plastic collectibles speak to my brood—as do the massive herds of hideous-looking (and disturbingly pointy) dinosaurs that I've grown accustomed to finding with my feet in the dead of night. It's a small price to pay, though, given that I get to witness all manner of drama unfold before me as I eavesdrop on the disjointed conversations that the aforementioned beasts evidently have. (i.e. "My dear, you've already had THREE stegosauruses today, which is entirely shameful. I'm afraid you've become a glutton—so there will be NO PIE for you this evening.") That is, of course, if I remain quiet and still for the duration of said performances— invisible almost—to a select pair of pretenders who are, at times, embarrassed to be pretending at all.

There are stuffed animals here, too—ones that fairly transcend the bounds of meaning for my children. As one might expect, they're threadbare from years of love and being dragged, hauled and/or carted virtually everywhere. Of course, they belong to our family now, having adopted a certain humanness that, oddly enough, even my husband and I recognize. Surely it makes sense to buckle them in when we travel, to kiss them good night at bedtime and to include them as we hold hands during grace. They are the very same creatures for whom search and rescue missions are orchestrated and vigils are held when, inevitably, they are lost...the ones that my daughters feel compelled to dress in doll clothes and toddler underwear...the ones who may well journey to a faraway place one day—like college or perhaps a first apartment.

Needless to say, if that ever comes to pass, I wouldn't be disappointed.

Planet Mom: It's where I live (hoping that my children's imagination never truly dies).

The Remains of Summer

With a mere whisper of July remaining, I cannot help but flip through the calendar feeling as if I've failed spectacularly yet again. Alright, maybe it's simply a profound measure of disappointment and/or a mild case of mommy angst that I'm feeling and not failure per se. At any rate, there was so much more that I wanted to accomplish in the forty-seven days since the school year ended. Things that would make the summer exceedingly memorable for my children. Remembrances that would gather in the corners of their minds for decades to come. Happenings that would surely find their way into the mother-of-all writing assignments come September (i.e. the celebrated back-to-school narrative that practically every student has ever faced): My Summer Vacation was Special Because....

Granted, my youngest charges have had immeasurable fun thus far in the season of suntans and sweet corn, however, if I hope to achieve the brand of joy and the volume of memories I had envisioned cultivating before the thrum of crickets finally dies, I'll need to hasten my step. That said, I've compiled a fairly impossible (yet impressive) list of that which I hope to do with my family during the fleeting time that remains—thirty-four days and counting.

For starters, we must seize an enormous cardboard box, one that begs to be transformed into a house of sorts—complete with doors, an abundance of windows and skylights, a child-sized escape hatch and a mail slot that promises to give new meaning and purpose to the junk mail I loathe so completely. We should also spend at least one endless afternoon wielding chunks of sidewalk chalk, together giving rise to a bustling city upon our favorite concrete slab—the one that doubles as a canvas every summer. And when the rains threaten to destroy our self-proclaimed masterpiece, we ought to head inside to construct a behemoth-sized blanket fort that will envelop the entire living room for days on end. Just because. And once we've burrowed deep within the confines of either the cardboard cottage or the haven of blankets, we should then read books together—beginning, of course, with *Mrs. Frisby and the Rats of Nimh*.

Furthermore, it's imperative that we invite a forever friend to stay for a delicious wedge of time, rekindling the past and erasing the miles that now separate us. More importantly, we should do something completely outlandish (like pitch an 18x10 ft. tent in the living room) so as to make his stay wholly unforgettable. We should visit the ocean, too, pausing as its waves give chase and our lungs become filled with the unmistakably brackish scent of the sea. We need to bury each other in the sand, as well, and gather shells by the bushel, and build sandcastles of epic proportions, and walk on the beach at dawn—as there is nothing else on earth quite like it. We ought to visit a handful of historic places, too, and wonder aloud how it must have felt to live during such an era. Feeding our intellect and stirring our minds at a museum is a good idea, too—as is catching a drive-in movie on a whim and camping out at Grandma and Grandpa's in the aforementioned monstrosity-of-a-tent—as promised.

What's more, painting something together made my summer bucket list as well, not to mention teaching my brood the fine art of skipping stones, reading (and folding) an actual map and catching minnows with our bare hands. Oh, and cursive writing, too—a skill that the Department of Education apparently no longer deems worthy of inclusion in its curriculum—a decision that defies all logic and understanding.

And although it's unbearably difficult, I will try my level best to unplug from my dear computer for a time. Likewise, it is essential that we spend a goodly portion of the coming weeks devouring fresh garden tomato and cucumber sandwiches. Lots of them. Spontaneous picnics involving said sandwiches are of paramount importance for August, too, as is playing badminton until we can no longer see, except for the intermittent flashes of fireflies as the dark of night slowly swallows the yard, the thickets and trees in the distance and, eventually, what remains of summer.

Planet Mom: It's where I live (lamenting the finite quality of summer and knowing all too well that we'll be plunked on the shores of September long before we are ready).

The Sum of Summer

I'm fairly certain that my children hate me—mostly because of their workbooks. The ones that I insisted they complete this past summer, come hell or high water. And although there were vast stretches of time during which reprieves were granted from the toilsome task in question (because of vacations, because of friends who came to call, because I was plagued unmercifully with guilt), I still managed to clinch the *Mommie Dearest* nomination. That said, whenever I needed a reminder as to where I fit on the Tyrant Scale, I simply opened the aforementioned workbooks and read some of the asides my dear charges had scribbled in the margins (i.e. "I'm dying!" "This is horribly annoying and boring!" and "Once upon a time, two innocent children were forced to do big, stupid, unpleasant workbooks which were eternally evil. The end.")

Naturally, this brand of condemnation called into question the wisdom behind my decision to sully the summer by thrusting academics upon individuals who clearly weren't interested in the inherent beauty of word problems or in the quiet joy of crafting short stories. Looking back, I now see that it really didn't matter—that making my brood exceedingly miserable for far too many days in June, July and August (no matter how fleeting or insignificant the time seemed to me), was of little consequence in the grand scheme of things. Evidently, my heathens would have acquired a boatload of knowledge with or without the wretched workbooks. *Real world* knowledge that probably has more practical merit anyway. Indeed, my entire family benefited from that which summer seemed more than eager to impart. Together, the following pearls of wisdom represent our harvest.

Despite what may seem perfectly sensible to a child, snow boots don't function particularly well in the rain. Nor do playing cards or peanut butter sandwiches. On a similar note, science experiments gone awry don't belong on anyone's kitchen counters, cicada carcasses have no business sitting on anyone's sweater (*Look, Mom! It's a brooch!*) and favorite stuffed animals should never, ever linger in the vicinity of an unoccupied, uncovered toilet.

Considering the coefficient of friction and the gravitational pull of the Earth, sleeping bags are ideally suited for sliding down carpeted staircases. Scooters, by contrast, are not. Furthermore, objects in motion tend to stay in motion unless and until they collide with solid matter—like oak trees, unsuspecting craniums and steel-clad doors, for instance.

In related field studies, Frick and Frack discovered that hamsters do not enjoy dental examinations—nor are they especially fond of massages. They will, however, tolerate being placed within the confines of a tiny plastic car. Frogs, on the other hand, will have no part of such foolishness. Dogs, conversely, have no shame and will therefore concede to virtually anything a ten-year-old might be inclined to dream up—to include video cameos and fanciful excursions to exotic places like the Canine Islands.

Some other summertime observations I made: Apparently those who wear bandages festooned with cutesy pictures are no longer cool. *Who knew?* Badminton and Frisbee injuries (of the parental variety) don't garner nearly the sympathy that they deserve. However, kids are fairly obsessed with *their* hodgepodge of injuries and insist that parents become equally fascinated for the duration of the healing process.

Furthermore, Captain Vacation found that it's easier to locate one's lodgings if he actually remembers to jot down the name and address of the hotel where reservations have been made. I learned that the brackish scent of the sea, while deliciously intoxicating at the shore, isn't nearly as pleasant when it fuses to clothing, resulting in a lovely eau de dead fish that will likely trigger fond memories of the beach coupled with an overwhelming desire to retch. Together, we ascertained that hotel shampoo smells better than it tastes, that some kids simply won't share their shovels despite a deluge of diplomacy and that the warm sands of the shore are soothing beneath one's feet, yet wholly unforgiving when wedged in one's swimsuit. Moreover, seagulls are hostile creatures with a penchant for fresh pastries and fries—a point I duly noted for future reference.

Curiously, none of the abovementioned lessons of summer had anything to do with a workbook. As it should be, I suppose.

Planet Mom: It's where I live (summing up summer).

M is for Motherhood

While it's true the term "motherhood" is a simple collection of ten letters, specifically arranged for ease of pronunciation, it is suggestive of so much more. In sum, I regard it as a wholly intangible, behemoth-like affair that effectively upended all that I thought I knew about life as a decidedly callow twenty-something. Needless to say, the experience continues to shape and mold me, schooling me day and night in the curious ways and means of children, wowing me with the inherent remarkableness of the aforementioned creatures and rendering me forever changed as an individual. As it should be, I suppose. That said, here's how I spell motherhood.

M Motherhood is a *messy* beast-of-a-thing—with its suffocating mass of sippy cups and sidewalk chalk, lemonade and lunch boxes, bicycles and building blocks. Never mind the ubiquitous nature of stuffed animals and the profusion of refrigerator-worthy masterpieces that inhabit our homes, marking time as our progenies progress along the winding path of childhood. And let us not forget all the lovely shades of gray with which we must contend: the tangled complexities of teens, the relentless questioning of toddlers and the soft underbelly of the headstrong child—the one we try desperately to govern without stifling. Indeed, motherhood is a messy business.

O Motherhood is *overwhelming* to be sure—a seemingly insufferable, plate's-too-full collection of moments that, when taken together or viewed within the prism of the unattainable ideal, beat us into submission, the thrum of parental failure ringing in our ears. That said, there's nothing quite like comparing oneself to the façade of perfection—holding our harried selves up against those who appear to be getting it right, the moms who keep all the plates spinning as if flawless extensions of themselves.

T Motherhood is *timeless*—an eternal post to which we are assigned, willing or not. From the moment our writhing infants, ruddy-faced and wrinkled, are placed upon our chests, motherhood begins in earnest. And although our parent/child relationships shift and season over time, they remain inextricably woven within the fabric of our lives. Not even death can end the appointed role, as a mother's counsel is sought long after she has been eulogized.

H Motherhood is a *humbling* experience. Ask anyone who has ever faced the stinging truth as it relates to intolerance and hypocrisy—delivered by a six-year-old, no less, soundly putting those who ought to know better in their respective places. So often kids eclipse our academic abilities, too, reminding us how important it is to embrace change. Never mind that every fiber of our being screams in protest. Moreover, becoming a parent means a humbling loss of identity to some extent, punctuating the uncertain nature of our so-called significance in certain circles. We are simply so-and-so's mom now—maker of sandwiches, applier of sunscreen, gracious recipient of dandelions. But somehow the title feels right, as does finding a pretty vase for the dandelions.

E Motherhood is *edifying* in that literally every day we learn something new—most of which is harvested from conversations at the dinner table or at bedtime, from diaries that beckon unremittingly or from tiny notes we discover wadded up in someone's pants pocket. We spend a lot of time watching, too, realizing that our mothers were right all along. Children will, indeed, cut their own hair, shove peas up their noses and breach late night curfews to test both boundaries and our resolve. Arguably, the lessons of motherhood never truly end.

R Motherhood is *real*. Good, bad or indifferent, it is palpable, inimitable and exceedingly enlivening. It is the stuff from which memories are made and so much purpose is derived. For me, anyway.

H Motherhood delivers nothing less than a *heady* rush— an intoxicating dose of awe wrapped in the sheer rapture of having had a hand in creating life, not to mention having been called upon to shape one or more future citizens of this world. Mothers are, without question, difference-makers.

O Motherhood makes us swell with *omnipotence* now and again—a grand and glorious surge of I'M THE MOM, THAT'S WHY sort of sway that leaves us feeling all-powerful, if only fleetingly. But nothing makes us puff up more than hearing censure as priceless as, "Dad, did you get Mom's permission to do that? She makes the rules, you know."

O With motherhood comes *obsession*. And spiraling panic. And unfounded fear. And, of course, debilitating worry over that which will probably never occur anyway. In sum, we fret about bumps and bruises, unexplained rashes and fevers that strike in the dead of night…about report cards and recklessness, friends we cannot hope to choose and fast cars that will whisper to our charges, inevitably luring them within, despite our best efforts to forbid such foolishness.

D Motherhood is *delicious*—a profoundly gratifying slice of life we would do well to savor. Never mind its patented swirl of disorder and wealth of doubts, fears and impossible demands. Indeed, motherhood threatens to swallow us whole, while at the same time allowing us to drink in its goodness, gulp by gulp.

Planet Mom: It's where I live (reflecting on the many facets of motherhood).

CHAPTER 6

The Seven Habits of Highly Defective Parents

In Praise of September

I love this time of year—the wedge of weeks during which the succulent remnants of summer collide almost seamlessly with a taste of autumn. Aside from the perfect marriage of warm days and cool nights, I suppose it's the patented swirl of excitement surrounding the start of school that I find so completely intoxicating. Call me crazy.

I blame the mechanical pencils, mostly, in all their steely glory, and the pink erasers that beckon to me unremittingly from the shelves of office supply stores and beyond. The three-ring binders sometimes get to me, too, shouting above the tumult with their palette of delicious hues and fancy-schmancy features. Never mind the throngs of rugged backpacks, endowed with a profusion of zippered compartments and pouches, fueling my quiet obsession with organization, or at least some semblance thereof. And now that my progenies have joined the ranks of middle-schoolers, there are cavernous lockers to adorn as well—with chandeliers, plush carpeting and wallpaper, apparently.

Oh. My. Hell.

Granted, the inherent madness of the back-to-school rush, with its deluge of frenzied purchases, fiscal misery and impossibly giddified children, threatens to consume me each and every August. But it adds a much-needed dose of structure to my life as well and a certain rhythm to mothering—one that I suspect I'll lament when I no longer have school-aged children in my charge.

There is something quietly reassuring about restoring our routine come September—even if it involves unpleasantries like bedtimes, alarm clocks and the evils of homework. In a sense, I think it's the predictable nature of things that grounds me, and hopefully my children. Knowing what's expected and what's to come, at least in theory, encourages preparedness and some measure of assurance. Like calendars with the tiny squares filled in, a table of contents with more than a mere fragment of clarity and sock drawers with the suggestion of order.

Okay, maybe not sock drawers, so much.

At any rate, swarms of yellow school buses now inhabit the land as if commanded by the tides—a cadence and pattern by which a great many lives are governed. Mine is no exception. Mornings are now filled with the hustle and bustle of shepherding my brood out into the world of books and pencils—with shoes tied (mostly), lunches in hand (occasionally) and backpacks clattering and jouncing as they dash across the dew-laden lawn to the bus stop they've frequented since the early days of kindergarten. Of course, it was only yesterday that we sat side by side on the curb together, reading *Stuart Little* while we waited for the bus to round the bend and groan to a halt. But I digress.

Mornings are slightly more hectic now, and by the same token, afternoons with my sixth-grade daughters are the embodiment of chaos—the latest news of the day spilling from their mouths in a flurry of words from the moment they make landfall until they pour themselves into bed each night—a collective heap of exhaustion. Which is not to say that is a bad thing necessarily. Part of me truly enjoys the debriefing process I have come to know and expect as a parent at the close of each school day, and as I ferry them (ad nauseam) here and there throughout the entire year. And no matter how many stories I hear (ranging from angsty to the bounds of absurdity), I'd daresay the gemlike commentary I've gathered and the genuine connections I've made with my daughters will never grow old.

But somehow, the harvest of September is special—perhaps because it smacks of newness, in sharp contrast to August's comparatively uninspired crop of parent-child conversations. Perhaps because of the sense of possibility the celebrated season of new beginnings engenders within each of us. Or perhaps, very simply, it is the omnipresence of tall pencils and full erasers that makes the month so special, suggesting the notion of a clean slate and starting over, anew.

Or maybe that's why I hold September so dear.

Planet Mom: It's where I live (in praise of September).

A Sacrilege of Sorts

There are but two kinds of people in this world—those who brazenly read the endings of books before the endings are actually reached and those who would never dream of a crime so heinous. I myself fall with the masses into the latter category, always mindful of the tenets we must uphold: Thou shalt not spoil the endings of good books no matter how dire the circumstance or how great the temptation.

Of course I've been so bold as to glance at the last page while contemplating a purchase in the aisle of a bookstore, allowing my eyes to sweep across the fuzziness of passages, to graze but not actually rest on hallowed words, erasing all hope of ever being rewarded for my ability to resist said allure. If nothing else, I can be proud of that.

However it wasn't until I was deeply immersed in *The Miraculous Journey of Edward Tulane* (Chapter Seven of this scrumptious read-aloud, more specifically) that I became painfully aware of a terrible truth: My children would (and, in fact, *had*) flipped ahead twenty chapters in said prized piece of literature, to the very last page (gasp!) "...because I wanted to know what would happen to Edward, Mom. I was worried about him. He lives, you know."

Of course, I was horrified. And profoundly disappointed. I had higher hopes for my progenies—hopes that they would grow to become upstanding citizens, embodying all-that-is-righteous-and-good. Principled people who knew better than to commit sacrilege. Instead, it appears, my wayward bunch has embraced the dark side of life. Even my oldest daughter has admitted to that which is a sheer disgrace—she reads the very last sentence of every novel—as a rule. Needless to say, such a divulgence rendered me dumbfounded.

"Why?! Why would you *do* such a thing?!" I had to ask finally, eyes fixed upon the creature I thought I knew.

"I don't know. To pique my interest I guess."

"*To pique your interest?!*" I shrieked, shaking my head in disbelief. "Good grief! Where's the mystery in that?! Where's the long-awaited pleasure that a grand culmination promises?! The delicious sense of satisfaction derived from having journeyed far and wide across the vast and uncertain terrain of a narrative gem?!" I demanded to know.

She shrugged her shoulders as if to say, "What's the big deal, Mom? It's just a book."

Of course, this was wrong on so many levels that I couldn't begin to wrap my mind around the unspeakable atrociousness of which it reeked. Nor could I forgive the other two ratfinks for having stolen my joy. I wanted to discover for myself Edward Tulane's fate—to continue devouring the book, page after succulent page, and eventually, to drink in the magnificence of the grand finale that surely awaited me.

But it was not to be. Those unmerciful beasts continued to fill my ears with details of the story, doling out bite-sized blurbages just to watch me writhe in pain. "No! NO! Don't tell me a syllable more!" I pleaded, wondering from whence this penchant had come. I don't remember anyone bursting at the seams to tell me about *Goldilocks* or *Little Red Riding*

Hood. Back then it was a non-issue. The end was something that would be revealed in due time upon turning the last page. As it should be.

I'd almost rather my heathens wantonly fling caterpillars across the living room and stuff them inside their backpacks (oh wait, they've done that!), saturate thirsty bath rugs at will (done that, too!), or festoon the dog with lipstick "...because we wanted to give him purple-ish lips, Mom!" than to rob themselves of the parting gift of a fine book.

Sadly, this represents yet one more area of life I cannot control. I must come to grips with the fact that my children will choose friends, careers and eventually mates—almost entirely devoid of my (infinitely sagacious) input. And ultimately they will decide whether to continue as card-carrying members of the Flip-Ahead-to-the-Last-Page Club. Oy.

Planet Mom: It's where I live (beside myself with indignation).

The Beauty of Mismanagement

As I type this, it's two-thirty in the afternoon on a weekday and everyone in my household is still wearing pajamas. No one has brushed his or her teeth, not one hair upon one solitary head has been coifed and thus far, exactly zero sit-down meals have been served. All concerned parties have opted to graze through the day like cattle, raiding the fridge and cupboards at will. Myself included. That being said, dishevelment abounds and lethargy has rained down upon us like a scourge.

Indeed, the *Supernanny* would be horrified. And because I recognize the magnitude of my deplorableness, I can envision her disapproving glare—the way she'd scowl and shake her head at me. Like a taskmaster, she'd stand amidst my chaos with a big, fat marker in hand, fervently filling a white board with a host of solutions for dealing with the disorder and mismanagement that permeate my world. It's likely that a complete overhaul of my parenting system and skills (or lack thereof) would be recommended if not demanded, necessitating the summoning of nanny reinforcements. Legions of them, quite possibly.

Naturally, we'd invite them in for imaginary tea—to be served within the confines of the not-so-imaginary blanket fort now consuming my living room. The one I allowed to be constructed. The one littered with cracker crumbs. The one from whence we viewed the antics of *Tom & Jerry* because I simply couldn't bear to hear one more syllable emanating from Rush Limbaugh.

Granted, there is no school today, so the death of structure (which I condoned and perhaps orchestrated to my benefit) could, in fact, be deemed appropriate. Maybe even welcomed in some circles. Okay, tiny circles. Few in number. But quantifiable circles nonetheless. Even still, I ought to be ashamed of the sorry state of my domestic affairs. My ducks are undeniably in disarray. And that cannot be good.

I suppose it's no secret that I don't run a very tight ship. Admittedly, I pilot the *Titanic* most days—struggling to avoid the icebergs that pepper my hectic mornings. The women in the school office could attest to that fact. The ones who see me traipsing in to deliver forgotten lunchboxes and misplaced jackets—telling indicators of my ineptitude as a parent. Helen knows the score, too. She drives the big, yellow bus that we race to meet each morning—backpacks bouncing, shoelaces flapping and bellies sloshing with breakfast as we dash through the wet grass, my mind flying through the anxiety-driven Mom Checklist at warp speed: Is everyone wearing shoes and clean underwear…did they brush their teeth…did they actually EAT something…did I remember to pack their snacks…their library books…their homework…and so on.

The high schoolers sitting at the back of the bus know the awful truth, too. The ones who've forever peered through the clouded panes and watched me schlepping around the same silly book, *The Tale of Despereaux*—a wonderful story, I'm sure, but one I've failed to finish reading aloud since Christmas. I planned to share this literary gem with my brood at the bus stop, where we'd sit together on the curb and devour page after page as the gray morning skies surrender to the sun. I suppose I lug it there because I'm holding out hope that somehow we'll find time to move past Chapter Three.

For whatever reason, I think I managed mornings better when my charges were kindergarteners. Back then we actually finished books together and even had time to discuss colorful characters—proof that my time management skills were at least reasonable and my mornings, less hectic. I hardly ever had to deliver a lunchbox or a coat because someone forgot it and I honestly don't remember racing across the lawn to catch the bus—ever.

Then again, my memories of blanket forts and lazy days in pajamas are a bit fuzzy. It's possible I embraced the notion of disorder back then more than I'd care to admit. Perhaps that's the beauty of mismanagement—we conveniently forget the less-than-perfect-looking stuff of parenthood, yet savor every delicious moment while we're living it.

Planet Mom: It's where I live.

Necessity is the Mother of Clean Closets and Tidy Drawers

I used to be obsessed with neatness—a strange sort of child who, completely unprompted, would devote an entire Saturday to the rearrangement of my bedroom furniture, organizing drawers and eradicating dust with wild abandon. Much to my parents' chagrin, I'd lug large and unwieldy dressers across the floor in fits and starts, nonplussed by the unremarkable nature of my progress, the uncooperative penchant of my carpeting and the very real possibility that the dozen or more wooden legs involved would weaken and eventually snap like Mom and Dad had warned so many times. But I was driven, filled with an overwhelming desire to bring order to my world and a fresh, new look to my 10x10 foot haven of personal space—a canary yellow cube I called my very own.

What's more, there was something deliciously liberating— perhaps even cathartic—about wrestling with a chest of drawers that sought to undermine my every effort to muscle it ever so deliberately and in embarrassingly small increments without a bit of assistance. I was ambitious if nothing else. Never mind daft.

Needless to say, untold hours were spent drafting floor plans and analyzing my decisions—as if the placement of each and every souvenir-inspired trinket, shoebox stuffed with collectibles and cumbersome piece of furniture mattered. Because it did. Never mind that I knew next to nothing about feng shui or its inherent wonderfulness. Apparently, I was born with an innate appreciation for the spatial relevance of objects that surrounded me. Or maybe my curious obsession with moving furniture and shuffling the contents of drawers in a quiet state of panic was fueled by an intolerable degree of boredom and/or a desire to avoid stubbing my toe on the way to the bathroom in the dead of night. I don't pretend to know what spurred my impassioned efforts; however, I am wholly convinced that that industrious soul is nowhere to be found today.

Decades of amassing that which I clearly couldn't live without (to include an irreplaceable, yet hoard-happy, family) has resulted in a hideously cluttered existence. That said, virtually every corner of my home has been sullied to some extent—a byproduct of living with people who are physically incapable of returning anything to its rightful place in the universe, much less, throwing it away. Villages composed of Legos, like tiny clumps of crabgrass, creep into crevices and occupy tabletops for weeks on end, as do legions of Barbie dolls that lie about the place, shamelessly nude. And let us not forget the shoes (oh, my hell, the SHOES) and the train-wreck-of-a-dresser that a certain someone has refused to purge since kindergarten. Not to be outdone, my husband marks territory with coats and hats and, of course, the trappings of projects in various stages of completion, all of which I find patently unforgivable. Furthermore, the unsightly mass atop *his* dresser is only slightly less offensive than the one detailed above. I wish I were making this up.

No longer do my Saturdays involve frenzied cleaning missions, the reordering of an otherwise obscure set of drawers, or a compulsion to move my coffee table somewhere else...just because. I simply don't have that kind of luxury, never mind the initiative required to act upon it. Instead, my days are rife with failed attempts to keep all the plates spinning (i.e. the psyches nurtured, the homework vanquished, the inexorable bickering at bay). That is not to say that tiny bursts of inspiration never occur, but my domestic priorities have shifted markedly since the advent of motherhood and my tolerance for household squalor has risen to an unprecedented level.

Basically I clean, purge and/or organize for three reasons: when someone spills something and that something is categorically vile, when the laws of nature regarding storage capacity have been irreparably breached or when the arrival of guests is imminent. Indeed, necessity is the mother of clean closets and tidy drawers, while shame is the mother of purged refrigerators. It's a far cry from my neatnik days, but for the most part, practicable.

Planet Mom: It's where I live (probably not cleaning my refrigerator).

Fixing What Isn't Broken

Forever I've been astounded by the stupidity with which I approach parenting—in particular, the tenet I uphold that involves fixing what isn't broken. Like the blanket fort that would be "so much better" (read: on the fringe of collapse) if only it were larger. Or the refrigerator masterpiece that would surely sing if only it had more glitter and macaroni (never mind that it will no longer stick to the fridge without duct tape and divine intervention). And let us not forget the idiocy that routinely falls from my lips wherein I suggest upgrading to a life filled with rainbow sprinkles and hot fudge, when the child in question was perfectly content with a vanilla sort of existence. It's what I do, apparently.

More than once my dear husband has reminded me how counterproductive this is—as if I needed to feel worse about my failures in the realm of motherhood. Clearly, I want my kids to appreciate what they have as well as the circumstances that surround them now and in the future, but for whatever reason I seem wholly incapable of leaving well enough alone— attempting to supersize their happiness as a matter of course.

Pets are a perfect example. I've known for quite some time that my children have had a desperate longing for a big, hairy dog. Something golden retriever-ish or perhaps a black lab with manic tendencies. But I'm allergic to dogs. And slobber, not to mention the notion of gargantuan tails on a quest to whack the bejesus out of anything and everything held sacred and dear. As a result, my brood has conceded defeat on their dog agenda, opting to be satisfied with a tiny, hypoallergenic lap dog that does, indeed, possess manic tendencies and (thankfully) a smallish tail.

But I felt bad (read: horrible) about not being able to give them the dog of their dreams, and I wanted to somehow make it up to them. So one summer not long ago it made perfect sense to promise that we'd adopt two hamsters, but I emerged from the pet store with *five* of the furry beasts—a moment I now recognize as having been inspired by sheer madness. It began innocently enough: "If one hamster per child was good," I reasoned, "two per child was even better!" "And how could we possibly live with ourselves if we left behind the only remaining hamster in the big, scary tank, tragically separated from its brethren for all eternity?" It was unconscionable.

Who knew the stupid things would later morph into belligerent creatures with a propensity for cannibalism, indiscriminate pooing and nighttime revelry on par with Bourbon Street? Not that our dear rodents have ever visited New Orleans, but you get the idea.

Roughly one year later, the very same guilt-induced debacle transpired, although this time it involved lizards. *Two* were obviously better than one. Furthermore, I regarded the fact that lizards could potentially grow to be two feet long (necessitating a forty-gallon tank!) as inconsequential. Never mind the very real possibility that we could wind up with two males—ones that would eventually consume one another's tails and toes. And because the gods apparently hate me, we do, indeed, own two males. Once again, I am reminded of how completely contented our children would have been with just one lizard.

At no time has my proclivity for fixing what isn't broken become more apparent than now...as I recall the sundrenched afternoon during which I needlessly wrestled with websites and special sales codes, product details and compatibility charts all in the name of procuring a greatly coveted electronic gadget for my child—the one who was frolicking outside with her sister, wholly engrossed with a stick, a couple of foam swords and a giant tent they would later enshroud themselves with and careen around the yard, shrieking like banshees. Naturally, I interpreted this as a desperate cry for a new-fangled techno-device without which she would surely wither and die.

Apparently, my idiocy knows no bounds.

Planet Mom: It's where I live (attempting to supersize happiness).

Be Careful What You Wish For

"If wishes were horses, then beggars would ride." I remember hearing that expression as a child, but I never fully understood the particulars of its meaning. Needless to say, my charges are equally baffled by such utterances, shooting me that patented Mom-is-slightly-deranged look whenever I make mention of horses and beggars.

"We're not asking for a *pony*, Mom—just a golden retriever and a hotel thingy for our hamsters." Odds are, I reach for such an idiom because I've grown weary of my brood's ceaseless petitioning. Indeed, I've become fairly intolerant of the phrase, "I want…" or "I wish…" when coupled with anything even remotely frivolous.

I suppose that my plight in this regard is not all that uncommon. Whiny children are ubiquitous, and the allure of summoning hope in the face of impossibility is simply too delicious for any of us to resist. That said, we all wish for things we cannot have—if only to taste, ever so fleetingly, what could be. It's as if we forget our practical selves and instead indulge in unbridled possibility. At least I do.

So I guess I shouldn't expect anything less from my progenies. Nor should I be appalled to learn that one of them had the audacity to make a desperate plea for something entirely self-serving—like the abolishment of a certain brand of schoolwork. Technically speaking, she didn't actually MAKE the wish (or so I was later informed), but its merits were heavily weighed against the drawbacks. Thankfully, she came to her senses.

"I've been thinking about my wishing stone, Mom…" (i.e. the perfectly wonderful keepsake harvested from the shores of Nova Scotia by two of the most thoughtful neighbors I've encountered in recent memory). "I really *hate* math and I almost wished that math homework were NEVER INVENTED!"

Of course, I gasped for dramatic effect.

"But then I realized if I didn't have math homework, I'd probably never learn how to cash my paychecks and stuff—which would be horrible," she continued.

"Good point," I acknowledged. "Luckily, you didn't follow through."

"Yep. I saw a shooting star once and wished that I could see my third grade teacher AND THE VERY NEXT DAY I got to visit her. Shooting stars really work, Mom…if you wish hard. I'm pretty sure this stone will work, too, so I might wish I could fly next—which would be *awesome*, but it's sort of silly, isn't it? People can't fly."

And at that, I was silenced. All my mothering instincts and kernels of wisdom abandoned me, rendering me incapable of responding. A wish is still a wish, right? Whether exceedingly outlandish or pitifully sensible. Whether it's spelled out in great detail upon the pages of one's diary or whispered earnestly into the folds of one's blankets, long after tuck ins are complete and the shroud of night has fallen. Perhaps I would do well as the appointed curator of my kids' beloved supplications to handle them with more care, resisting the urge to dismiss them as trifling or unworthy of anyone's time.

Indeed, nothing serves to ground me more than being privy to their cache of profoundly compassionate longings—the ones so completely unrelated to that which is fanciful or imprudent.

"I wish Freddy didn't have to move away."

"I wish everyone in the world had a house to live in."

"I wish Grandma's cancer would go away."

More than once I've made the mistake of assuming that the "I wish..." portion of their plea would be followed by something entirely foolish. Shame on me.

Likewise, I distinctly remember wishing my oldest daughter would grow up sooner—because it seemed vastly more impressive to parent a child whose age in years could be expressed with *two* digits, as opposed to something as unremarkable as an eight or a nine. Naturally, it followed that having a teenager trumped having a twelve-year-old, and so on. So many years later, it is plain to see that my wish was granted—a wish I now lament ever having made.

Planet Mom: It's where I live (ever-mindful of the gravity of wishes—great and small).

The Color of Bizarre

Of all places, it began in an obscure corner of a local pharmacy, with child in tow. My incapacitating infatuation with a certain hue of green paint, that is. Who *does* that? What sort of deranged mother follows a late night visit to an urgent care facility (due to excruciating ear pain of the youth variety) with a spontaneous and completely self-serving foray into the realm of household décor? *This* sort of deranged mother, apparently. One who was less concerned with the prospect of obtaining a curative pharmaceutical for her dear daughter than with the intoxicating possibility of acquiring said paint for a certain someone's writing lair.

For the record, I didn't intend to become smitten with the aforementioned hue whose algae-inspired essence was splashed over the entirety of the prescription drug enclave, beckoning to me unremittingly (like only pond scum pigmentation can). It just sort of happened and I could do nothing to resist. Indeed, the paint spoke to me.

Oddly enough, it spoke to my eleven-year-old, too, whose blinding pain somehow evaporated as she stood before the wall of green, mesmerized by what appeared to be the world's largest harvest of guacamole. Or seaweed. Possibly both.

"Mom, isn't that the most *awesome* color you've ever seen?! It looks like frog spit and it would be PERFECT for your office! Plus it would cover up that lilac you're so sick of, wouldn't it?"

And at that, I was silenced. For this was the child who had refused to embrace the notion of change for as long as I can remember. The child who, on occasion, had launched visceral tirades in response to the mere suggestion of rearranging our living room furniture, never mind reordering her sock drawer or straightening the cushions upon our cussed couch.

God forbid we PAINT.

This could possibly explain my addled state and why I then became a disturbing source of fascination ~~a terrible annoyance~~ to the pharmacist, likely creeping her out with my shameless curiosity involving, of all things, latex paint.

"Can you tell me, ma'am, what shade of green that is?" I asked, pointing at the celebrated wall. "I know this sounds crazy, but I *have* to know. I've been wrestling with everything from *gecko green* to *almost avocado*, and now that I've gotten the go-ahead from our self-appointed Rule Captain," I said, gesturing to my daughter who was clearly convinced that we should drop everything and paint, "I'd be stupid not to." Translation: If I don't jump on this project in the next ten minutes, my child, who is frighteningly obsessed with sameness, will forget she ever expressed an interest in said endeavor, dooming me to the horrors of a purple workspace for all eternity.

For a time, the woman stared blankly at the wall and then at me, probably wondering how I had eluded security at the mental hospital from whence I undoubtedly had come. She then shook her head (possibly making me appear less deranged and more pathetic), picked up the phone and dialed someone who might be inclined to house peculiar data involving the whereabouts of little known paint swatches. Naturally, I was taken aback, yet mildly intrigued by her willingness to help.

Then things got weirder. She began firing a barrage of questions in rapid-fire succession. What sort of room did I intend to paint...how many windows were contained therein...what sort of ambient light existed...had I ever considered using a complimentary color? Of course, this rendered me patently delirious. Here was a woman who recognized the desperation in my voice—a woman who could sense the dysfunction in my home—a woman who, at least on some level, understood what it was like to live with a tiny tyrant who stifled my every whim. Whims related to change, that is.

So when she actually tore a small chunk of paint off the wall, I was aghast—but in a good way. "Here, take this to the paint store. Maybe they can match it," she offered, defining for me in so many glorious ways, the color of bizarre.

Planet Mom: It's where I live (poised to paint).

Ode to Odor

I'm sure there are worse smells than the one that enveloped the entirety of my home last week, only I can think of none. Except maybe that time in chemistry class (heretofore known as the Bromine Incident) wherein it seemed that every available molecule of oxygen had been sucked through the stratosphere and deposited somewhere between Saturn and Uranus. Translation: I thought I would die, which was largely unsettling because everyone would then learn of my secret crush whose picture was taped inside my locker—an inevitable discovery in the event my parents would empty said locker while classes were changing.

At any rate, the odor was horrific. Both times. This time, however, the source was puzzling and, as most disasters go, it befell our happy home in the dead of night. To add to our merriment, we were hosting a sleepover at the time, which meant that a profusion of kid-paraphernalia was strewn everywhere, to include wayward DVDs, hairbrushes that waged a personal assault upon my feet and lumpy sleeping bags—ones that ought to have contained lumpy children at such an ungodly hour. But no. Nearly everyone was awake and milling about, perfectly distraught by the suffocating fog that hung heavy in the air—aside from the time we huddled together watching bad TV and cupping our hands over our noses in a futile attempt to breathe.

Of course, I became convinced that this was how we'd die, curled up in a corner or an abandoned blanket fort, leading crime scene investigators to embark upon a frenzied mission to solve the case. And after wandering around the yard like a fool, inhaling the stench that lived there as well, it became apparent to me that a foreign power had gathered the most godawful-smelling skunks on the planet, coaxed them inside a giant warhead and dropped said abomination directly upon my home. Since there was no other logical explanation, I turned on the news, fully expecting to see video clips of Pepé Le Pew-inspired creatures invading my neighborhood. A call to the State Police came next, as one might expect. I can only hope the officer who answered the phone wasn't injured when he likely fell to the floor, seized with laughter.

In the midst of my catastrophizing panic, however, I flung open windows and doors, combed the attic and garage, crawled in closets and thrust my head inside the dishwasher—in hopes that I would find that which sought to corrode my sorry soul, one singed nose hair at a time. Eventually, I ordered my husband to the dreaded basement—to slay the fetid beast that surely lurked there, but not before I instructed him to stand in roughly seventy-three different places and sniff.

"Is it worse here…or over here? How about next to the stereo? Go stand over there and report back." The absurdity of this exercise cannot be underestimated, nor can the nauseating toxicity of our air quality that night.

And like so many infinitely obtuse ideas I contemplated during the wee hours in question (to include encapsulating myself inside the refrigerator to escape the horribleness), I toyed with the notion of ordering hazmat suits for everyone. However I stopped short since a) I knew the expense would be obscene b) by the time they arrived, no one could sign for them because we'd either be dead or comatose and c) I was overcome with guilt, knowing that adequate protection for our pets would be virtually impossible. Needless to say, I got teary-eyed just envisioning hamsters dressed in tiny, yellow suits. Or maybe it was the wall of stench that made my eyes burn and tear. I can't be sure.

In any event, the culprit was, indeed, an ill-tempered skunk—one inclined to target the air intake gadgetry of unsuspecting heat systems. Translation: The foul aroma plagued our home and every cussed thing in it for roughly eighty-three hours—not that anyone counted. Okay, we counted. In the end, vinegar was our saving grace.

Planet Mom: It's where I live (avoiding skunks...and singing the praises of our pest control people for the vinegar tip).

Captain Underpants

As I type, I'm envisioning the disjointed discussion likely taking place in my brood's fifth-grade classroom right about now, spawned, of course, by the events surrounding Saturday's cleaning fest at our home. Like most frenzied attempts to rid my world of filth and clutter, this one involved the impending arrival of guests, errant food particles and a shameless violation of child labor laws. I'm guessing the conversation unfolded thusly:

Child One: "My Mom made my sister and me dust the whole living room this weekend WITH A PAIR OF MY DAD'S UNDERWEAR and it was *entirely horrible*."

Teacher: (rendered speechless, except for the chortles she probably choked back in an effort to appear genuinely empathetic and professional in the midst of kid-generated absurdity).

Child One: "Yeah, my Mom was running the vacuum practically ALL DAY, which she NEVER does...because we were about to have some company visit and we had to move the couch...because there was a big mustard stain on the carpet she was trying to hide (with said couch) and because my sister and I were standing around doing nothing except eating old candy we found under the couch, Mom handed us a pair of Dad's underwear...so we could 'dust something' and make ourselves 'useful' (likely scarring the aforementioned youth for life), and then later on she told us to go upstairs and clean our bedroom, too, which was a *total* disaster. You've probably heard about it. It's *legendary*."

Teacher: "Oh. Dusting. With your Dad's underwear. To make yourselves 'useful.' Disastrous bedroom. I think I understand."

Child One: "Yeah. Mom calls our room a 'train wreck' but there are parts of it that are really more like an *avalanche* because a certain someone, who will remain nameless, hasn't cleaned her dresser since kindergarten and everything slides off in a ginormous heap about once a month. It's funny because all you have to do is add a paper clip or something incredibly small to the top of the pile and the whole thing crashes to the floor, which doesn't make Mom very happy."

Teacher: "Train wreck of a room. Avalanche-like dresser. Mom's not happy. I see."

Child Two: "But she's happier now because I FINALLY cleaned my dresser. So it's not a train wreck anymore. Or an avalanche. Or a disaster area. Or anything especially horrible. The only problem is what happened in the living room. I spilled a glob of mustard on the carpet last week. And then on Saturday morning, my beef barbecue sandwich accidentally flew out of my hand when I jumped over the footstool and into Mom's favorite chair. She went ballistic, like she always does. So we ended up helping her clean, and move furniture, and pick up about a million toys—only we didn't do it right because she found little pieces of my sandwich underneath the cushion and embedded in the carpet EVEN AFTER we scrubbed. Well, actually THE DOG found little pieces of my sandwich and I knew it wasn't going to be a very good day. So she handed us a pair of Dad's underwear and told us to dust. I thought I was going to hurl."

Teacher: "Mustard. Beef barbecue. Underwear. Urge to hurl. Uh huh. But the underwear was just a dust cloth, right? One your mom has probably washed a thousand times?"

Child One: "That's what she told us, but I don't believe it. She was probably so mad about the carpet and the chair that she wanted to punish us by grossing us out. Well it worked. When I grow up and get my own house, I'm *never* going to make my kids dust with anyone's underwear. That's just plain wrong."

Planet Mom: It's where I live (likely amusing teachers every day).

The Hieroglyphics of Family

The unthinkable has happened. I've become one of those women who puts stick figure people on her car. You know—to broadcast procreative talents in a manner that even cavemen could readily grasp (or perhaps *mock*, because said portrayal is so embarrassingly unoriginal, not to mention self-absorbed).

At any rate, it was inevitable that I would succumb to the mass marketed, frippery-inspired family car sticker craze, especially given my penchant for oversharing. Indeed, the huddled mass of people and pets now emblazoned upon my rear window qualifies as such—a telling distillation of my life, rendered plainly and simply, as if by a child, with what appears to be sidewalk chalk. I'm not entirely sure what drove me to acquire such foolishness, though I suspect it was my fascination with the notion that an entity as complex and hopelessly entwined as a family unit could be readily reduced to something that seems almost entirely manageable. An abbreviated version of one's motley crew, as it were, all neat and tidy, smiling for the camera, not an angsty adolescent or overtaxed adult in the bunch.

The frazzled and woefully imperfect parent within me, of course, *had* to have it—even if it smacked of impossibility, painting what could only be described as "the delicious illusion of order" upon the canvas of my disordered world. But I digress.

I threw the silly thing in my cart, delusions and all, and went home a happy woman. Naturally, on the first sunny day following my purchase, I made the joyous trek to my car—stick figures in one hand and window cleaner in the other. And because I couldn't bear to discard a single sticker included in the set, I used them all, plastering an entire corner of glass with a parade of modern-day hieroglyphics.

That said, each twig-like personage is now depicted with some sort of accessory that seemingly defines him or her (i.e. the trappings of life without which we would surely wither and die). Shopping bags and sports gear. Backpacks and briefcases. Sadly, and despite a great deal of rummaging through the lot, I failed to find a graphic representation of a computer, a jigsaw puzzle or anything remotely suggestive of chocolate, all of which epitomize the essence of my being. Instead, I settled for a golf club and a whiskered cat at my side.

And although my charges were quite satisfied with the soccer ball and the tiny tennis racquet I outfitted them with, a tower of books and a much-adored electronic device would've made far more sense (for Child One and Child Two respectively). Likewise, my husband would have been thrilled to be pictured with the big, hairy dog I will probably never agree to adopt, although the baseball gear (he assures me) "is just fine" and the neurotic little dog we *actually* own is "just fine, too," both of which appear in the same crowded corner of glass. Yet our sticker-fied family dynamic is still left wanting.

More specifically, my search for a woman-child/college student stick figure proved fruitless and I cannot begin to express my disappointment. Thank you very little, gods of inane car stickers.

Okay, maybe I didn't look hard enough. Or perhaps I should have added my own pitifully rendered stick figure, so that *all three* of my progenies could have appeared there as a cohesive whole. I suppose I could have sketched our dear lizards and wee hamster, too, at the insistence of a certain couple of somebodies. Instead, I addressed the perceived injustices by caving to their demands that I include two stick figure boys. Boys who have taken part in our pets' funeral services and rock-paper-scissors battles. Boys who have been bandaged and fed here more than a few times. Boys who are practically family anyway, and rightly belong with our so-called sticker family.

Here's hoping they're okay with that.

Planet Mom: It's where I live (joining the ranks of stick figure people everywhere).

Home Alone

It's rumored that I need to have a little more faith in my children as autonomous creatures—at least when it comes to being levelheaded, resourceful and not remotely interested in summoning the fire department unnecessarily. Although, maybe it's just that the opportunity has yet to fully present itself. I can't be sure.

At any rate, for a very long time now, and almost reflexively, I have viewed my brood's emergent ability to handle situations completely on their own as largely deficient, characterizing their fledgling methodology for dealing with life's inevitable difficulties as irreparably flawed. Shame on me for not believing in them more and criticizing less—for dooming them to failure even before they can imagine success.

Everything from tying shoelaces and crossing the street to shepherding expensive instruments and irreplaceable flash drives to and from school has been met with unwarranted skepticism and/or a healthy dose of catastrophizing, which I've pretty much perfected at this juncture in my parenting career. Never mind entrusting them with tasks like walking our neurotic little dog (the one inclined to hurl his smallish body into the path of oncoming cars) or remembering to snugly latch the lids of hamster cages, lest the wily beasts escape. Suffice it to say, I have issues with control, punctuated by a host of irrational fears and an unwillingness to fully embrace my children's ever-increasing level of maturity. As a result, I've doled out independence in embarrassingly small chunks.

So when it came time to broach the subject of staying home alone, with nary the suggestion of parental supervision, I became consumed with a quiet sense of dread. My dear progenies, who have longed for freedom seemingly forever, couldn't *possibly* function without me hovering over them, issuing a barrage of directives for the duration: "Keep the doors locked. Don't let anyone inside under any circumstances. Answer the phone, but don't suggest that you're HOME ALONE. Find a pen and actually take a message. Write legibly. On something besides your hand. Furthermore, don't even THINK about cooking anything. Or shampooing the dog. Or calling your friends who are probably home alone, too, toying with the notion of climbing onto the roof because that seems like a perfectly rational thing to do. *Yes*, I climbed onto my roof as a kid. That doesn't mean *you* should. Also, the security system will be armed, so don't go outside."

Despite my reluctance on the matter, I recently caved and allowed Frick and Frack to hold down the fort. Alone. For several consecutive hours. Oddly enough, no one died or had been abducted by aliens. The dog bore no visible signs of trauma, the house was fairly intact and there were no bicycles on the roof. However, upon entering, I noted that our newfangled security system had been curiously disarmed. Naturally, this led to a discussion, one that unfolded thusly:

Me: "So why isn't this thingy (read: the hi-tech-alarm-gizmo-I-don't-pretend-to-understand) beeping?"

Frick: "I disarmed it."

Me: "Why on earth would you do *that*?!"

Frick: "Because it was beeping. Annoyingly. Plus, I knew the police and fire department would show up any minute if I didn't."

Me: "Oh, right. And why was it beeping?"

Frick: "Because Sadie went outside."

Me: "I thought I told you guys NOT to go outside...or to even open the door."

Frick: "Yeah well, she did. She thought she heard your car."

Me: "Okay, why is this (key holder) box empty?"

Frack: "Because I lost the key."

Me: "You lost the key. Terrific. Why would you even NEED the stupid key?!"

Frack: "Because Taylor wouldn't let me in."

Me: "Why wouldn't you let your sister back in the house?!"

Frick: "You told me not to let anyone inside, under any circumstances. But I had to. She kept banging on the door and it was really annoying."

At this point, I had no words. Nothing I had conjured in my deranged little mind had prepared me for what apparently had transpired. In any event, I found comfort in the knowledge that my brood had, indeed, demonstrated responsible behavior. Sort of.

Planet Mom: It's where I live (eating my words).

The Island of Misfit Parents

I'm a poor tool when it comes to holiday décor. A mere handful of days remain on the calendar before Christmas and I have yet to string a single light on shrubbery or hang a solitary stocking from the banister, now cold and bare. Never mind erecting an oversized tree in our living room, one that may or may not stand entirely straight. That would require ambition, the ability to govern the impossible-to-govern and an exhaustive search for our less-than-functional tree stand. What's more, its assembly would consume an inordinate chunk of time, devoted primarily to hauling the artificial wonder from the bowels of our attic (hopefully, without incident), dragging its dead weight down a narrow staircase and around impossibly tight corners and then piecing the beast together, branch by color-coded branch, all the while exercising civility and decorum.

A tall order, indeed. It's no wonder I put it off each December. Although maybe it has something to do with the fact that my kids are far more interested in climbing inside and atop the monstrosity-of-a-box and barreling down the staircase than in helping to build the cussed tree that said box has housed for nearly a decade and a half.

Every year, though, I vow to improve—to embrace the Yuletide more than ever before, to rouse a spirit of goodwill and cooperation among the elfin creatures who reside here, to deck the halls in a more timely fashion, *to actually mail our Christmas cards before Groundhog Day.* Of course, I make such a pledge so that my children might refrain from reinforcing my holiday-related ineptitude (i.e. Mom, I hope you know that PRACTICALLY EVERYONE ON THE PLANET has already put up their tree—except us—we're misfits).

Ouch. It's not as if I haven't *meant* to do all those things, and more. Aside from attending 487 Christmas plays, holiday concerts and craft-making sessions involving pine-scented whateverness, I've compiled an impressive to-do list—one that spells out in great detail what I *should* be doing to prepare for this season of seasons. If nothing else, I am well intentioned, as evidenced by my heartfelt promise to bake the giant Halloween House cookie that has mocked me since mid-October—the one I threw in my cart in a moment of deluded inspiration, never once believing that it might STILL be in my pantry two months later. I wish I were kidding.

Child: "We're NEVER baking that cookie, are we, Mom?"

Me: *Hangs head in shame.*

To add to the mélange of angst and discontent brewing beneath this roof, our tiny herd of reindeer has yet to be assembled in the lawn, an event that has come to symbolize a welcome committee for Santa, much like the gingerbread cookies and carrots we place in a tin made especially for that purpose. Naturally, I defend that which is indefensible. "There's no snow on the ground! Plunking reindeer in the grass, not to mention, '…plunking reindeer in the grass WHILE IT RAINS,' just seems *wrong*. And besides, one set of antlers is defective. And the lights are shoddy. And the neck swivel thingy lurches and jerks as if it were a sprinkler head. On crack. Remember how your dad had to cobble the stupid thing together with wires and screws…and the hideous-looking tangle of lights he wound around its belly? At least we have a Christmas wreath hanging on our door…and a pumpkin on the stoop. How many people can say *that* in December?" I foolishly boast.

Of course, commentary like that is never well-received, usually being met with a chorus of groans, a profusion of eye rolling and remarks that generally employ the word "lame." As in: "Seriously, Mom? That's so completely lame."

She had a point.

Admittedly, I am a poor tool when it comes to holiday décor.

Planet Mom: It's where I live (on the Island of Misfit Parents).

V is for Valentine

V is for the *valiant* deeds you do as a matter of course—like traipsing through our home in the dead of night in your underwear to find the source of a sound I've tried (and failed miserably) to adequately describe, except to say that it is "…most definitely not a normal 'house sound.'" Moreover, you've rushed to my aid on countless occasions to thwart the spillage of veritable pools of repulsiveness, unstopping the loo with remarkable aplomb, never once pausing to judge the ridiculous nature of my fear and loathing.

A is for your *appreciative* nature and for your inclination to express said appreciation in the form of chocolate. And almonds. Perhaps dark chocolate-covered almonds, if I were asked to more accurately define the essence of your appreciative ilk, my dear Romeo.

L is for *loveable*, given the endearing creature that you are. That said, you're kind and compassionate, thoughtful and engaging, generous to a fault and more romantic than you'll ever know. I never have to question your love for me or your ability to make me laugh even when the bottom falls out and the wheels fly off (think: projectile vomiting and flooded basements). You know just what to say and when to say it, reading me as well as any book you've ever held in your hands. Even your foibles (which, by many standards, should've made me certifiably insane by now) are marginally unobjectionable—something I never thought humanly possible.

E is for the *enthusiasm* with which you approach life—even in the face of my less-than-enthusiastic view toward tedious chores like cleaning the garage, weatherproofing the deck and planning the totality of every summer vacation we've ever been so fortunate to take. Furthermore, the restraint you demonstrated for the duration of my Orlando-inspired tirade (i.e. the one involving shameful histrionics in which I accused a certain airline of being patently tyrannical) was most admirable. For that alone, I love you dearly.

N is for your *nonjudgmental* nature. You don't care that I sometimes forget to cook. Or clean. Or shop. Or water plants. You accept me for who I am, unconditionally, and know that a lot of plants will likely die in my care.

T is for the *tolerance* you exhibit each and every day. Admittedly, I'm difficult to live with. I'm needy, erratic and I have a crippling aversion to spiders. I swill milk straight from the jug, my showers are of an interminable length and I've been known to mock your shortcomings with merciless precision (i.e. "Can't you at least *pretend* to be organized?") What's more, I am physically incapable of getting anywhere in a timely fashion, which I'm certain rankles you to the core. You'll never know how grateful I am for your tolerance in the abovementioned arenas.

I is for the *ingenuity* you routinely display when you're called upon to delve into our brood's unwieldy school projects—the ones that ought to warn parents of the perils of working with way too much glue and far too little direction. So clever and resourceful are you, utilizing an unlikely arsenal of duct tape, crusty pizza boxes and errant screws. You're perfectly selfless, too, embracing the celebrated and often untimely excursion to craft stores without the slightest objection or hint of frustration. After all, you reason, it gives you a chance to bond with other parents who have made the very same trek—to gather paint, to compare the circumference of various foam balls and to suffer the ill effects of pipe cleaner envy.

N is for the *novelty* you employ practically every time you pack someone's lunch, adding a touch of love and creativity to an otherwise banal event. Never mind that you've replaced me as the Sandwich Captain and Scrawler of Lunchbox Notes. Of course, I was envious at first, harboring a visceral brand of resentment for a time. But I've come to realize that you've taken on the task to lighten my load. What's more, I genuinely appreciate your flair for catering to creatures that are, at best, a challenge to nourish.

E is for your *emboldening* ways. In a word, you're my biggest advocate in this life—silencing my doubts, offering definitive proof that my cup runneth over much of the time and always, always providing a soft spot to land when I fall. Valentine, I love you more than words could ever say.

Planet Mom: It's where I live (spelling it out for my special valentine).

We Put the "Mad" in "Mad Scientist"

It's April—Weird Science Month, apparently. At least in *this* asylum it is, particularly given that my fifth-grade progenies were recently assigned a school project that was deemed categorically intoxicating. An exercise in academia devoted entirely to my brood's abiding love of science-y type stuff. One in which inane curiosities would not only be nurtured, but patently celebrated. Hence, the ensuing delirium.

That said, Jekyll and Hyde could barely contain their enthusiasm as they shared with me the sordid details of what would prove to be both epic in scale and absurd in nature. Like a clown car, droplets of insanity kept spilling from their mouths in giddified bursts, rendering me at once fascinated and horrified by their plans to test two of the oddest hypotheses I had ever wrapped my mind around. Fascinated, of course, because the notion of reading aloud to a houseplant (to compare growth rates) and/or sniffing fetid socks among other things (to determine what makes people sneeze) is, well, *fascinating*. I was horrified, by contrast, because I was certain I'd be commissioned to read aloud to said plant on occasion as well as sniff the aforementioned socks. Good grief.

For the record, the socks were egregiously foul and the reading-aloud-to-the-stupid-plant gig bordered on disturbing—particularly when I found myself pausing to check for understanding and apologized more than once for mispronouncing a word. I can't begin to express how utterly wrong (read: foolish, awkward, nay, *deranged*) it felt to do so, but I persevered—in the name of science and in the name of making my child happy (aka the Plant Whisperer). In a similar manner, I humored her cohort by shoving that-which-was-clearly-ill-advised (read: house dust, cinnamon and obscene quantities of black pepper) up my nose—once again, to further the field and to please my child (aka the Sneeze Captain).

Granted, there's nothing new beneath the sun. Bizarreness—especially as it relates to the many and varied experiments my children have conducted for the sake of scientific discovery—has lived and reigned here for a very long time. I suppose I should be used to it by now, unfazed by my charges' compelling desire to marry ingredients that have no business being together, to test the limits of things that ought not to be tested and to boldly go where no man (or inquisitive child) should go—namely, within the confines of a dryer, an occupied dog crate and a certain basement crawl space. I could go on.

Admittedly, I've been the chief curator of a fair number of studies described above, inviting substances of undetermined origin and wide-ranging viscosity to sully my windowsills, sinks and countertops for interminable stretches of time. Never mind the Shrine to Vileness (read: insect-related captivity) housed in the garage and the noble causes I've adopted over the years "…because so-and-so's mom won't let him experiment at *his* house." Needless to say, I don't know what it's like to live in a home without some sort of glorified laboratory-fest gong on. I'm surrounded, it seems, by creatures with a crippling affinity for that-which-is-repulsive-yet-wholly-intriguing. If nothing else, it's familiar—and probably vital to my kids' development.

Lord knows how important it is to test the validity of theories that involve decomposing food, fermented dandelions and the microwavable nature of chocolate bars. Or so I've been told. Likewise, the gravity of pioneering research on the half-life of plastic toys currently buried in our lawn cannot be underestimated. Nor can the monumental body of data my charges gather almost every summer, which definitively answers the question: "How many ants does it take to haul away a single potato chip?"

With any luck, such studies may change how we view the world, possibly enhancing our understanding of community-based synergy—or perhaps enlightening mankind relative to the hazards of exploding chocolate. Which isn't such a bad thing—during Weird Science Month and every other moment devoted to the wonderment of discovery.

Planet Mom: It's where I live (channeling all-things-science).

Juneuary

I love this time of the school year, as we straddle the delectable months of May and June—quite literally on the cusp of summer. Translation: The celebrated death of structure is nigh and I can almost taste the deliverance from order and obligation—especially as it relates to parenting a pair of wily fifth graders. Far and away, it's my favorite wedge of weeks on the academic calendar; although September's nice, too, with its bustling fleets of bright, yellow school buses, towers of textbooks and freshly sharpened pencils. Trendy backpacks and lunchboxes abound, too. Everything, it seems, is awash with newness come September, just as it was so very long ago when I headed back to grade school with the swarming masses.

But the *present* chunk of time is downright edible—a delicious string of days that meld together like the final pages of a good book. Needless to say, the sundrenched afternoons and scrumptious evenings filled with games of tag and the ever-present thrum of crickets woo me into thinking that nothing on earth could possibly be better—except maybe a moratorium on homework, which is pretty much what we've been granted of late. That said, there is no substitute for this season's splendor—and the fireflies we are eager to chase at dusk. Nor is there any match for the grand finale my kids revere more than life itself (i.e. the culmination of school, with its patented swirl of delirium-inducing celebrations and jammed-to-capacity schedule of events). Indeed, it is a frenzied cluster of weeks that threatens to claim my sanity, but it passes all too quickly and I find myself pining for more.

If I had my druthers, another thirty-day chunk of time would be sandwiched between the fifth and sixth months, infusing the school calendar with that which is righteous and good (namely, science projects that don't necessitate the summoning of a marriage counselor, sports schedules that are very nearly practicable and weather forecasts that typically include blue skies and balmy temperatures). Juneuary, I'd call it. Of course, it would contain a perfectly frivolous holiday during which people would pause for three consecutive days to pay homage to squirt guns or pet toads. Possibly both. You're welcome, said the maniacal visionary and curator of whimsy.

Alas, there is no Juneuary, and a mere handful of days remain in my children's school calendar—a woeful reality that is, of course, punctuated by the fact that this week will officially end their grade school years. That said, my brood is poised to enter middle school in the fall—where the likelihood of being trampled by a herd of eighth graders is nearly equivalent to that of being stuffed inside a locker (incidentally, a locker that no one will figure out how to reliably lock and unlock without divine intervention and/or the acquisition of at least one superpower).

Never mind the inevitability that I will fail to locate their classrooms on Back to School Night, at which time I will surely forego the opportunity to meet their new teachers because I'll be too busy wandering aimlessly through the labyrinth of hallways that appear disturbingly similar. Make that COMPLETELY INDISTINGUISHABLE, except for the smallish numbers printed near the doors that I may or may not fully discern, given the addled state I expect to be in at that time.

Maybe I should just stow my kids somewhere in the bowels of the elementary school for the summer, so they might stay a bit longer, tethered to the people and things they know best. A place where an embarrassment of items were lost and subsequently found (read: library books, lunch money, a certain someone's clarinet, eleventy-seven sweatshirts, a beloved rock and an errantly placed baby tooth). A place where scrapes were tended to, psyches were nurtured and curiosities were fed since the early days of kindergarten. A soft spot to land these past six years—a refuge that has made all the difference this June.

Planet Mom: It's where I live (searching desperately for the pause button).

A Kinder, Gentler Sort of Summer

I don't remember my summers as a kid being the least bit hectic, never mind structured. As I recall, summer was an exercise in deliverance and spontaneity—an intoxicating river of endless days and weeks, blurred at the edges, verdant at its core, punctuated by dozens upon dozens of delicious remembrances that pool in the corners of my mind even still.

There was no glorified schedule or master plan that bound me to times or places, unless you consider the regularity with which my dad and I watched late-night ball games together in our living room, the ceaseless drone of the big box fan humming in the background like a raspy biplane. There were no obligatory to-do-list items I felt necessarily compelled to realize before heading back to school either, except, of course, the ones that involved harvesting baseball cards, tooling around on my banana seat bike and acquiring a new pair of sneakers. Low-tops. Black.

Summer was a time to relax, recondition and, on occasion, run away from home—an impulsive act of stupidity, inspired largely by gypsies and like-minded eleven-year-olds who felt stifled by boundaries of the parental variety. But I digress. Of all the seasons of my childhood, summer was far and away the most delectable.

That said, my younger brother and I practically lived in our backyard swimming pool, until the laze and haze of August segued into the rush of September, its bright yellow school buses and freshly waxed floors jolting us back to a different sort of reality. When we weren't paddling around in big, rubber inner tubes or diving to the bottom in search of stones or coins, we could be found at the water's edge immersed in a game of checkers on a giant beach towel, an island of sundrenched bliss. Other days we'd disappear deep into the woods, climbing trees and cobbling together all manner of poorly constructed forts with a motley crew of neighborhood kids, hammers and nails we pilfered from our fathers and wood scraps we managed to haul there, one armload after another. Brambles and poison ivy be damned.

We logged countless hours of basketball and badminton, too, threw Frisbees at dusk till no one could reliably see and lay in the cool grass, pausing just long enough to watch the vermillion skies fade to purple, then to wooly gray and eventually, to an inky black canvas dotted with a smattering of stars—some bright, some barely discernible as the shroud of night consumed every tree, thicket and barefoot child in its path. Multitudes of fireflies took center stage then, materializing out of nothingness it seemed, ushering in the goodness of many a summer's night.

Shortly thereafter, we assembled the masses for hide-and-seek, a spirited game hopelessly devoted to perpetuity and the governance of an ungodly amount of acreage, encompassing the far reaches of one's neighborhood long after the woods grew thick with mosquitos and alive with a chorus of crickets. Sweat-soaked and breathless from giving chase, we eventually headed home, having heard the familiar thwack of a certain screen door coupled with our parents' demands to come inside, signaling an end to this and so many good nights of summer. But our bedrooms would soon be dappled with the morning sunlight, and the promise of yet another endless day of summer beckoned unremittingly.

By today's standards, I fear what I've described above would qualify as dreadfully dull. There were no cell phones to speak of, no tablets in existence and not a single app had been so much as imagined. By and large, moms didn't run taxi services for their children in the summertime. Nor did they farm them out to an embarrassment of camps or overload their schedules with a glut of culture and tutelage and the insanity that fuels organized sports.

Times were simpler then. Less harried, and more memorable, methinks. Perhaps because the tapestry of summer was woven at a kinder, gentler pace, helping us all to find joy in the ordinary.

Planet Mom: It's where I live (remembering when summer was really summer).

Vacation Schmacation

I didn't even want to go on a stupid cruise. People get seasick on cruises. Agoraphobic. Claustrophobic. Aquaphobic. Lilapsophobic. At times, they suffer the unmerciful wrath of foodborne illnesses, they become preoccupied with rogue sharks and ill-mannered pirates and they often lament a dearth of trees. At least I did. Miss the trees, that is. Worse yet, seafarers fall victim to that special brand of withdrawal—the one associated with not being able to send text messages obsessively or to check one's email ad nauseam without shelling out obscene sums for Internet connectivity. Never mind the very real possibility of hitting an iceberg while sailing the ocean blue or, God forbid, capsizing in waters that are disturbingly deep.

Of course, we *know* the waters are disturbingly deep because the nifty little televisions in everyone's impossibly small staterooms conveniently display the current depth (measured in thousands of feet!) in a continuous loop, along with a relief map of the western hemisphere illustrating how godawful far from land said ship is presently situated. After Day Two of our eight-night Bahamian cruise, I simply stopped dwelling upon such foolishness and tried to imagine a scenario in which Poseidon would save me if I fell overboard. Naturally, I was convinced that *someone* in our party of six would fall overboard during the course of our epic journey to the tropics, or that my directionally-challenged children would at some point vanish inside the fourteen-story, 964 ft. vessel or that my husband would fall for an insanely gorgeous redhead with little or no neurotic tendencies. Who could blame him?

Aside from the voyage itself, I had no idea how involved preparing for a cruise would be. There were on-shore excursions to plan well in advance of the trip, most of which I stupidly accomplished in the wee hours of a hellacious night, a mere handful of days before we left. There was also the matter of transporting our motley crew (to include my parents, our youngest children and an embarrassment of luggage) through the uber-congested Lincoln Tunnel to Manhattan's 88th pier, a place where Conestoga wagons and horse manure would surely be frowned upon.

This, of course, led my dear husband to the pure genius of renting a fifteen-passenger van, heretofore known as our $832 carcass on wheels, the dilapidated nature of which cannot be overstated. As I recall, three of us might have been properly belted in, there was a mere suggestion of shock absorption present for the teeth-jarring journey and a repulsive pair of safety glasses beckoned to my brood from the backseat. *Gak!* But because the gods were smiling upon us, the air conditioner functioned flawlessly and each time we skittered across an exit ramp, we somehow failed to collide with a guardrail. And while the circus-like event of obtaining passports and the tirade-infused meltdown associated with my packing frenzy on the eve of our departure very nearly necessitated a small team of marriage counselors, my husband and I remain very much in love.

It's true; I didn't want any part of the cruise my parents so graciously bestowed upon us on Christmas Day. But somewhere, between the lazy catamaran ride to our dolphin encounter on Blue Lagoon Island and lolling in the pristine waters of the Caribbean at Castaway Cay with my family, I surrendered to the notion of leisure. No longer would my irrational fears about our summer vacation consume me. From that moment on, I refrained from inviting worry and dread into my otherwise harried world. Instead I let the warm embrace and gentle caress of the surf erase every trace of anxiety I had harbored since we boarded the ship in New York.

Granted, some of us did, indeed, become lost on that behemoth-sized boat. Reading glasses and hearing aids were misplaced, too (the latter of which were recovered), a tooth was broken at dinner, a seagull wreaked havoc at the beach and a rollercoaster at the park went on the blink. But for the most part, our time together was imbued with goodness and punctuated by dozens upon dozens of delicious remembrances—many of which involve being pampered beyond all imagining.

I miss the chocolates on my pillow each night, the towel origami and crisp linens that awaited us as we returned from a myriad of daily exploits, the live entertainment, indescribably attentive servers and meals that qualified as delectable if not superb, the inimitable wedge of time I spent with my family that I will treasure forever and ever.

Thanks, Mom and Dad, for a wonderful vacation.

Planet Mom: It's where I live (joining the ranks of cruisers).

The Seven Habits of Highly Defective Parents

Sarcasm aside, Stephen Covey should have written a book with the abovementioned title. Not that he failed spectacularly as a father, but because people tend to more readily grasp what *doesn't* work, as opposed to what does. Like tightrope walking, for instance—without a net. In a practical sense, *Seven Habits* would've been an invaluable guide for parents, highlighting the antithesis of good advice as it relates to the uncertain nature of raising children. Countless individuals, myself included, could've then avoided seven of the biggest pitfalls of child rearing—all of which I've shamelessly embraced since the advent of motherhood. So in the true spirit of generosity and irreverence, I've compiled a list of that which you would do well to eschew.

1. STOCKPILE EXACTLY NOTHING IN YOUR DISCIPLINARY ARSENAL, rendering you categorically ineffective (read: deplorable) when it comes to dealing with ill-mannered children and/or defiant teens. A sign that you're on the right track in this regard can be clearly demonstrated if you lack any discernable ability to assign logical consequences to a wayward grocery cart, let alone an unruly child. Moreover, if you think "positive reinforcement" is just a bunch of psychobabble and you have absolutely no idea what will happen if and when you actually reach the count of three (i.e. at the climax of your hackneyed threat: "One…two…two-and-a-half… two-and-three-quarters…two-and-seven-eighths…"), you're well on your way to becoming a highly defective parent. However, you've truly arrived in said capacity

when you scream at your brood, "Stop screaming!" and it actually works.

2. DO EVERYTHING FOR YOUR CHILD/ CHILDREN, lest they become discouraged, frustrated or palpably incensed as a result of their futile attempts to do for themselves. Heaven forbid you let them fail. At anything. Nor should your dear progenies be held accountable in this life. For anything. Never mind their longings for independence and ownership as they grow. Continue on the path to martyrdom by picking up their shoes, making their beds and triple-checking their homework day after day, right through college and into grad school. Fight their battles for them, too, paving the way on every imaginable front. In this manner, you can insure their dependency (and your sense of purpose as a slack-picker-upper) for a lifetime.

3. SAY "YES" TO YOUR CHILD/CHILDREN FAR TOO OFTEN, even if it spells emotional/financial ruin for you, or reckless endangerment for them. A happy upbringing is all about instant gratification and leniency, after all—not to mention, keeping the peace. Indulge them daily—hourly if need be, so that you might satisfy their every whim. Translation: Let your charges pitch a monstrosity-of-a-tent in the living room for weeks on end, perilously slide down staircases in sleeping bags and adopt more pets than the Animal Control Board thinks you can readily accommodate. Note: If your house doesn't smell like hamsters or wet dog, you're not trying hard enough.

4. COMPARE YOUR CHILD/CHILDREN TO OTHERS at every opportunity (especially those involving hyper-successful peers, siblings and

well-mannered house plants)—a practice that serves to solidify feelings of inadequacy and self-loathing. Kids simply adore being held to an unattainable ideal, relishing the notion of not-measuring-up in all avenues of life.

5. MODEL IMPROPRIETY AT EVERY TURN. Launch tirades, throw shoes and by all means, refuse to share your sand shovel. Additionally, hold grudges, damn politicians and say incredibly vile things about the Everyday Math you've been expected to embrace since your oldest entered kindergarten. Better still, demonstrate the beauty of white lies, offer your brood an abundance of inappropriate ways to deal with bullies and hang up on a telemarketer at least as often as Rush Limbaugh says something stupid.

6. ALWAYS SPEAK BEFORE YOU THINK. Enough said.

7. INTRODUCE THE CONCEPT OF PANIC TO YOUR CHILD/CHILDREN BY ROUTINELY INVITING FEAR AND WORRY INTO YOUR COLLECTIVE CORNER OF THE WORLD. The more irrational the fear/worry the better. Histrionics are good, too, especially as they relate to obscure maladies involving parasites native to Tasmania, the horror of being struck by a sofa-sized chunk of space debris and, of course, the Mayan apocalypse.

Planet Mom: It's where I live (in all my defective glory).

Words Matter

I didn't even know the woman, but I bristled when she spoke. Of course, her words weren't even intended for me and I'm sure she had no idea how capably they would seize my joy and take me back in time to a day I'd rather not remember.

I was standing in the card aisle of a local department store of all places, wrestling with indecision famously. As I read and reread each of the selections I was considering (encouragement for a woman battling cancer and a birthday wish for a dear friend who had moved a world away), I weighed the words contained within each heartfelt message carefully, recognizing their power to connect souls in good times and in bad.

"CARDS DON'T MATTER," I heard her grouse through clenched teeth, chiding her children who were likely picking out a birthday greeting for a friend or a favorite cousin. "We've already gotten a gift, now choose a ninety-nine-cent card and let's get out of here," she spat, indignation spilling from her lips. "He'll just throw it out anyway," she reasoned.

Though a towering wall of greeting cards separated us and I could see exactly *none* of what had transpired in the adjacent aisle, the exasperation that wafted over the transom was palpable and left little room for misinterpretation. Without question, it had been a long day and patience was nowhere to be found. Clearly the novelty of traipsing around a store with kids in tow had long since worn off.

Granted, I had been there and done that as a parent, patently consumed by a simple yet impossible wish to be somewhere else in this life besides searching for the perfect gift for yet another kid-themed birthday party. That said, I have frequented the brink of insanity while shopping with my brood more often than I'd care to admit, shamelessly enraged by something as ridiculous as a rogue wheel on a cart from hell coupled with my children's irksome demands: "But we have to smell the smelly markers before we buy them, Mom. We have to make sure they smell juuuust right. And then we have to look for a birthday card with a little dog on it. Wearing a pink tutu. Maddy likes little dogs. And tutus."

Frustration, I understood.

What rankled me to the core was the premise of this woman's argument. That "cards don't matter." Because sometimes they do.

Like most people who learn of things that are unspeakably difficult to handle, I unearthed this little pearl of wisdom mired in grief and plagued by guilt. As if it were yesterday, I remember rummaging around my brother's house in the days that followed his suicide, searching for answers or perhaps a tiny glimpse into his troubled world. Granted, I didn't know him nearly as well as I could have...and probably *should* have. As I sifted through his CDs and thumbed through his books, eager to gain even a modicum of insight, I stumbled upon a drawer with a handful of cards neatly stacked within. Cards he had saved. Cards that likely meant something to him. Cards filled with words that apparently mattered.

It was at this point, I'm quite certain, that I felt a deep sense of regret and shame, for none of my cards were among those he had harvested. Surely, I had sent him a birthday greeting (or twenty), a congratulatory note regarding his beautiful home or his wonderful job, an irreverent get-well card to brighten an otherwise unenjoyable hospital stay, a wish-you-were-here postcard from Myrtle Beach or the Hoover Dam. Hadn't I?

Incomprehensibly, I couldn't remember. All I could wrap my mind around were the missed opportunities and the paltry thank-you note I had written that lay on his kitchen counter. Unopened. The one my four-year-old daughters had drawn pictures on as a way of offering thanks for his incredible generosity at Christmastime. The one that mocked my ineptitude and chided me for failing to mail it sooner...so that he might have read it...and felt in some small way more valued than perhaps he had before. The one that reminded me that words left unspoken are indeed the worst sort of words.

I'd like to think he occasionally sat on his couch and sifted through that cache of cards on a lazy afternoon, warmed by the messages scrawled within—a collection of remembrances worthy of holding close. Likewise, I hope he knows of the countless times since his death that I've been overcome with emotion in the card aisle of many a store, pausing in the section marked "brother" to read and reflect on what might have been—an odd yet cathartic sort of behavior.

So as one might expect, the horribleness of that day flooded my mind the very instant I heard CARDS DON'T MATTER. But instead of letting it swallow me whole, I turned my thoughts to why I had come—to find the most ideally suited messages for two special people, knowing they would feel special in turn.

Planet Mom: It's where I live.

CHAPTER 7

Training Wheels

The Dog That Came to Stay

It was his eyes that got me. Deep pools of espresso dappled with specks that reminded me of caramel. I hadn't even reached through the cage to caress his indescribably soft ears yet, a practice I would come to revere more than practically anything since it brought as much calm to me as it did to him. Never mind his sleek, black coat and grizzled eyebrows—the ones he could move independently, effectively conveying his mood, which was almost always agreeable.

The plan was to adopt a rescue dog for my dad, one that would serve as a loving companion for him as he grappled with Alzheimer's disease. Something that would ground him as his world fell apart. The trouble was that I needed grounding, too.

Needless to say, I didn't intend to fall in love with such a dog. Nor did I think I would be incapable of delivering on a promise I had made to my dad.

"I'll find you the perfect dog. Just give me a little more time. I think you'll love the one we end up with, but we have to be sure it meets all the criteria first."

Unfortunately, none of the candidates we considered passed muster for a variety of reasons: too lively, not lively enough, too disinterested in people, too apt to jump on people, too aggressive and so on. It seemed as though we were doomed to fail.

Then Jasper appeared as my husband and I meandered through the SPCA for the umpteenth time, peering into cages in search of an answer to our prayers. Our eyes locked with the aforementioned black lab mix and the rest was history. Originally, he was supposed to stay with our family only until we felt he was ready to transition to my dad's home. "We'll keep him for a week or so—long enough to adjust to life outside a kennel," I told my kids. "He's old and needs some TLC," I reasoned to myself.

Weeks stretched into a solid month and by then I was hopelessly smitten. Jasper had quietly wheedled his way into our family and had become a part of our lives we didn't even know was missing. Indeed, there was no mistaking the bond that had formed between us and there simply was no turning back. That said, he stepped with ease into our crazed schedule and house filled with teenage drama, noise and angst, despite his dog years and inability to recognize his own name—the one the Rescue had fittingly assigned him.

Against all odds, he learned to love our yappy, fourteen-pound Bichon and, in the process, made the latter less prone to anxiety attacks and barking seizures involving delivery trucks and unsuspecting joggers. At every turn, he modeled good behavior for our not-so-compliant, curly-haired pooch—the one we thought was beyond hope for ever acting like a normal dog. Almost daily they now play together, tossing their toys into the air and racing around the house like a couple of deranged squirrels—something that makes my heart smile. Every. Single. Time.

Not surprisingly, it wasn't long before I discovered how comforting it was to have a big-ish dog place his head or warm muzzle in my hand as I awaken each morning. Or the soothing effect he has on all of us as he wedges his box-like body next to ours on the couch at the close of a long day, somehow sensing our need to decompress. By contrast, he embraces our clamor and chaos—celebrating both the disorder and the abundance of joy that resides within our home.

Needless to say, there's something extraordinary about having this dog, in particular, around—and by "around" I mean that he has become my shadow, following me everywhere but into the shower. What's more, he reluctantly bids me farewell when I have to leave and greets me in the doorway when I return, tail wagging wildly, reminding me that *all* dogs are inclined to smile. You just have to look for it.

As a result, I never feel unappreciated or truly alone no matter how empty my house happens to be—the kids running in seventeen different directions and their dad expertly manning the taxi or holed up at his office. Looking back, I think it's during those quiet times when I value his presence the most. He's there for me day in and day out, keeping me from dwelling on the sadness that lies beneath the surface of every joy—the ever-present sorrow related to having lost my dad not in the physical sense, but by every other definition.

Somehow, I know my dog understands. It's in his eyes.

Planet Mom: It's where I live.

Exhaust the Little Moment

Without question, I am the most incompetent individual using Snapchat on the planet today, a Neanderthal when it comes to hi-tech forums for sharing photos and videos via smartphones and the like. I know this to be true because my teenage daughters broke the devastating news to me. Thankfully, I'm not particularly devastated by it—just discouraged, and slightly annoyed by my failure to embrace yet another trend in social media.

According to my brood, it seems that I've missed the whole point of said craze. While I'm fixated upon sharing my treasured photographs, clever memes and the occasional video clip with friends and family on Facebook, Instagram and Twitter, I'm passionate about preserving them as well. Like seashells I've culled from the miles of shoreline I've trekked, I want to enjoy them later, slowly turning them over in my hands, feeling the grit of sand between my fingers, revisiting the memory that was created in the gathering process.

Such is not the case with Snapchat, however. It's a transient beast. A keyhole view of life that self-destructs within mere seconds. A way of capturing the gloriousness of an instant (serious or silly as that might be), and then letting it die, just as the ephemeral traces of fireworks fade into the dark of night.

Needless to say, the whole thing seems completely foreign to me and I'm having great difficulty wrapping my mind around the concept, despite the fact that Teen One and Teen Two have spent upwards of FIVE WHOLE MINUTES trying to help me understand. Of course, how could I expect them to invest more time, given the fact that they're terribly busy Snapchatting with their inner circle of cyber friends? However, I'm part of that inner circle now, so it's all good.

At any rate, I'm fairly certain that neither of the aforementioned teenagers have read any poetry by Gwendolyn Brooks. But somehow they've managed to apply a smattering of her most storied words to their lives.

"Exhaust the little moment. Soon it dies. And be it gash or gold it will not come again in this identical disguise."

Apparently, the beauty of this particular form of media sharing is in its impermanence, forcing would-be recipients to attend to the content of what is sent. Naturally, I can envision a host of opportunities for abuse among teens and tweens in this venue, but at this juncture in time I choose to focus on what is positive about it. Perhaps I can even learn to love that which is decidedly temporary—a lesson that can surely be applied to life itself on a grander scale, much as Brooks opined. Indeed, our hearts are only beating—temporarily, so we may as well make the most of it.

Further, Snapchat has afforded me a tiny glimpse into the colorful teenaged world in which my daughters currently reside, beyond taking note of which books, movies and YouTube tripe happens to intrigue them at the moment. Crazy as it sounds, it gives me the chance to connect a little more, too, engaging on their level, joining in their fun, speaking their language for a time—albeit clumsily. I get to look on as they revel in the art of just being themselves as well, which is a gift in every sense of the word, especially as they begin keeping me at arm's length more and more with each passing year.

Granted, Snapchat may not be as endearing or prized as hearing firsthand about a certain someone's latest crush, perceived injustice or small victory, but it's something, and that something is good.

Planet Mom: It's where I live. Snapchatting. Sort of.

You Might Be a Band Parent...

Fall is upon us. Time for corn mazes and jack o' lanterns, flannel shirts and apple cider, football and marching bands. But let us not forget, 'tis the season for band parents, too. In the spirit of identifying with the tireless role that they play in support of their music-loving, instrument-lugging progenies, I've made a handful of keen observations so that others might avoid entering the future ranks without first knowing what's in store.

You might be a band parent if...

1. You shop for vehicles based primarily on their capacity for cramming large and unwieldy musical instruments within a given square footage—as well as additional band members of varying size who may need a ride home on occasion. Having the extra cargo space for a six-foot color guard flag also comes in handy when your daughter announces she'd rather flip a flag than march around on a football field while playing a clarinet. *Hello...that's marching band, dear.*
2. You come to expect desperate phone calls and/or texts following drop offs, informing you that an item of vital importance was somehow forgotten (i.e. money, dot sheets, guard gloves, sweatshirt, socks, nude-colored strapless bra, etc.). Naturally, you're expected to come to the rescue. Every. Single. Time.
3. Your car knows the way to the band room, to every football stadium within three-hundred square miles and to the beloved concession stand—where you will spend an estimated quarter century of your life. Or

maybe it just feels that way, since you emerge from each of your eternal shifts there totally spent, smelling much like a French fry and reflexively responding to dietary requests with, "Would you like cheese on that?"

4. Forget singing along like a banshee to Sam Smith tunes on the radio. Instead, you find yourself drumming out the beat of *Seven Nation Army* on your steering wheel and chanting its hypnotic mantra because you've heard the band play it roughly SEVEN MILLION TIMES. Why do you engage in such foolishness while cruising around town? Because it now inhabits your subconscious mind. And you love it. Almost as much as you love the marching band as an entity and the kids who embody its spirit.

5. On the eve of band competitions, you lose precious sleep and become all but consumed with performance anxiety—despite the fact that the performance in question isn't even yours. Which makes no sense at all.

6. Never mind your career, hobby or favorite sitcom. You now spend the bulk of your days and nights either engaging in or thinking about fundraising for the marching band. If you could train your dog to help you achieve your financial goals for the season you'd do it in a sixteenth note (translation: almost instantaneously).

7. There have been great multitudes of discussions in your household that begin with the words, "One time, at band camp…" and not once have you freaked out. Well, maybe one time, but that's because you couldn't stop thinking about that line from *American Pie* and you were paralyzed with fear over the issue of having to discuss the topic of sex at the dinner table.

8. It's barely October and already you've spent enough money on the concession stand to fund a mediocre political campaign. But if *you're* the one running for office (based on your track record of providing hot, nutritious meals for your family during marching band season), don't bother. Everyone's grabbing dinner featuring soft pretzels and chili dogs an average of two nights a week. At least it's hot. Probably.

9. You hate to admit it, but you don't really care much about watching football anymore. The team is undoubtedly great, but now it's all about THE BAND. And HALFTIME. Or the PREGAME SHOW that happens prior to kickoff. Heaven forbid you're still in the parking lot loading up like a pack mule or stuck in line for cheese fries when your school performs. Your kid will NEVER forgive you. So if that happens, be sure to lie well and don't miss it next time.

10. You witness something special every single day— namely the warmth and acceptance with which the band welcomes one and all into the fold. You recognize the band director and his or her associates as gifts from above and you look on with wonder as your child blossoms in an atmosphere of positivity and inspiration, ever so grateful that you heard the words, "Mom, I joined the marching band!"

Planet Mom: It's where I live, loving my experience as a second-year band parent at Loyalsock High School, despite all my whining.

All Hallows Eve...The End is Near

I've been informed it's over—my brood's love affair with trick-or-treating, that is. I knew it would happen eventually. I just wasn't expecting it to happen now, seemingly minutes before Halloween. It's possible I'll need weeks of therapy in order to cope with such tragic news. Please send candy.

I guess I was kidding myself to think my kids' enthusiasm for harvesting gobs of chocolate and fistfuls of candy corn would last forever. And I probably missed some important signs last October when my progenies disguised themselves to the nth degree (one wore a disturbingly realistic horsehead mask while the other donned a ginormous set of bat wings), but then sort of dragged their feet when it came to traipsing all over the neighborhood, treat bags in hand. At the time, I simply pushed it out of my mind. Denial, as it were.

As the stages of grief are classically defined, I suppose I haven't progressed much since then. I *still* reject the idea that the fun is over, defending the fact that "...even *adults* like to dress up in ridiculous outfits and solicit candy. Who wouldn't?"

Almost immediately, I learned how incredibly stupid that question was. In no uncertain terms, I was enlightened as to how "completely *done* with that" they were.

"We just want to stay home, answer the door and scare little kids to death."

Egads. I wasn't prepared for that sort of response. I guess I just want to hold on to the past, or maybe even live it a little longer if possible. I liked it when my twin daughters were just babies—most of the time anyway. They were pumpkins their first Halloween, kittens their second, and burly lumberjacks their third year I think. I remember dotting their cheeks with dark eyeliner, giving their faces the suggestion of stubble. I also fondly recall piling warm layers of clothing beneath red and black-checkered jackets to complete the look.

For the first several years, my husband and I lugged them around the neighborhood in their little, red wagon, using blankets and coats to prop them up and cushion the bumpy ride. Hats and mittens were a must, cleverly incorporated into the ensemble. At each house we visited, friends would crowd around the door to see how adorable our children looked, each year's costume topping the last.

As they grew older they were able to walk with us, tightly gripping one of our hands while clutching their coveted treat bag with the other. Each year we journeyed further and further away from home, eventually canvassing the entire neighborhood in one night—which was no small feat.

More recently, they've met up with their friends on All Hallows Eve, eager to wander the streets of our close-knit community, a smallish herd of mask-toting teens and tweens in the dark of night, some carrying flashlights, some entirely too cool to carry a flashlight, their raucous laughter filling the autumn air. By evening's end, they would return home, sweaty and utterly spent, usually hauling all or part of their costumes—either because they were too hot or they broke somewhere along the way. Treat bags bursting with candy. Smiles all around.

But this year will be different. No more ambling from house to house. No more bags of loot to dump on the kitchen floor to better sort and ogle. No more little, red wagon or mittens. At least my kids have assured me there will still be the wearing of costumes, however. So there's that. I guess I'll just have to accept reality and embrace a new and different Halloween tradition—as scary as that might be.

Planet Mom: It's where I live...lamenting the end of All Hallows Eve (sort of).

The Great Sock Abyss

Some time ago my daughter cleaned her bedroom, and in so doing resurrected an embarrassment of items that she had ostensibly given up for dead. Things that she hadn't seen in such a long period of time that she forgot about them almost entirely. There was a pair of earbuds that had been MIA forever, more than a year's worth of allowance and at least nine coffee cups, one of which still contained what could only be described as a fermented atrocity.

Lovely. Just lovely.

Most notably, she unearthed an ungodly number of socks. Tall ones. Short ones. Socks with stripes. Socks with dots. Socks that will never again be suggestive of clean and socks imprinted with teensy-tiny foxes. My personal favorite.

Admittedly, on more than one occasion I felt compelled to rummage around in her hovel, intent upon gathering all the lone socks in order to pair them appropriately—because it makes me insane to know that the socks in question are, for lack of a better term, estranged. Never mind wadded up, inside out and appearing as though they had been shot from a cannon.

How hard could it be? I remember thinking. *You just look around, find the right patterns and put them together. It's not rocket science.* Truth be told, I found such an endeavor to be virtually impossible each time I tried—and subsequently failed—to locate matching pairs. It was as if her room had transformed into the Great Sock Abyss—the place where perfectly wonderful socks go to die, or, perhaps more tragically, become separated forevermore.

Like a fool, I had to ask my daughter the obvious question: WHERE DO THEY GO?

"I have no idea where the lost socks go, Mom. No clue."

At any rate, when she cleaned her room (see paragraph one) I was patently euphoric over the news of her sock discovery, since their mates had been hanging on a rack in the laundry room since the dawn of time, in hopes of being reunited at long last. Imagine my surprise (read: PROFOUND GLEE) when she produced a dozen or more of the missing socks. It was categorically off the charts and almost as joyous an occasion as the time she found her favorite pair of dilapidated sneakers. Sneakers so pathetic, and yet so dear, she more affectionately refers to them as *dead*—as if the term "dead" were somehow a good thing. Technically speaking (she's quick to remind me), they're still functional. Sort of.

That said, in the past I've questioned her dead sneakers as well as the bizarre logic that would support a decision to NOT keep socks and their mates together. Who *does* that? And why on earth does it happen month after month?

"I don't know, Mom. I guess I take them off and tell myself that I'll put them together later, and then I don't. Honestly, it's just too much work."

At that, I shook my head in disbelief and perhaps disappointment. Then I began to wonder if I had driven my mom crazy in much the same way. I couldn't reliably recall my specific behavior as it relates to the pairing of socks, although all signs pointed to having been a neat freak, so they were probably ridiculously ordered. Perfectly aligned in neat and tidy little rows when clean. Turned right side out and paired properly when dirty.

Now that I think about it, it's entirely possible that I drove my mother to distraction by spending an inordinate chunk of my teenage years organizing my closet and drawers. It's also likely that my obsession with rearranging my bedroom furniture by myself at all hours made her nearly certifiable on occasion. In fact, I moved my dressers and bed around so often that their spindly legs were on the verge of snapping—something that would make any parent implode.

So maybe I should consider myself fortunate, only having to deal with lone socks for a decade or two. Not the annihilation of furniture. As an added bonus, my daughter's bedroom gets cleaned. Occasionally.

Planet Mom: It's where I live, probably looking for missing socks.

Mission Impossible

Next time around, I'm having sons. Know why? Because then I won't have to fret over nail polish spills, exorbitant water bills or bathroom counters filled to capacity with every unnecessary beauty product under the sun. But it's bigger than that. When it comes time for each of them to shop for that momentous high school semi-formal occasion, we'll hit just one store, fall in love with the first tuxedo we stumble into (which will fit like a dream), pay the man and live happily ever after. Okay, okay, maybe we'd get hung up for thirty seconds or so choosing just the right cummerbund hue (honestly, how tough can THAT be). But we'd still be in and out of there in a flash—comparatively speaking, of course.

With three daughters, I've pretty much accepted the fact that I'm doomed—at least in the bathroom category and in the shopping-for-apparel (and shoes, and purses, and trendy jackets) arena. And the list goes on. So why would searching for a formal gown be any less exasperating than all the other girlie-things I deal with on a day-to-day basis? If anything, this maddening little event may outrank all the back-to-school shopping fiascos I've ever endured. Perhaps, though, such experience will gear me up for the inevitable—the mission of helping them each choose a wedding dress. No need to rush things, however. Life is perfectly complicated already.

Thankfully, our two youngest girls currently have no interest whatsoever in spending an eternity pursuing the perfect addition to their wardrobes. Nothing on earth would bore them more. Furthermore, they couldn't give a hoot what their friends think about their taste in clothing. That's because they're three—and totally oblivious about the existence and influential nature of "fashion police." Who knows what kindergarten will bring, however. I dread the day they refuse to wear an outfit because so-and-so mentioned that it had gone out of style the week before. Just shoot me now.

No doubt, those aforementioned impressionable youths positively adore their big sister; and sooner than I'd care to imagine, they'll long to follow in her footsteps—which, I'm sorry to say, often lead directly to the mall. Did I mention that I'm doomed? But at least I'm not alone. On my valiant quest to help my teenage daughter find THE dress for her upcoming semi-formal dance recently, I encountered swarms of frazzled parents—some too exhausted even to speak.

Most of them were moms, carrying heaps of slinky, colorful, sequined garments in their arms, and wearing completely sapped-out, "get-me-out-of-here" expressions on their faces. A few mumbled something about wanting to be put out of their misery. Believe me, I felt their pain. I, too, had an armload of sequins and a look that mirrored theirs. I figured it was only a matter of time before the mumbling would begin.

After half a dozen or more stores and countless trips to the oh-so-uninviting dressing rooms, I began to seriously doubt that THE dress even existed. There appeared to be a direct correlation between my aching feet and pessimism. In my opinion, plenty of dresses she had tried that day looked fabulous on her (as did the stiletto heels she'll ditch after the first dance). Not that my opinion MEANS anything, mind you (and apparently it doesn't). Finally, I thought, "Hey, let's ask this perfect stranger, or better yet, this lovely mannequin how gorgeous you look in that dress!" If it wasn't the color, it was the cut. If it wasn't too short, it was too shimmery. If it wasn't too racy, it was definitely dowdy. I thought it would never end.

So imagine my surprise when she emerged from the dressing room wearing a smile from ear to ear and a stunningly beautiful gown. If I hadn't been so caught up in the moment and thrilled over the news that we had finally succeeded, I would have gone looking for my little girl in that dressing room. It seemed as though she had disappeared. No doubt, a son would have done the same. So maybe in spite of everything, I'll discover that having daughters suits me just fine—even when it comes to the "S" word—shopping.

Planet Mom: It's where I live.

Merry and Bright. Sort Of.

I love indoor Christmas lights. Tiny white ones, more specifically—the sort that cast a soft glow at dusk, filling a darkened room with ambient warmth, reminding me that it was totally worth risking life and limb to hang them atop windows and French doors as I foolishly balanced on a step stool, the meaty arm of a sofa and once, even upon a tall stack of pillows that were strategically placed upon said sofa. Yep. Totally worth it.

My husband, by contrast, adores such festive trappings, but is less than enamored with the idea of wrestling with them for more than twenty-seven minutes—the average time it takes to retrieve the tangled masses from the attic, arrange them in clumps on the floor and then wrap them around a Christmas tree in a manner that is both geometrically and aesthetically pleasing. What's more, he can't stand it when he makes the inevitable discovery in the thick of decorating madness (i.e. lights that won't light, bulbs that are broken or flicker with the slightest bit of movement and entire strands of lights that are sporadically lit at best, a far cry from merry and bright).

Of course, these are the very same lights that functioned perfectly *last year*—the ones we tested before boxing them up and shoving them into the deep recesses of the attic. I'm convinced that something criminal happens in there between New Year's and Thanksgiving. Something that can probably be traced to Elf on a Shelf, or an equally reprehensible little creature inclined to tamper with our trimmings. However, we don't own any of the aforementioned elves, nor would I feel compelled to put them on a shelf or anywhere else because they creep the cranberries out of me. Nevertheless, it's clear that *something* goes on in that attic that would explain our less-than-functional lights.

Yes, it's possible they're just chintzy, and that we're too cheap to care.

At any rate, we are then faced with a dilemma—the one my husband and I experience each and every year. Do we ditch the strands of lights that refuse to cooperate completely, effectively ridding ourselves of the headache that is defined by tightening and checking ALL of the bulbs individually? Or do we stuff the dysfunctional segments of strands into the tree, where we hope no one will notice and subsequently judge our character?

And let us not forget the problem of what to do with the strands that won't light at all. If you're anything like my husband, you'll keep plugging them into the wall socket and jiggling the wires, repeating the idiocy that is wrapped in denial. Admittedly, I am slightly amused by his antics, so I encourage him to continue trying. Again. And again. Eventually, though, he decides to part with the wretched strands, leaving them for dead. Meanwhile, I cram yard upon yard of half-functioning light strings into the tree, doing my level best to disguise the ones we've determined to be misfits this Christmas—because a) I'm too lazy to go to the store to buy more and b) I'm too stubborn to unravel what I worked so hard to position on the boughs in the first place.

"It's fine," I rationalize. "We'll manage with the ones that DO work and no one will be the wiser."

I have to wonder, as I cruise around town at dusk, peering into yellow squares of windows at fir trees and mantles aglow with twinkly, white lights—do rogue trimmings plague their households with the same ferocity as ours? Maybe we're an anomaly. Or maybe the universe hates us. Or maybe, just maybe, our Christmas spirit is being tested. I suppose it stands to reason that we continue to pass since we rise to the occasion each year, making our home merry and bright in spite of the intolerable struggle that has become familiar if nothing else.

Planet Mom: It's where I live, probably messing with Christmas lights.

New Year...Same Old Resolutions

It's January—time to make a comprehensive list of all the areas in our daily lives that desperately need improvement, or at the very least, tweaking. For many of us, that means the list we made LAST year. I, for one, have taken an inventory of my shortcomings these past few weeks and pledge to keep at least a handful of the New Year's resolutions I've made AGAIN, despite the unlikely nature of lasting success. Here are the highlights.

For starters, I'll be kinder. More specifically, I'll stop harboring ill will toward the people who seem to take an eternity to put air in their tires at the gas station. No longer will I wish that a chunk of space debris would fall upon their heads, effectively ending their stint at the pump, making my wait that much shorter. Perhaps instead, I'll use the time to meditate or make a grocery list. Who am I kidding? I'll play the bazillionth game of solitaire on my smartphone or count the appalling number of *Trump for President* bumper stickers I see in the vicinity.

Secondly, I'll stop enabling my kids. Even though it pains me greatly, I'll refrain from harvesting gobs of toothpaste from their bathroom sink each morning, followed by removing wads of hair from their shower because, quite frankly, this practice has done nothing but teach them how to be unaccountable in life, not to mention, horrible at housekeeping. Instead, I'll ignore their domestic failings (as intolerable as that might be) and bank on the notion that eventually they'll become SO GROSSED OUT they can't help but be inspired to do the job themselves. Probably.

Related: I'll try to be a better parent. Translation: I vow to stop yelling, "THE YELLING IN THIS HOUSE HAS GOT TO STOP!" Please reference the previous paragraph for insight as to why such behavior might be warranted (i.e. my teens DRIVE me to it and my parenting tools are decidedly defective). Needless to say, the irony here isn't lost on me and I recognize fully that I won't be nominated for Mother of the Year anytime soon. However, I'd be thrilled if I could simply spend less time yelling about the yelling I do.

In addition, I resolve to spend less time using my smartphone and more time interacting with humans. More specifically, I'll curb my penchant for texting and sending instant messages to those who happen to be in the same room with me, sometimes within arm's length. In lieu of that, I'll engage in actual face-to-face conversations with the people I love, allowing words and phrases to fall from my lips in a cascade of spontaneity. Technology be damned.

What's more, in the new year I'll attempt to rid my world of unnecessary stress. No longer will I feel guilty about sleeping in or taking a mental health day on occasion, which, of course, will be defined by watching an embarrassment of old movies while spooning my dog on the couch. All day, if circumstances warrant. Don't judge.

Furthermore, I promise to finish at least *some* of the projects I start, beginning, of course, with hauling our artificial Christmas tree and outdoor lights to the attic. With any luck, that will transpire before Groundhog Day. The most challenging project I'll likely tackle in the coming year, however, will be indoctrinating my dear husband on the finer points of organization. Pray for me.

And because no one's list of New Year's resolutions would be complete without referencing the pathetic nature of a diet and exercise routine gone awry, I pledge to walk more in the new year as well as add more greens to my plate. I won't give up my dear frappés, however.

I haven't gone COMPLETELY mad.

Planet Mom: It's where I live (welcoming a brand new year, striving to achieve the same wretched resolutions).

Valentine's Day in the Trenches of Parentville

Somewhere in the great continuum of life, my children evolved from toddlers to teens—seemingly overnight. And although I don't miss the blur of early parenthood, projectile vomiting or the abundance of pointy, plastic dinosaurs I trod upon in the dead of night, I *do* miss delicious experiences like shopping for valentines with my brood. Stop laughing.

Never mind that it was a painstaking process, watching them pace back and forth in store aisles attempting to choose the ultimate design from the hoards that were available. Even *more* painstaking was the process of helping them fill out dozens for classmates and beloved teachers, since the children in question had yet to master the art of writing their own names. But that was part of the fun—witnessing their determined efforts and the care with which they tackled the task year after year. In the end, it was always worth it.

So it's sort of sad that the celebrated valentines-exchange-gig is over for my kids. Sadder still is the fact that mass marketers never seemed to have capitalized on consumers like parents—an enormous segment of the population that could potentially benefit from trading sentiments related to being in the trenches together. Just for fun, I came up with a handful of ludicrous valentines that moms and dads might find fitting for the occasion.

1) You look ravishing, Valentine...especially when you find time to shower and brush your teeth after a harrowing day with the kids.

2) Can't wait to be alone with you, Babe...right after we read forty-seven bedtime stories and wipe the pasta off the dining room walls.

3) You had me at "I'll go to the parent/teacher conference this time. You just make yourself comfy on the couch, have a big glass of wine and read a great book."

4) There's nothing that says LOVE like offering to fold our brood's laundry (the *right* way) and find all their missing socks.

5) You're never sexier than when you're unplugging the kids' toilet or helping them with their godawful homework.

6) Be mine, Valentine! The kids are at a SLEEPOVER!

7) I'll be yours always and forever...if you promise to let me nap on the beach while you keep our youngest from drowning and/or pooping in the sand.

8) You're my soul mate and I can't imagine life without you as we tackle sleep deprivation, sibling rivalry and teen angst together.

9) You take my breath away, my love—even when I'm NOT yelling at the kids.

10) I'll love you till the end of time, Valentine, or until our children stop asking unanswerable questions.

11) Nothing sounds more romantic than you, me and grocery shopping WITHOUT the kids.

12) Dance with me, tiny dancer—even though the floor is littered with potato chips and naked Barbie dolls.

13) Kiss me, you fool—never mind that our children are conducting a science experiment in the kitchen—possibly with flour, glitter and glue.

14) I'll love you to the moon and back…if you'll plan the kids' birthday parties and the next six vacations.

15) You complete me, my dear, but never more than when you're taxiing the kids all over the damn place.

16) Oh, how I adore thee, my hero…especially when you traipse around the house in your underwear because I heard a strange noise at three a.m.

17) Valentine, you make my heart race, even more than when our children play in traffic or ride their scooters through the house.

18) Love means never having to explain why you let the kids eat ice cream for dinner.

19) I'm hopelessly devoted to you—just like I'm devoted to posting stuff on social media that may or may not make our teens cringe.

20) My love for you is unconditional, much like my love for the pieces of bacon our kids discard.

Planet Mom: It's where I live, with my special Valentine.

Namaste for Dummies

Here we are, in the thick of February—a time at which I should be comfortably settling into the exercise routine I ostensibly adopted on New Year's Day. But such is not the case. For whatever reason, I found Groundhog Day to be a more inspiring square on the calendar—possibly because *Groundhog Day*, the movie, made me realize what a horrible rut I had fallen into with regard to my physical self. Each day I repeated the same bit of idiocy—that of exercising an undying devotion to being sedentary. More specifically, the pathetic nature of my fitness program had come to be defined by walking my dogs, followed by the rigors of channel surfing.

At any rate, seeing the movie sparked within me the impetus to put down the remote control and to crawl out of the burrow of blankets I had built on the couch so that I might unearth one of seventeen Yoga-for-Beginners DVDs I currently own but have rarely viewed. Of course, I chose yoga because apparently I enjoy pain. And I chose to work out in the privacy of my own home because I'm enough of an embarrassment to myself, let alone to others. The struggle is, indeed, real. I don't need an audience to attest to that fact.

To say that I am inflexible and ill equipped to bend and twist in a manner that many would consider insufferable is an understatement. My limbs are decidedly defiant and my muscles practically scream in protest each time I reach for my toes. Admittedly, I'm a poor tool when it comes to contorting my body into that which is suggestive of a pretzel. What's more, I'm unbalanced, I don't breathe properly and I incorporate far too much wincing into my half-hour routine.

I'm quite sure that yogis everywhere cringe as I lurch around my coffee table, attempting to clear my mind of distractions. What am I saying? I AM A DISTRACTION. I think about the mounds of laundry I ought to be sorting, the toenails I should have trimmed and the fact that I'm out of ideas for dinner. Again.

Besides, who wants to deal with the misery of pushing one's body to the extreme and far beyond its comfort zone when one can instead Google the bejesus out of absurd Super Bowl commercials? Confession: Each time I haul my yoga mat from the bowels of the closet, I have to walk past my computer and fight the very real urge to sit down and type in the words "Best Super Bowl Commercials."

Let us just say that sticking to my daily yoga regimen has been difficult at best. But I'm managing so far. Today will mark the fifteenth consecutive day I've hit the mat and groaned audibly. Meanwhile my dogs look on from their perch on the couch as if to say, "Enough with this foolishness. It's time to turn on the tube and spoon with me." Likewise, my cat monopolizes my mat space, deciding it's a fantastic place to loll around and give himself a bath—never mind that I'm busy failing at yoga here.

And because I'm *completely* mad, I invited my family to practice the routine with me one morning, thinking they might make the experience less of an effort and possibly more fun. When they finished rolling their eyes and/or laughing hysterically at the suggestion, my husband agreed to humor me, "…just this once." Of course, he divided his time between mocking the instructor, blowing in my ear to derail my tenuous state of concentration and moaning in pain. Admittedly, however, it did make me feel better to know there was at least *someone* on the planet less flexible than myself.

Namaste.

Planet Mom: It's where I live, often failing at yoga.

Ten Ways to Say "Thank You, Mom"

Thanksgiving Day is almost upon us. Time for family, feasting and a well deserved respite from the impossible demands and harried pace of life. Time for bribing my kids to wear dress clothes, for hiding the abomination of clutter that exists within my home and for treating the reluctant gravy stains that will inevitably occur. Time for snapping wishbones, smoothing tablecloths and clinking fancy silverware. Together.

It's time for pies, pictures and parades, too, as we reconnect with loved ones, near and far. Mostly, though, it's time to gather and to give thanks for harvest and health, just as it was at Plymouth in 1621. Indeed, it is time to give thanks for the many people and things deemed instrumental in our lives.

I, for one, recognize the wealth of goodness with which my life has been blessed. But on this particular Thanksgiving Day, my thoughts rest on my mother—perhaps because her world came crashing down this past June, perhaps because of the battle she's now fighting, perhaps because she's always been there for me—even still. So thank you, Mom, for so many things…

…for being a good listener in spite of the vat of foolishness I'm sure to have delivered over the years…for reminding me that you can never have too many friends or woolen blazers…for emphasizing the importance of pausing when a child speaks, allowing the void to be filled with what's really on their minds.

…for letting me do stupid (yet exceedingly edifying) things—like putting all kinds of time and energy into a less-than-seaworthy raft, like chewing gum in bed, quitting band, forgoing French and studying till three a.m. for a physics test…

like getting a disastrous perm, allowing gossip to consume me and dating boys with long hair and fast motorcycles.

...for tolerating my imprudence and forgiving my mistakes—like burning our water pump, which transformed our swimming pool into a pond overnight...like tormenting our sitters unmercifully, forgetting your birthday and breaking God-knows-how-many windows and flower vases...like betraying your trust by filling our house with teens and booze while you and Dad vacationed in Florida.

...for encouraging me and inspiring a sense of belief in myself, teaching me to accept what I have and to handle disappointment when it visits...for helping me recognize the inherent value in power naps, mental health days and a good, long cry.

...for letting me go...on the mother of all road trips with eleventy-seven of my closest friends...to the lake with the aforementioned motley crew...to an insanely large university where I would surely be swallowed up in lieu of finding my path in life...for biting your tongue when I quit my job in the city and when I married the wrong man.

...for introducing me to the almighty crock pot, to the concept of saving money and to the notion of waiting for the real prize instead of grasping desperately for the veneer of gratification.

...for underscoring the importance of writing thank you notes, of spending time with my grandparents, of talking to babies and of liking myself—even when I'm least likeable.

...for teaching me how to sort laundry, to deal with a loathsome roommate, to make a mean pot of chicken soup, to soothe a grexy baby, to contend with a rebellious teenager, to find a great pair of black flats…to appreciate the patina of a genuine antique and the untold merits of a good iron…to instinctively know when to opt for eggshell (as opposed to ecru)…to own my decisions, to list pros and cons and to always weigh my options carefully.

…for loving your grandchildren with as much ferocity as you loved me, for implanting within me the seeds of faith and for instilling me with the impetus to seek solace within the pages of a good book and nurturance within the arms of a good man.

…for letting me be there for you and Dad this past summer— likely fouling up your checkbook and misplacing things in your kitchen forevermore, but being there nevertheless.

Planet Mom: It's where I live (giving thanks).

The Lingo of Parenthood: A Curious Addendum

I'm convinced there aren't enough terms in the English language to adequately reflect upon my harried life as a parent. More specifically, there ought to be words that, when cobbled together, help us to more effectively define the indefinable and/or express the mélange of exasperation, angst and joy we sometimes feel throughout the course of a typical day. To that end, I've developed a handful of new terms to expand upon the current vernacular.

CELL PHONE CIRCUS: The crazed barrage of texting/phoning that takes place in order to arrange for a friend or relative to pick up one's child/children after school or an activity in the event you can't possibly do it. Of course, you don't realize you can't do it until it's almost time to pick up the aforementioned waifs, at which point you become panic-stricken, not to mention mortified by your failure to anticipate such a circumstance. Out of sheer desperation, you then phone or text seventeen different people, highlighting your stupidity, spelling out the logistics involved with the proposed pick up and promising a pony to anyone who says "yes." With any luck, someone will come to your rescue and haul your brood home.

PARKING LOT PURGATORY: The indeterminate wedge of time (i.e. roughly a century) during which parents sit in their cars in the parking lot at school, at the soccer field, etc. in anticipation of the emergence of one's child at the conclusion of the event in question. Naturally this happens because the *scheduled* end time isn't remotely related to the *actual* end time. Invariably, we are the last to know. To add insult to injury, our kid clearly has a knack for being dead last. Every. Single. Time.

FESTIVAL OF MOODS: The kaleidoscope of emotions our progenies (especially of the teen and tween variety) demonstrate, ranging from the pinnacle of euphoria to beyond the point of surly. Over time, we have come to expect the unexpected, yet we never quite know which disposition will be featured at any given moment—which makes dealing with it even more thrilling (not so much). The only thing we can be sure of is its highly changeable nature. And drama. *Lots* of drama. Like so many things that fall under the umbrella of parenthood, it goes with the territory.

DREAD-MONGER: A parent who is routinely plagued by an overwhelming sense of irrational fear as it relates to an unfounded belief that something horrible has happened to one's child. The trigger could be the text you receive informing you that he or she might have incurred a concussion. Of course, your child assures you there is no reason to be alarmed—unless you find certain statements disturbing such as: "I'm a little confused and nauseous because a huge shelf fell on my head and IT FELT LIKE MY BRAIN BOUNCED." It could also be the itchy rash that mysteriously shows up three weeks into a course of antibiotics—the rash your child cleverly documents with a series of photographs, texting them to you in succession from school ~~to make you INSANE with worry~~ to brighten your day. Making matters worse, you Google the symptoms and brace for impending doom. It's what you do.

EMBARRASSMENT BY ASSOCIATION: The act of offending one's offspring simply by being alive. More specifically, when your kids reach that magical age we all know and love, they become completely mortified by your presence—to include the way you walk, talk and breathe. Heaven help you if you happen to sing in front of their friends, set foot in their classroom or step within four hundred yards of their school bus.

NEW AND IMPROVED WALK OF SHAME: The familiar excursion you make from your car to the school office, delivering yet another item your child forgot—something vital to his or her existence. Like so many times before, you hang your head as you place said item on the counter, vowing that it will be the last time you behave like a helicopter parent. Probably.

RANDOM HUG FEST: Spontaneous displays of affection in the form of hugs, given freely by one's child/children for no apparent reason whatsoever. The impulsivity and genuineness of such an expression of warmth, if nothing else, reminds us that we are loved despite our innumerable flaws. Savor each and every one of them.

Planet Mom: It's where I live.

Say Yes to the Dress—Maybe

I have not-so-fond memories of my high school prom, most of which stem from having worn a dress that felt as if it were lined with burlap. It was a white, floor-length eyelet gown, cinched unmercifully at the waist, making the thought of dancing almost unbearable. Never mind walking, talking and breathing. However, *not* going to the dance was out of the question. I went because all my friends would be there. I went because the hype leading up to the event was intoxicating. I went because prom night was a rite of passage—apparently, so was wearing obscenely uncomfortable shoes and stuffing myself in a dress that was two sizes too small.

Cutoffs and sneakers were more my speed. If only I could have convinced the Prom Committee to allow everyone to dress as if they were going to a backyard barbecue, not a stodgy affair where herds of adolescents would spend much of the evening shuffling around in stiff formalwear, feeling both awkward and insecure. Or maybe that was just me.

The only thing less enjoyable than the prom itself was the gown-shopping marathon my mom and I endured beforehand, my angst superseded only by my negativity. I remember thinking I would *never* find the perfect dress, because it didn't exist. Designers, it seemed, didn't have flat-chested prom-goers in mind when they created styles for the masses. Instead, the racks were spilling over with plunging necklines and slinky, strapless numbers I couldn't wear on a bet—not without hours of alterations and/or divine intervention. Lo and behold, we stumbled upon a gown that would work. Besides, I reasoned, I only had to endure it for a few hours. Then I could ditch it for jeans and a t-shirt—my garb of choice. Not surprisingly, that's exactly what I did.

So when my youngest daughter announced that she would need a prom dress this year I was speechless, my mind swimming with enough pessimism for six people. But, I reminded myself, she is a different kind of creature—a fun-loving free spirit, one who thrives on adventure and feels comfortable in her own skin, worlds away from me. That much I know.

That said, virtually everything about our shopping excursion was unlike my own of decades ago. For starters, we found heels long before we looked for a gown and she systematically broke them in over a period of weeks. On the day we finally set out to find a dress, my daughter brought the aforementioned shoes along so she could put them on to see how they looked with each gown she tried. Brilliant.

We then proceeded to haul massive amounts of silky, sequined whateverness into the dressing room, banking on the premise that more was better. Itchy tags and tangled hangers be damned. Despite the fact that we both fell in love with the very first gown (in which she looked stunning), she soldiered on—just in case she would discover something even *more* irresistible. There were black ones and red ones. Dresses without straps. Dresses without backs. Each one distinctively elegant. Each one with its own special charm, making the decision-making process fairly impossible.

After what seemed like forever, we were able to narrow it down to two favorites. And when I say "we" I mean my daughter and myself, an exceedingly helpful sales woman, a handful of patrons who happened to be in the vicinity and hordes of my daughter's friends who offered instantaneous feedback via social media. Who knew that shopping for a prom dress would necessitate input from one's Snapchat tribe, which apparently was present in the dressing room? I kid you not.

Needless to say, it's a different world than it was some thirty odd years ago. Stranger still, we actually had fun searching for *the* perfect dress—so much fun, that we bought BOTH of her favorites. And because the gods were smiling, they were remarkably affordable, surprisingly comfortable and oh-so-beautiful.

Already it's looking as if she won't need decades of prom-related therapy.

Planet Mom: It's where I live, gearing up for Prom Night.

Training Wheels

My oldest daughter, more affectionately known as the woman-child, recently adopted a hamster—which is all well and good I suppose. She's away at college, so, theoretically speaking, the whiskered beast won't add appreciably to the chaos that lives and breathes here. To date, we house a pampered dog, a self-absorbed cat and, ironically, *five* smelly hamsters—which is plenty, given that a number of children and house plants also reside here, making demands and a profusion of noise as a matter of course.

Well, not the plants so much.

At any rate, the aforementioned co-ed is a fairly responsible twenty-something who has waited a very long time to welcome a pet of her own—to feed and water said creature without fail, to scrub away stench and eradicate poo with glee, to know the horrors and complexities of cage assembly and the sheer panic of "misplacing" the dear rodent in question. But, in all fairness, she couldn't be happier or more eager to embrace the notion that such a tiny (and admittedly adorable) being is now entirely dependent upon her ability to perform such tasks. There's something to be said for delayed gratification.

However it has come to my attention that a certain couple of somebodies have a problem with their big sister's new role as a bona fide pet owner. It seems that someone's panties are officially in a bunch over the matter of obtaining (or not) parental consent for the purchase of the abovementioned hamster.

Once the news broke (i.e. the furry beast was deposited upon the coffee table for one and all to behold), the ~~vociferous rant~~ conversation unfolded thusly:

"Does MOM know you got this?!" Child One fumed with indignation.

"Yeah! You can't just walk into a store and BUY A HAMSTER without Mom's permission! She'll absolutely FREAK when she finds out!" Child Two barked, visibly disturbed by her sister's alleged failure to follow family protocol.

"Hellooooo, I'm an *adult* and Mom will be perfectly fine with this. You'll see," the woman-child defended, almost comically.

Indeed, I *was* perfectly fine with it, but I was then faced with a thorny task—that of explaining to my youngest charges the particulars that encompass perhaps the grayest of parenting areas: *when, how and under what circumstances should we relinquish authority—great or small—to our children*, especially to those on the cusp of adulthood. In so doing, I found myself wrestling with the intangible nature of age as it relates to maturity, struggling mightily to define the indefinable and ham-handedly muddling through the whys and wherefores that drive nearly every decision that ultimately leads to the conferral of independence.

Somehow I managed to field the barrage of unanswerables and all concerned parties under the age of twelve seemed reasonably content with the outcome of the Great Hamster Debate. Translation: They were decidedly enthralled to learn that one day they'll likely be carrying smartphones and able to adopt a herd of llamas, with or without my blessing.

However, it made me think about the process itself, about the supreme challenge of knowing when and how much to surrender in the way of sovereignty, about what an inexact science it truly is. It's not enough that our grasp on the vestiges of control is tenuous at best; we must also deal with the uncertain nature of *when* to give it up.

Naturally, the training wheels are the first to go, then it's our presence they no longer require as they careen around the proverbial block, oblivious to the fear we routinely invite. Finally, they rush headlong into the enormity of the world, eager to make their own way and to cast aside the likes of training wheels forever.

I'd like to think I'm on the right track, no matter how inordinately awkward I feel at times, doling out freedom in embarrassingly small chunks, gauging success one child and one liberating event at a time. Loosening the reins, as it were— perhaps the most difficult task of all.

Planet Mom: It's where I live (lamenting the finite quality of childhood).

If the Sock Fits, Marry It

I've been married some twenty-seven years, nineteen of which to the same wonderful man. In that span of time I've come to the conclusion that a successful marriage doesn't have as much to do with an abiding love as it does with an ability to tolerate a disordered sock drawer.

That said, my husband's socks are in a pitiful state of disarray much of the time. Again and again, I've tried to bring a sense of order and uniformity to the unruly heaps in his dresser by employing a variety of tactics (i.e. ditching the socks with holes, pairing those without mates and grouping them according to style or color), to no avail. Somehow the huddled masses return in a less-than-tidy fashion, yearning to breathe free. And because I've grown to understand the psyche of the disordered male, egregiously flawed as he might be, I've become a more compassionate mate.

By the same token, my husband accepts my flaws, and the fact that *my* sock drawer is a ridiculously organized space—complete with separate compartments for sweat socks, woolen socks and dress socks, nary a rogue in the bunch. The only thing it lacks is a coordinated cataloguing system inspired by Dewey Decimal. Needless to say, I recognize how difficult this must be for him, coming to grips with the sad reality that he lives with a closet neat freak. Of course, no one knows I'm a neat freak because there are no outward signs, unless you happened to be present on the day I purged our linen closet, hurling a disturbing number of blankets, towels and obscenities into the yard during a brief yet memorable fit of rage. Most of the time, however, I suffer in silence, allowing the tide of paraphernalia that comes with marriage and a family to consume me.

Admittedly, since the advent of children I've drifted from my well-ordered life and neatnik tendencies, much like growing apart from the distant relatives we stumble across at a funeral, decades later, squinting hard to try and remember who they are and how they once fit into our lives.

That said, everything in my world used to be neat and tidy. There was a place for everything, and everything was in its place. Even the food in my pantry was logically aligned, tallest to smallest, labels facing out. To this day a tiny part of me dies whenever I peer inside our supersized refrigerator, the contents of which rest on shelves indiscriminately, as if they had been violently launched from a cannon across the room. But I digress.

Getting married and having kids changed everything. After years in the field, I've determined that about ninety percent of parenthood involves finding lone socks in obscure places. Plus there are even *more* sock drawers to deal with. Indeed, there is more stuff in general—stuff that is piled in our attic and garage, beneath beds and atop closet shelves, in cedar cabinets and the musty basement. Stuff that has no business being stuffed where it gets stuffed. Apparently, appliance garages aren't just for blenders anymore. They're for lunchboxes and dog vitamins, too, leftover popcorn and tubs of butter that may or may not be encrusted with the remnants of a week's worth of toast. And let us not forget the crumbs that gather there en masse. The ones that no one wants to clean.

What's more, it's been so long since we could park two cars in our garage I've forgotten what that even feels like. I suspect it would feel wonderful, much like it would to put china *and only china* in my china cabinet. Instead it houses prized artwork from my kids' grade school experience and a decade's worth of snapshots. Likewise, my refrigerator holds newspaper clippings, report cards and pictures of my favorite people and pets in the world. It holds vacation keepsakes and magnets with phrases I find particularly meaningful, too. Because that's what families do—they fill their homes with tangible reminders of the love that lives there. And they tolerate the disorder, sock drawers included.

Planet Mom: It's where I live, with way too many socks.

Life is Good...Mostly

I own a handful of trendy t-shirts emblazoned with the slogan: LIFE IS GOOD. I wear them because they're ridiculously soft, they feature stick figures with infectious smiles and, quite frankly, because I like the upbeat message they send to the big, bad world. Often times, people will stop me in the grocery store or post office, point at my shirt and nod in agreement: "Yeah, life *is* good, isn't it!" which is great, because sometimes I'm the one that needs a reminder.

That said, sometimes life is downright ugly—like right now, as the wheels fly off this crazed election and increasingly hateful rhetoric spews from otherwise civilized and compassionate people. I am no exception. Life is not only ugly, it's also heartbreaking and undeniably unjust because senseless violence continues to ravage the globe, hurricanes, floods and fires strike unmercifully and so many people I love grapple with cancer, or Alzheimer's or any number of other devastating diseases. Neighbors move away. Parents and beloved pets die. Friends endure unspeakable adversity—including, but not limited to financial ruin, crippling addictions or, heaven forbid, having to bury a child. What's more, marriages fail, suicides happen and people I care about become broken for a host of reasons.

I suppose that loss—sometimes more than people can bear—comes with the territory, an unwelcome side effect of this thing called life. Strangely enough, the more sorrow I experience, the more difficult it seems to manage on a personal level, each event affecting me more deeply than the last. You'd think that by now coping with it would be a walk in the park for me—something distinctly unpleasant, yet easy to accept because, if

299

nothing else, it's familiar. Admittedly, I sometimes stay in bed and hide from the world—especially on days when sadness and negativity threaten to consume me, convinced that by avoiding reality somehow it will cease to exist.

Of course, avoidance is only temporary. It does nothing to change what is real. So I shake my fist at God, infuriated by the fact that bad things happen to good people each and every day—despite denial, despite rage and despite prayers.

And then, as the sun rises, a funny thing happens. My dog ambles over to my bedside and shoves his head and warm muzzle into my hand, demanding to be petted, acknowledged, and eventually, fed since it's time for breakfast. I then crawl on the floor and spend a few moments rubbing his impossibly soft ears and talking with him about all the important things in his life—the walk we'll take later, his renowned affinity for squirrels and how great his scrambled eggs will taste. Yes, my dog eats scrambled eggs. Don't judge.

At any rate, somewhere between hugging him and caressing the leathery pads on his feet my mind is flooded with what can only be described as gratitude. Indeed, I can't imagine life without the rescue dog my family and I decided to adopt more than two years ago—our black lab-mix with the grizzled face and unsteady gait. Nor can I take for granted the other loveable beasts that reside here, never mind that our curly-haired, pint-sized yapper is decidedly neurotic and that our cat gives him plenty to be neurotic about.

From there, it mushrooms into recognizing all the good that has come into my life—all the people for whom I am thankful and all the experiences I'm glad to have had. I think of my husband, a man who has been my best friend for more than twenty years, the love of my life and my soft spot to land when the universe spirals out of control. I think of my three children who are talented, bright and most importantly, kind—ever so grateful that I get to be their mom. I think of all the people who touch their lives daily and I can't help but feel an overwhelming sense of indebtedness. I think of my treasured friends, my church family and how fortunate I am to have the lot of them in my life.

Of course, I'm happy to have a roof overhead, food in my pantry and the sweet refuge of music and books, too. But mainly it's the *people* that remind me that life is, indeed, good…mostly.

Planet Mom: It's where I live (probably wearing a LIFE IS GOOD t-shirt).

Apron Strings

I am a mediocre cook at best, perhaps an unlikely one as well, since I never was much for the kitchen—even as a kid. I have a handful of recipes in my repertoire that I feel comfortable with, most of which have been handed down through family over a number of years. Mastery came only as a result of determined effort and decades of repetition—certainly not from talent or inclination. That said, I almost never stray from the recipe, sticking to the formula that has worked for me time and again. There's always the chance I'll burn or undercook something, so I suppose that's all the adventure I need.

Occasionally, I'll branch out and try new things that I've seen on television, but only if I can pronounce the ingredients and find them easily in the grocery store. I'm not one to traipse around looking for something completely obscure that one of those celebrity cooks went on and on about. That's just not me. The degree of difficulty matters, too. Chances are if a third grader couldn't prepare it, blindfolded with a whisk tied behind his or her back, I'm not likely to tackle it anytime soon.

I realize this isn't the sort of example I ought to be setting for my daughters—always playing it safe, unwilling to step outside my comfort zone in order to reap the benefits that sometimes come with taking risks. As adults, I'm hopeful they'll be more adventuresome than I, delving into cookbooks, experimenting with new recipes they find online, crafting their own from scratch.

I'm sure if I had sons I'd feel the same way.

Nevertheless, I don't pretend to know what my children will glean from me as it relates to culinary skills. Lord knows I've tried to lure them into the kitchen, because, of course, I'd feel like a complete failure if I didn't at least teach them *something*. I'll admit it was easier when they were small. We'd pull the heavy mixing bowls out of the cupboard, shove wooden chairs up against the counter and sort through the drawer for favorite aprons—the ones that practically swallowed them so many years ago, two tiny sets of feet peeking out at the bottom. Together we'd bake cookies, scooping mounds of flour, cracking eggs in a less-than-efficient manner and eating chocolate chips straight from the bag. Not surprisingly, my kids were greatly invested in anything that involved making a terrible mess and/or eating sweet stuff.

Over time, I coaxed them into learning how to make some of their favorite dishes, banking on the idea that they'd be inspired by the outcome. For the most part, this has worked, evidenced by the fact that they feel comfortable enough to make their own dinner once in a while and no one has burned down the house as of yet. No small feat.

I suppose it doesn't really matter whether they fall in love with the kitchen and all that it entails. I won't be disappointed if they fail to fully embrace it, nor will I be displeased if they do. I just want them to continue to enjoy spending time with me there—even if I have to bribe them with chocolate chips or having free rein to make an enormous mess of my kitchen, something that's still very popular.

What's more, years from now I hope I'll see that I've managed to impart at least two things to my daughters, neither of which has anything to do with properly sautéing vegetables or peeling a hard-boiled egg without destroying it. I want them to recognize the importance of making a meal for someone who really needs to feel pampered or just plain loved—to know that comfort food is a godsend when someone is grieving or recovering or stressing about life in general.

I also want them to remember how special it made them feel to have someone bake them a birthday cake, slathered with their favorite icing and/or sprinkles. If they can in turn bake someone happy on their special day, that would, indeed, make me smile.

Planet Mom: It's where I live.

Beautiful Mess

Sometimes the stuff we need to hear from our children is muddled or falls to the floor, silent as snowflakes. Other times, those gems of communiqué are deafening, delivering messages that are both unfiltered and unapologetic. Still other times, the meat of the message is sandwiched in-between layers of fluff, artfully disguised as something unimportant. As a stunningly imperfect parent, I've been on the receiving end of each of these, although the sandwich-y variety is especially popular with my motley crew.

"Mom, please don't sing in the car. You're ruining Ed Sheeran for me. And by the way, I had a horrible day at school. Don't even ask. Now you're ruining Adele. Please stop."

Occasionally, I'm thrown off course by such commentary (i.e. harsh critiques of my musical abilities, or the lack thereof) and, consequently, fail to attend to the nugget of truth nestled within the statement: "I had a bad day, ergo I will pummel anything and everything in my path to relieve my pain and angst."

Thankfully though, messages of that ilk usually snake their way through the tangle of thoughts crowding my mind and I actually address what's bothering the daughter in question. It's only taken me twenty-seven years of parenting to figure that out.

If I've learned anything at this post, however, it's that the learning never ends. And that more often than not, the most valuable lessons are the ones taught by the children I'm attempting to raise.

Case in point: Not long ago, at the close of a very long day, I was in the thick of admonishing one of my teenagers for the disgraceful state of her bedroom—which is more like a burrow than anything. Over the past few years, I've grown accustomed to keeping her door shut in order to avoid a rage-induced tirade, since it's a battle I'd rather not have.

That said, her clothes are nearly always strewn like carnage, the dirty ones rarely making it to the hamper, the clean ones arranged in tired heaps on the floor, almost never finding the drawers or closet because that would make entirely too much sense. In all honesty, I can't remember the last time her bed was made, nor can I accurately recall what the top of her dresser looks like without the hodgepodge of stuff piled on it—an avalanche in the making.

Not surprisingly, I've been known to unearth remnants beneath her bed such as discarded bowls, coffee cups and the earbuds that had been MIA forever. Admittedly, and on occasion, I break down and mate the socks I stumble across and pair the shoes that I might have hurled into the aforementioned hovel because I simply can't stand that they aren't together, let alone in their rightful place in the universe.

So when I discovered her rain soaked hoodie, balled up in the corner of the dining room AGAIN, I began to seethe, marching upstairs to deliver it in person. And since she was standing in the doorway of her lair-turned-shrine-to-epic-disorder I couldn't resist the urge to chide her about that, too.

"Your room is a DISASTER," I spat, completely fed up with having to have the same conversation. Again.

"Yes, but *I'm* not," she answered as she looked me straight in the eye—then hugged me tight and headed off to bed for the night.

It's what I needed to hear—a tiny reminder that the really important things in life aren't disastrous, one of whom was standing squarely before me, growing into a remarkable human being, one who is loving and kind, joyful and generous, hopeful and bright. It was a message both loud and clear that helped me remember that the ultimate goal (mine anyway) is to embrace parenthood and to recognize it as the beautiful mess that it is.

One day, not long from now, she'll leave that room behind, box up her favorite treasures and cart them someplace new. And I'll help her pack—sure to salvage a lone sock or something to remind me of the days that were filled with chaos but with joy as well.

Planet Mom: It's where I live, mastering the art of defective parenting. Spectacularly.

Motherhood Anew

When I first became a mother, it felt as though time stood still, my days and nights never-ending, woven together into an unfamiliar tapestry that defined my upended world. I remember thinking the infant stage would endure forever and that I would surely be driven mad in the process. Sleep was a commodity I craved with fervor beyond all imagining, as were hot showers without the constant worry of being responsible for a tiny human 24/7.

My mother, of course, assured me that the sleepless nights, inconsolable crying and umbilical cord awfulness would eventually abate. Things would get better and my life could be reclaimed to a degree. A new normal would emerge in due time, largely contingent upon my child developing some level of independence. Turns out, she was right.

Granted, as my oldest daughter grew, my days were still filled to capacity and mostly blurred at the edges, although at the core they were remarkable and good, making me grateful to be a mother. Again and again this happened as another child joined the fold and I reminded myself that the inaugural stages only *felt* like a train wreck. I would muddle through, somehow. Motherhood would not consume me.

Eventually there would be sand castles and building blocks, baby dolls and baking cookies, blanket forts and, of course, endless summers in pursuit of the yellow-green flashes of fireflies. Days would be spent creating entire villages with sidewalk chalk and devouring favorite books together nestled on the couch—hours of being present with my children, moments that I now struggle to remember in perfect detail. If I sift through old photos and squint hard, however, I can often return to what was—tethered to a time and place when I was a different kind of mother.

At the time, I never imagined longing for those things, assuming they'd always be there—the books, the sandbox, the fireflies and so on. I hadn't considered that a day would come when my children no longer crawled into my lap for a story or begged me to build a teetering tower with blocks or allowed me to rock them to sleep. Back then it almost seemed a bit inconvenient, having to stop what I was doing and be present with my daughters, never mindful that eventually there would be "a last time" for engaging with them in that way.

I often wonder which book was the last to be read aloud. I have no way of knowing, but I suspect it happened at the bus stop, a place where we turned hundreds of pages together as we sat on the curb waiting for the school bus to groan to a halt. And when did we last chase fireflies, our bare feet skimming the cool grass at dusk, mayonnaise jars in hand? I can't reliably recall, although it might have been the same year I helped them climb trees or build a snow fort in the backyard.

By design I suppose, childhood has a season—an indeterminate yet finite number of days we get to watch our progenies move through the stages of development. If we're lucky, we remember to etch upon our minds the moments of pure perfection immersed within the tumult, when time is suspended and we can drink in the joy we happen to experience. So many ordinary moments as a parent wind up being extraordinary because we remembered to actually live them—to savor the goodness in the midst of madness.

If nothing else, this is the advice I'd like to impart to my children—especially to my oldest, who just became a mother. And although she struggles to get enough sleep and spends far too much time doubting herself, I *know* she feels a wealth of gratitude and has embraced the concept of unconditional love, as has everyone who has ever nurtured something.

Needless to say, I am beyond grateful that I'll get to relive so many of the moments that make motherhood special—even if I'm called Grandma.

Planet Mom: It's where I live, revisiting motherhood as a newly minted grandmother.

ABOUT THE AUTHOR

As a member of the National Society of Newspaper Columnists, Melinda L. Wentzel, aka Planet Mom, is an award winning slice-of-life/humor columnist and author whose primary objective is to keep mothering real on the page while maintaining some semblance of sanity on the home front. Her work has appeared in the *Atlanta Parent Magazine*, the *San Diego Family Magazine*, the *Kansas City Parent Magazine*, *Twins Magazine*, *Chicken Soup for the Soul*, *A Cup of Comfort*, *Mountain Home Magazine*, *Life in Altamonte Springs City Magazine*, the *Khaleej Times Weekender*, Dubai, UAE and a host of online publications to include *Mamapedia*, *BetterWayMoms*, *MomStuff*, *HybridMom*, *MomBloggersClub* and the *Huffington Post*.

For more than a decade, her newspaper column, *Notes from Planet Mom*, has appeared in *Webb Weekly* (Lycoming County, Pennsylvania), where she offers parents who subsist at various stages of lunacy a sanity cocktail in the form of gloriously irreverent and, at times, surprisingly tender pieces about marriage and life with kids. She and her husband live in north central Pennsylvania with their twin daughters, two pampered dogs and a self-absorbed cat. Visit her website at www.melindawentzel.com, follow her on Twitter at www.twitter.

com/PlanetMom or join her in the trenches of Parentville on Facebook at www.facebook.com/NotesfromPlanetMom.

Other titles by Melinda L. Wentzel aka Planet Mom:

Deliverance: A Survival Guide to Parenting Twins: 10 Field-Tested Tips to Navigate the First Year

CPSIA information can be obtained
at www.ICGtesting.com
Printed in the USA
LVHW051518240719
625190LV00001B/24